Ethics in Governance in India

Governance and ethics are intertwined. A government functions within certain broad moral and ethical parameters, integrally linked with the sociological foundation of the polity in which it is articulated. The importance of ethics in governance has acquired a significant place in contemporary theoretical discussion.

This book situates ethics in governance in India in the national frame and incorporates the context of globalization, allowing for the increasing importance of non-state global actors in national decision making. The author argues that a lack of ethics quickly turns into corruption and leads to governmental efforts to deal with it. He proposes that ethics are a set of standards that a society places on itself to articulate its responses to societal needs, and discusses the efforts of the Indian government to eradicate corruption and its failure to do so.

A theoretical approach to the issues of ethics in governance and corruption, this book is of interest to academics in the fields of Asian Politics, in particular Indian politics, and political philosophy.

Bidyut Chakrabarty is Professor in Political Science at the University of Delhi, India.

Routledge contemporary South Asia series

Ethics in Governance in India

Bidyut Chakrabarty

Routledge
Taylor & Francis Group

LONDON AND NEW YORK

First published 2016 by Routledge

2 Park Square, Milton Park, Abingdon, Oxfordshire OX14 4RN
52 Vanderbilt Avenue, New York, NY 10017

Routledge is an imprint of the Taylor & Francis Group, an informa business

First issued in paperback 2019

British Library Cataloguing in Publication Data
A catalogue record for this book is available from the British Library

Library of Congress Cataloging in Publication Data
Names: Chakrabarty, Bidyut, 1958– author.
Title: Ethics in governance in India / Bidyut Chakrabarty.
Description: Abingdon, Oxon ; New York, NY : Routledge, 2016. | Series:
Routledge contemporary South Asia series ; 110 | Includes bibliographical
references and index.
Identifiers: LCCN 2015040387 (print) | LCCN 2015050352 (ebook) |
ISBN 9781138100244 (hardback) | ISBN 9781315657783 (ebk) |
ISBN 9781315657783 (ebook)
Subjects: LCSH: Political ethics–India. | Civil service ethics–India. |
Public administration–Moral and ethical aspects–India.
Classification: LCC JQ229.E8 C53 2016 (print) | LCC JQ229.E8 (ebook) |
DDC 172.0954–dc23
LC record available at http://lccn.loc.gov/2015040387

ISBN: 978-1-138-10024-4 (hbk)
ISBN: 978-0-367-32225-0 (pbk)

Typeset in Times New Roman
by Wearset Ltd, Boldon, Tyne and Wear

Dedicated to
Those fighting for justice and fair play

Contents

Preface and acknowledgement

The decline of ethics in public life and its inevitable consequences continue to be intriguing to scholars and policy makers alike. Regardless of ideological differences, opinions converge on the point that corruption is an impediment to national/global growth. So it needs to be effectively combatted to secure the future of human civilization. But who will bell the cat, especially if those who are given the responsibility to capture it allow the cat to freely roam around! As the present study has shown, public authority breeds corruption and most of the institutional devices seem to have been handicapped given the growing vested interests in governance. Nobody seems to be serious in the containment of corruption and malpractices, because of the selfish motives of those who remain critical in dispensing public services. Corruption is said to have become inevitable in a rigid administration; nothing seems to move unless one dishes out monetary or other benefits in exchange for what one receives from the government. This was the scene in the context of the License–Quota–Permit Raj, as various studies of how the government functioned have shown. The impact was felt, though the social climate was such that no serious campaign was launched to challenge the system that seemed to have encouraged corrupt personnel to abuse public authority for personal enrichment. Attempts were made, as shown in the book, to weed out corruption by creating new public institutions and strengthening the existing ones. Despite putting these new mechanisms in place, the results did not seem to have been encouraging; that, however, raises a bigger question by suggesting that, without adequately changing the social climate, mere tweaking of the system by creating/strengthening institutions was futile. This is one side of the story; the other side is about the attempts, repeatedly made by the ordinary masses, to challenge the system and also the beneficiaries. The 1974–5 Total Revolution campaign by Jayaprakash Narayan (JP) is illustrative here. It was a spontaneous campaign that soon built into a nation-wide mass movement against those who abused authority to fulfil partisan ideological and also gainful missions. The JP movement may have failed to achieve its goal; nonetheless, by catapulting the issue of corruption onto the centre stage of Indian politics, it not only built a new political trend, but also created an environment in which people got a voice. The 2011 Anna Hazare-led *India Against Corruption* continued this, though the context was remarkably dissimilar. Like the 1974–5

JP assault on corruption in public life, the Anna Hazare campaign, despite having succeeded in creating a mass support base, gradually fizzled out without attaining its proclaimed aim of having a Lokpal. But that it triggered a mass momentum against corruption was undeniable. Both these movements reinforced the importance of creating a propitious social climate, in which tendencies supporting corruption and corrupt practices are considered anathema for healthy social growth.

I have been toying with the idea of writing a full-length monograph on ethics in governance since the publication of *Confluence of Thought: Mahatma Gandhi and Martin Luther King Jr* (Oxford University Press, New York, 2013), which I wrote to emphasize the importance of ethics in politics. Both these apostles of peace fought hard to prove the point that ethics, once sacrificed, resulted in a complete debasement of public life. In my 2013 book, I focused on ethics as a powerful conceptual category that inspired fearless campaigns in India under Gandhi's leadership and later in the US, which King Jr spearheaded. In this book, I have endeavoured to show the dialectical interpenetration between the decline of ethics and its consequences in the Indian context since the acceptance of the state-led planned economic development with the approval of the first Five Year Plan in 1951. Given the dramatic socio-political changes following the adoption of the 1991 New Economic Policy, the story cannot be told in the same unilinear fashion. Hence the book takes into account the changing context while articulating ethics in governance in India in the transformed socio-economic milieu. Although the book is selective in its treatment of the theme, it has nonetheless raised a fundamental point that the ethics deficit and its adverse consequences are society driven, which also confirms how critical a propitious social climate is in creating and also strengthening the roots of ethics in public life.

I owe a great deal to Dorothea because without her support it would not have been possible for me to go ahead with the project. I remember Jillian who encouraged me to carry on with the project when I was not sure about its future. By efficiently handling the e-correspondences for preparing the contract for the book, Sophie also helped me a great deal in sorting out difficulties. I also acknowledge the academic help that I had received from those who made extensive comments on various talks that I gave on this theme in different campuses in India and abroad. I am thankful to Professor Paul Heywood of Nottingham University, a friend of mine since the LSE days, for having shared relevant texts on corruption with me during the preparation of the manuscript for the book. Two of my former graduate students – Dr Prakash Chand and Dr Arindam Roy – were always helpful in procuring those useful government reports that allowed me to further streamline the argument. I am grateful to them. I also fondly remember Surender who helped me a great deal by arranging some of the important documents for my research. I am fortunate to have a very endearing family that always stood by me, especially when I was immersed with my work at home. By always being creatively distractive, our kids – Barbie and Pablo – always remain a source of unblemished joy and happiness. Finally, I would not have been academically proactive without my students here in Delhi and elsewhere where I taught at different phases of my teaching career because of their constant probing and inquisitiveness which never allowed me to become intellectually 'fossilized' or to nurture the usual instinctive human tendencies to remain complacent or violently dismissive of creative efforts.

Bidyut Chakrabarty
Delhi, 2016

Introduction

I

Governance and ethics are intertwined. A government functions within certain broad moral and ethical parameters, integrally linked with the sociological foundation of the polity in which it is articulated. The importance of ethics in governance has acquired a significant place in contemporary theoretical discussion, more so because of the growing decadence in governmental practices largely owing to a decline of ethical values in public administration which is perhaps singularly responsible for the rise of 'corruption' in a virulent form. The possible reason is located in the overgrowth of the state through which bureaucracy has become a 'rent-seeker', ignoring its Benthamite role of being 'a benevolent guardian'. The World Bank-sponsored solution is to downsize the state and allow free play of the market and civil society – consolidating the ideology of neo-liberalism. Whether this is an appropriate strategy for the developing and also underdeveloped nations is a challenging question that needs to be addressed, underlining the importance of 'public' in public administration. This is a challenge that involves a thorough analysis of the circumstances and also the outcome in a historical context because the dwindling of ethics in governance is not an overnight phenomenon, but an offshoot of a long-term process.

It is difficult to conclusively define the term ethics, which is usually a context-driven conceptualization. Nonetheless, on the basis of the literature on administrative ethics, one can derive a meaningful definition of what ethics is all about. One of the prominent thinkers F M Marx, in his 1949 article in *American Political Science Review*, sought to conceptualize the idea by linking it with the prevalent political ideology that the machinery of government is expected to translate into social reality. Public administration is thus an instrument in attaining the purpose of the political order. 'The core of administrative ethics [thus] lies', argued Marx, 'in the ideas that nourish the political system', implying thereby that the administrators are not free to follow their own personal values in the course of their professional activities, but are obligated to be 'conscious agents of a democratic community' and to direct their action 'toward promoting the healthy growth of a free society dedicated to the common good'.[1] Ethics is therefore a set of standards that society places on itself to articulate its responses to societal needs. Mere adoption of rules cannot inject ethics in human behaviour; what is thus required in firmly promoting a culture of integrity in administration is also a set of mechanisms to execute rules and regulations by putting in place competent disciplinary agencies to investigate violations and deviations, and also to impose sanctions quickly.

Corruption is an important manifestation of the failure of ethics. The word – 'corrupt' – is derived from the Latin word *corruptus*, meaning 'to break or destroy'. The word 'ethics' is from the original Greek term 'ethikos', meaning 'arising from habit'. In defining corruption, the idea of ethics appears very critical. Although corruption represents 'deviation' from established norms, there is hardly a universal definition because of its contextual roots. Nonetheless, the definition provided by Carl J Friedrich seems to have captured its complex texture. For him, corruption is

> a kind of behaviour which deviates from the norm actually prevalent or believed to prevail in a given context.... It is a deviant behaviour associated with a particular motivation, namely that of private gain at public expense.... Such private gain may be monetary one, and in the minds of the general public it usually is, but it may take other forms.[2]

Corroborating what Friedrich suggests, a recently articulated definition further underlines the characteristics of corruption by stating that corruption

> involves the distortion or subversion of the exercise of public office so that it meets partisan or sectional rather than public interests, so that some people gain who should not and some lose (or fail to benefit) who should not.[3]

Key to a rising grip of corruption, as is evident in this conceptualization, is declining ethics in public life which encourages distortion of values. Public office becomes a space to gratify one's corrupt design and the system loses its vitality to combat tendencies striking at its foundation.

It is unfortunate that in India corruption has, for many, become a matter of habits, ranging from grand corruption involving persons in high places to retail corruption touching the everyday life of common people. The anti-corruption interventions so far made are seen to be ineffectual and there is widespread public cynicism about them. The interventions are seen as mere posturing without any real intention to bring the corrupt to book. They are also seen as handy weapons for partisan, political use to harass opponents. Corruption is so deeply entrenched in the system that most people regard corruption as inevitable and any effort to fight it as futile. The cynicism is spreading so fast that it bodes ill for our democratic system itself.

II

In any discussion of ethics in governance, corruption invariably forms an integral part. Containment of corruption, which is endemic in developing countries for historically ordained socio-political reasons, is thus a foremost administrative concern. In some form or other, corruption exists in every country regardless of the level of economic development; the degree may differ and its expanse may be limited. In developing countries, corruption seems to have become integrally connected with public life, which is certainly a source of irritation for everybody, and yet serious efforts at combatting corruption always receive relentless opposition. This is, however, not paradoxical because corruption is considered to be an enabling mechanism for works that cannot be accomplished otherwise. What is hypocritical is the prevalence of corruption and also a strong opposition towards mitigating its debilitating socio-political effects. Being aware of how corruption is weakening public administration, public authorities undertake meaningful steps to address the concern, which may sometime work miracles though gradually fizzle out on most occasions since mere institutional mechanisms may not always be adequate to effectively contain corruption. What is thus critically important is the citizens' involvement in governance; they should be vigilant enough to catch the wrong-doers and those who tend to bend rules to extend favour in exchange for material gains. This is easier said than done. Nonetheless, there is a clear sense in this endeavour which, in course of time, is likely to create an environment in which those who indulge in corrupt practices for personal benefit will be forced to behave because of the public vigilance.

What is corruption then? One of the most persuasive definitions, which is also easy to comprehend, happens to be the one given by the World Bank. Corruption is, to quote the World Bank, 'the abuse of public funds and or office for private or political gain'.[4] This confirms the contention that corruption is a failure in governance. The 1999 report on Human Development in South Asia thus contends that

> corruption is one of the most damaging consequences of poor governance. It undermines investment and economic growth, decreases the resources for human development goals, deepens the extent of poverty, subverts the judicial system and undermines the legitimacy of the state. In fact, when corruption becomes entrenched, it can devastate the entire economic, political and social fabric of a country.[5]

As experiences in South Asia reveal, corruption has a spiralling effect on society, which gradually loses its vitality. The state becomes a hapless entity and is meant to serve the powerful who have appropriated the system to pursue and fulfil private ends. Important institutions of governance remain peripheral as far as the majority is concerned; they are reduced to mere institutional functionaries that are there to uphold the interests of a selected few. As the Human Development report, while underlining the distressing impact of 'entrenched corruption' on human life, further adumbrates by stating, when corruption becomes entrenched and systemic, its negative influence on economic and social development multiplies. Trust between the state and its citizens collapses. Basic laws and contracts are not honoured. Vast amounts of resources are spent seeking bribes and corrupt gains rather than engaging in productive activity.[6]

The outcome is devastating for the poor in South Asia who hardly have a voice in governance except during an election when they have, at least in principle, the authority to decide the fate of those involved in electoral battle; otherwise, they remain mere numbers adding to the demographic strength of the countries in the region. This has been very succinctly stated by the 1999 Human Development Report by suggesting that

> despite a marked improvement in the lives of a few, there are many in South Asia who have been forgotten by formal institutions of governance. These are the poor, the downtrodden, and the most vulnerable of society, suffering from acute deprivations on account of their income, caste, creed, gender or religion. Their fortunes have not moved with those of the privileged few and this in itself is deprivation of a distressing nature.[7]

This is the stark reality in South Asia, and there has been a consensus that corruption is primarily a symptom of poor governance. Unless corruption is conclusively tackled, it will lead to 'an era of entrenched corruption'.[8] How to address this menace? As per the 1999 Human Development Report,

> unless the wider institutional environment that breeds corruption is radically transformed – through economic, electoral, judicial, parliamentary and bureaucratic reforms that restore people's trust in government, specific anti-corruption agendas are unlikely to meet with success.[9]

On the basis of the above discussion, two basic arguments can now be made: first, poor government breeds, inter alia, corruption. One of the major factors for poor governance happens to be the weakening of the institutions that are considered critical in fulfilling the cardinal aims of governance. The reasons for such institutional decline are to be located in the peculiar unfolding of the socio-economic and political processes of the region, during both colonialism and its aftermath. The second argument which, in fact, is implicit in the suggestion that the 1999 Human Development Report made while seeking to find a way out relates to the idea that a corruption-free society is not a utopia, but can be brought about by radical institutional changes in governance through popular movements, involving people cutting across social, economic and political barriers. The idea is not without substance, as innumerable illustrations can be cited to show that anti-corruption movements in India and elsewhere have led to significant changes in governance. The acceptance of the 2005 *Right to Information Act* which was constantly demanded as an effective means to combat corruption is illustrative here; there is no doubt that the campaign, led by the Mazdoor Kishan Shakti Sangathan since the late 1980s, resulted in the replacement of the archaic colonial *Official Secrets Act* of 1923 by an empowering *Right to Information Act* in 2005.

III

Corruption seems to be pervasive in administration as bureaucracy is usually dubbed as 'a rent-seeking organization'. This is not a modern phenomenon. In his *Arthasastra*, a text that is traced back to the fourth century BC, Kautilya provided a graphic illustration of corruption by saying that

> just as it is impossible not to taste the honey (or the poison) that finds itself at the tip of the tongue, so it is impossible for a government servant not to eat up at least a bit of king's revenue.[10]

For Kautilya, corruption and administration are integrally linked. In common parlance, corruption means embezzlement of any kind that is not justified by norms, practices or rules. This also includes the use of public office for private gains, whereby an official responsible for public office is engaged in activities for private enrichment. The Mughal administration was also sensitive to corruption and steps were devised to contain corrupt practices. In fact, embezzlement of public funds by those associated with governance was considered to be a serious offence that always invited stringent punishment. The system, however, collapsed when administration became terribly chaotic which was often the case especially during the transition from one administrative control to another. Nonetheless, that corruption drew adequate attention during the Mughal administration is beyond question. As Carl J Friedrich underlines, corruption is 'deviant behaviour' justifying private gain at public expense. Corruption is thus a transactional evil where a favour is extended in exchange for private benefits.

With this definition in view, this segment is devoted to analysing the corrosive effects of corruption in administration in two interrelated parts: on the one hand, the discussion shall concentrate on the possible roots of corruption in India; later, on the other hand, it deals with those instruments and mechanisms that India has evolved to combat corruption. This is not, however, to suggest that the entire administration is corrupt and vitiated; instead, the argument is couched in the form of queries relating to the insidious impact of the desire for private gains at the cost of taxpayers' money. It is difficult to carry out an exhaustive study of the phenomenon, given the space constraint. Hence our aim is to flag up the basic issues that we consider critical in conceptualizing corruption in the context of a developing country, such as India, which is simultaneously a booming economy as well.

Corruption is ubiquitous in India. In 2016, India ranked 76th out of 168 countries in the Transparency International's Corruption Preparation Index, along with Thailand, Brazil, Zambia and Burkina Faso, among others. In a study conducted by Transparency International, it was found that more that 62 per cent of Indians had paid a bribe or influenced the officer to extract work in public offices successfully.[12] Most of the largest sources of corruption are entitlement programmes and social spending schemes, attached to the central government, including the Mahatma Gandhi National Rural Employment Guarantee Scheme and the National Rural Health Mission. The other important source of corruption involves the transport industry, especially the vehicles that are used to ferry goods across the states, which are forced to pay cash in bribes annually to numerous regulatory and police stops on the interstate highways. This is an open secret and nobody seems to feel bad about it; owners of these vehicles willingly pay to ease their movement from one state to another.

While explaining the growing incidence of corruption in India, the Second Administrative Reforms Commission refers to three factors which are also rooted in India's historical past in colonialism: first, colonialism had created a mindset that had a propensity to exercise power arbitrarily; second, the prevalence of a huge unorganized sector in which those who work are not conscious enough to demand their rights while working – such a workforce can easily be manipulated by those who hold positions of authority in public offices; third, the factors responsible for a corruption-prone mindset are over-regulation, complicated taxes and licensing systems, numerous government departments with uncontrolled discretionary power, monopoly by government-controlled institutions on certain goods and service delivery and lack of transparent laws and processes.

How to combat corruption? This is too difficult a question to respond in categorical terms because, so long as the mindset remains unchallenged, no institutional/legal mechanism is adequate to uproot corruption and its myriad sources from the polity. However, attempts have constantly been made to weed out the roots of corruption. India since independence has set up more than 45 committees and commissions to strengthen administrative capabilities by making the administrative machinery efficient and accountable. What began with the 1946 Tottenham Committee report, which also focused on the decline of discipline in civil service, was reiterated by the 1948 Economy Committee which was appointed to review the increase in the civil expenditure of the central government since 1938–9 and to make recommendation for the promotion of true economy in the administration 'by the elimination of unnecessary, wasteful or extravagant expenditure'. The argument was forcefully made by N Gopalaswami Ayyanger in his 1949 *Report on Reorganization of the Government Machinery*, which recommended the establishment of an Organization and Method (O & M) division to be made responsible for continued efficiency in the government offices and public services and methods of transaction of public business. This recommendation did not receive a favourable response till the appointment of another committee in 1950 under the stewardship of A D Gorwala. Among the important recommendations, made by the Gorwala Committee, two stand out: (a) creation of an O & M branch in government and a board of two members to be set up to provide necessary drive and direction to administration; and

(b) training aiming at precision and surety in the conduct of business and improvement of staff morale and also to encourage the civil servant to see his work in its widest context and to persevere with his/her own educational development.

In pursuance of the objective of establishing a corruption-free administration, Jawaharlal Nehru, the then Indian premier, set up a Corruption Commission with J B Kripalani, Paul Appleby and A D Gorwala as members. While Gorwala prepared a report on the efficient conduct of state enterprises, Paul Appleby in his *Public Administration in India* (1953) commented on the sources of maladministration in India by stating that

> even as it is, the structure of government diffuses responsibility, it retards action before the fact that insufficiently evaluates its course after the fact. There are on the whole too much scrutiny and too many impediments to action before the fact and too little systematic review and scrutiny of action after the fact. The structure of administration restricts and inhibits formal delegation. But there is more unconscious than conscious delegation. The view of the man at the bottom of hierarchy who writes the first note on a file is all important in most instances. Imperfect and insufficient conscious delegation is an important factor in making the heavy overload that grievously burdens the ministers and secretaries.

In Appleby's perception, the administrative ills in India are largely due to internal weaknesses that can be meaningfully addressed by streamlining the staff agencies within the administration. In other words, an effective system of decentralization of administrative authority is necessary to take care of most of the problems crippling Indian administration. While Appleby expressed concern at the declining of efficiency within administration due to 'imperfect delegation', the Shanthanam Committee that submitted its report in 1964 examined the extent of corruption in India and came to the conclusion that corruption was not confined to the lower ranks of public service; the number of cases in which the higher rank officers were involved was alarming. The Committee thus recommended the setting up of the Central Vigilance Commission to look into charges of corruption against civil servants. A well-equipped institutionalized agency, the Commission is also authorized to punish deviant public personnel if it is executed through due process of law.

There is also no dearth of legalized mechanisms to address corruption and corrupt practices in administration. Of all the preventive steps, one of the most important is the 2005 *Right to Information Act* that legally makes it binding on government officials to provide information requested by citizens or face punitive action. This Act has considerably empowered the citizens, allowing them access to information that had until then remained the exclusive domain of the government officials under the archaic colonial *Official Secrets Act* of 1923. The other empowering act happens to be the Right to Public Service legislation that has already been enacted in 19 constituent states of India. By providing time-bound delivery of services for various public services rendered by the government to citizens and devising mechanisms for punishing the errant public servant, this act has been effective in containing corruption and enhancing transparency in public dealings and the accountability of those involved in public service delivery. Similarly, the *Prevention of Money Laundering Act* of 2002 is also an attack on corrupt public servants by authorizing the government to confiscate properties that are disproportionate to his/her income.

One of the major interventions in this regard was the adoption of the 2011 *Whistle Blowers Protection Act*, which provides a mechanism to investigate alleged corruption and abuse of power by public servants and also to extend protection to those exposing deviant behaviour of government officials getting private gain out of public responsibilities. Of all these mechanisms, the institution of *Lokpal* for the country as a whole and *Lakayuktas* for the states is perhaps a significant endeavour towards creating a corruption-free India. The *Lokpal and Lokayuktas Act* of 2013, which came into force in 2014, provides the establishment of Ombudsman-type institutions in India to enquire into the allegations of corruption against public functionaries. The *Lokayuktas* at the state have come into being in several states, though the appointment of a *Lokpal* for the country as whole remains a distant goal, because of the disagreement among the political parties which are not favourably inclined to create a mega-agency to combat corruption regardless of political consequences.

As shown, institutions for the eradication of corruption are in place in India. Yet, the incidence of corruption does not seem to have declined to a noticeable extent. The scene is disappointing, but not disheartening since the public voice against corruption is too powerful to ignore and forces the public authorities to address the issue. The outcome is the appointment of various commissions/committees, which may not be as effective as they are made out to be; nonetheless, the effort itself is worthwhile, since it exposes the nature and also the pernicious impact of corruption on governance. What is evident is the fact that, in combatting corruption, the role of public authority is as significant as that of an alert public. In fact, they are intermingled: a vigilant public acts as a strong shield against distortions in governance. In other words, constant public monitoring of governance is a deterrent for those in power that will certainly act as an antidote to corruption. Implicit here is the idea that the available institutional protections do not seem to be effective by themselves; they become meaningful in the presence of an alert public that cannot be easily bypassed.

Corruption in administration is an issue that can never be addressed conclusively for three reasons: first, this is a pathological syndrome, the root of which can be traced back to the colonial days when exercise of power by those at the helm of affairs was far more arbitrary than what is visible now. With its long reign, not only did the colonial state authoritatively consolidate such a design, it succeeded simply because the forces of opposition did not appear to be strong enough; second, the trend continued in independent India with the dysfunctional vigilance machinery, breakdown of organizational integrity, declining importance of accountability in public authorities, logjam of procedural chaos and vitiated environment of work;[13] third, corruption is rooted and also flourishes because of a mindset that challenges neither institutional nor individual delinquency; well entrenched and effective as a mechanism, corruption seems to have become integral to our governance and hence it is better to accept rather than quibble since the situation will not change soon.

Is corruption inevitable? If that be so, the discussion on integrity in administration seems to be irrelevant. In view of the growing consolidation of public opinion against corruption in India, it will be difficult, if not impossible, to sweep the issue under the carpet. A vibrant democracy along with an alert citizenry is perhaps the best shield against corruption. There is thus a need to develop a counter mindset to scuttle the other mindset which champions an immutable character of Indian administration that cannot function unless couched in corrupt practices. The argument that administration is static defies the fundamental laws of social change; this is further reinforced in the light of the recent happenings in India in which mass energy was released to integrate citizens with governance. The transformation is visible with the involvement of the stakeholders, including the press, which has played a very critical role in creating an environment in which corrupt practices receive immediate public attention. The role of the oversight bodies, acting as watchdogs, cannot also be undermined in the gigantic task of making India free from corruption, as the examples from other countries show.

IV

As is evident, corruption is an outcome of complex processes in which the fundamental pillars of governance do not remain as effective as they are expected to be. In principle, the Constitution of India is perhaps one of the finest legal documents in terms of the principles that it upholds. Yet, this is not adequate to build an edifice of governance that is free from corruption. This is a paradox of India's recent political history, which is usually explained by reference to the historical processes that led to the emergence of India as a politically independent nation. What is most puzzling is to note that corruption is always despised at one level and yet it is being encouraged at another level as perhaps the most effective tool to get work done. The scene in contemporary India does not appear to be as bleak as in the context of the erstwhile 'Licence–Quota–Permit Raj' because of the increasing importance of public services due to utilization of communication technology in governance. In other words, the publicness of governance appears to have been significantly sacrificed in an era when a socialistic pattern of society was eulogized as perhaps the most effective socioeconomic arrangement to effectively address the issues of poverty and maldevelopment. The socio-economic mission that the founding fathers so assiduously nurtured while battling for political freedom from British colonialism remained un-fulfilled and India's development did not take off to the extent it was expected to, despite having endorsed, rather enthusiastically, the state-led development paradigm. Public administration ceased to be public and was appropriated for private gains. Corruption was endemic, and bureaucracy, instead of being an aid to public well-being, became 'rent-seeking' and 'extractive'. This was never seriously challenged, notwithstanding the availability of institutional mechanisms to combat corruption. The scene had, however, gradually changed following the consolidation of a powerful public voice against corruption that gained momentum as history progressed.

A perusal of India's democratic polity confirms two fundamental conceptual assumptions of public administration: on the one hand, in terms of the hardware of democracy which includes those major institutions which uphold democracy both in spirit and content, Indian governance is clearly democratic in character; bureaucracy in India is, on the other hand, essentially instrumental, being confined to formulating policies on the basis of political values that the politicians carry to governance. Under these circumstances, governance thus becomes an interface between bureaucracy and its political bosses. As a deviant behaviour, the roots of corruption need to be located in this interface, in which both the permanent and the temporary executives seem to deviate from what they are expected to perform while discharging their role according to the rule book.

The visible aberration does not seem to attract attention, because of what is anthropologically described as a 'cultural deficit' in the polity. Culturally, the deviant behaviour, despite provoking criticism, may not be deviant enough to be absolutely socially 'despicable'. This is indicative of the visible weaknesses of software, to use another computer metaphor, of democracy that undoubtedly leaves an impact on Indian public administration. Corruption can thus be said to be clearly culturally rooted in the Indian context, notwithstanding the well-formed democratic structure of governance, especially in terms of the hardware of democracy. Given the view supporting the cultural rootedness of corruption, the argument that corruption is also contextual gains an easy acceptance. Embedded here is the idea of the context being critical in shaping socio-political views. Instances can be multiplied to show that corruption figures prominently in contemporary public discourse and the voice that is articulated is too powerful to be ignored so easily. Of all instances, the 2011 India against corruption campaign, led by the octogenarian Anna Hazare, is perhaps the most glaring example of a spontaneous people's mobilization against corruption. The movement that hogged the limelight was reduced to a campaign for the creation of an institution – Jan Lokpal – to eradicate corruption. Despite its apparent success in mobilizing support for the campaign, the Anna Hazare movement thus remained constrained with a very limited purpose because the formation of another institution, however strong it may be, does not seem to be adequate to take the bull by the horns since the roots of corruption are far more entrenched in our culture and cannot obviously be tackled successfully by adding one more institution to the prevalent outfits.

V

Ethics in governance is surely a casualty given the unearthing of scams at regular intervals. One of the factors that led to the defeat of the erstwhile government, led by the United Progressive Alliance in 2014 was its alleged involvement in cases of financial embezzlement of public funds besides misusing public offices for private gains. The National Democratic Alliance government that was formed in 2014 seems to be radically different because of the reported endeavour towards eradicating corruption. The effort is to create an environment, supported by the government, political functionaries and various non-government agencies, to weed out corruption by addressing the root causes. This is a difficult task to accomplish since the problem is, as a commentator emphasizes, 'systemic' in character and India has become, he further characterizes,

> a republic of greed [which is] about businessmen purchasing political elites and the political elites walking into wealth that their own entrepreneurship did not create; it is their power to grant permission and licenses that has generated wealth, not their innovative business ideas.[14]

This is an analytically useful (and also persuasive) formulation, since scams seems to have become integral to India's governance especially in the last few decades. The instances of the involvement of those in governance in scams are far more frequent than before. Is India going through what is conceptually characterized as 'a gilded age', a term coined by Mark Twain and Charles Dudley Warner in their 1873 novel, *The Gilded Age: a tale of today*, to describe how the rampant corruption caused massive inequality in the US? Satirizing greed and corruption in post-Civil War America in the era now referred to as the Gilded Age, the novel is a powerful statement on the pernicious effect of corruption in all walks of life. It has thus been argued that 'both in its rot and heady dynamism, India is beginning to resemble America's Gilded Age (1865–1900) ... [that] transformed an agrarian US into an economic and industrial giant'.[15] As in the US, the business tycoons resorted to all means, fair and foul, to expand their empire; their complicity with the government of the day enabled them to fulfil their desire rather easily. As is evident, similarly to the barons of America's Gilded Age, most of India's billionaires have used 'three methods to tilt the playing field to their advantage: securing rich natural resources such as mine and land; ensuring favourable regulations in various industries, and restraining the entry of foreign competition wherever possible'.[16] The task was made easier, because of the collaboration, often collusion, that these favoured business houses had with the government at all levels, as in late-nineteenth-century America. Examples can be multiplied to demonstrate that those in political power extended undue favour to a selected group of industrial and business houses in exchange for, it has also been proved, kickbacks. The political class in India, like its American counterpart, seems to have largely ignored the ill-effect that the massive corruption had on the government exchequer, in particular, and society, in general. In other words, the moral fabric of Indian politics appears to have crumbled to a significant extent.

By drawing attention to the uncanny similarity between America's Gilded Age and what is happening in India now, an analyst thus graphically illustrates the point by saying that, despite the fact that

> historical analogy is tricky,... India today broadly resembles the earlier American experience, both in the rapidity of economic growth and structural transformation from an agrarian to a modern economy, and the accumulation of staggering fortunes, often through illicit means, with the attendant widening gaps between rich and poor.[17]

Is it thus fair to argue that unregulated and market-based capitalism generates corruption? A global survey of the processes of growth from Bismarck's Germany to that of contemporary East Asia confirms the contention. What happens simultaneously is also the consolidation of politico-ideological forces championing redistribution of wealth and concomitant social policies to correct the prevalent socio-economic imbalances. As history shows, America's Gilded Age led to the rise of 'the Progressive Era, marked by cleaner politics, a bipartisan fight against corruption, more honest business practices and a channelling of private wealth into philanthropy'.[18] An analysis of the socio-political processes in the Gilded Age thus reinforces the fact that decline of ethics in governance is clearly contextual; it further endorses the idea that forces challenging the business–government nexus emerge as natural byproducts in circumstances when the hapless victims mobilize themselves against the mighty as perhaps the only means for their survival. In this fight, they are likely to get comrades-in-arms: in the case of the US, the journalists, known as Muckrakers, who exposed through their writings in the highly influential new medium of national magazines, the unholy alliance between the crooked businessmen and equally debased political authority which led to public outcry, government and legal investigations and also enactment of specific laws to address their concerns. The present situation in India does not seem to be different: notwithstanding the gloomy scenario in governance, the fact that scams are being unearthed also confirms the vitality that the system retains despite consolidation of the forces striking at its foundation. Despite the fact that a republic of greed has, in other words, spread its tentacles, rather abrasively, there is a silver lining because the politico-ideological forces opposed to the collusion between business and politics seem to have become too powerful to be ignored so easily.

As the above discussion reveals, two important ideas seem critical here: first, in some respects, India appears to have entered a Gilded Age which cannot approximate to what America witnessed in the mid-nineteenth century for obvious historical reasons; the processes that account for significant decline of ethics in governance in India have different historical trajectories because of the nature of independence and also the structural continuity of public administration from its colonial past. India became politically free following the British withdrawal in 1947 though the institutions of governance were allowed to remain, because of her uncritical acceptance of the Westminster form of parliamentary democracy. The second idea is linked with the growing consolidation of a voice for ethics in public life that is being jeopardized because of the rising corruption especially at the behest of those holding political authority. While corruption seems to have gripped the entire political system, there is, however, an equally powerful conglomeration of forces that are opposed to the unholy nexus between the government and corporate houses. Just like the Muckrakers in the Gilded Age in the US, these forces are a powerful aid to the consolidation of opposition in India. In the changed scenario, it may not be easy for the industrial houses to manipulate government machineries according to their personal whims and selfish priorities. On most occasions, it was the public outcry against the misuse of the system for private gain that sustained the anti-corruption tempo to a significant extent. So, scams are the price that one has to pay to bring about the inclusive development that India is aiming for by crafting a developmental alternative to the state-led development paradigm that was so zealously nurtured by the founding fathers and their ideological successors till it was dismantled in 1991 with the acceptance of the New Economic Policy.

VI

There are two major arguments along with one supplementary argument that the book seeks to pursue. Conceptually articulated, the first major argument suggests that the query – ethics in governance – cannot be comprehensively understood within the available parameters of public administration. As is conceptualized conventionally, lack of ethics is attributed to a lack of administrative accountability. This is a very narrow conceptualization, since ethics in governance is also linked with the wider socio-political environment in which ethical considerations do not seem to receive as much attention as is required under normal circumstances. So, the argument that the book offers is derived from the broader socio-economic and political processes shaping differently textured responses to the issues of ethics and also tendencies towards its eclipse. To put it differently, ethics in governance needs to be grasped politically, given its roots in a wider social milieu that may not be entirely supportive, but fail to conclusively challenge forces encouraging corruption because of the peculiar historical circumstances. The second argument, drawing on the distinct US experience of the original Gilded Age, is about those processes that gain momentum once voices against the decline of ethics in governance acquire strength and direction. This has two aspects: on the one hand, it delves into the sustained movements/campaigns against abuse of political authority for private gain; it also draws, on the other hand, upon endeavours at protecting the institutional sanctity of constitutional democracy, which is considered to be an empowering device despite the hopeless situation that appears to have been consolidated due to the scant respect of those holding political power for democratic ethos and practices. The basic idea that this argument seeks to convey refers to the apparent incompatibility between the institutions in their original form and manifestation and what they gradually became in the course of the unfolding of India as an independent state, while seeking to translate into reality the socialistic pattern of society through state-driven economic development. Along with these two major arguments, the book also articulates a supplementary argument highlighting the contextual nature of efforts towards seeking to reaffirm the ethical roots of public governance amid apparent decadence in all walks of life. This suggests, on the one hand, that there cannot be a universal theoretical design to conceptualize ethics in governance, because of its location-specific nature; nonetheless, the growing consolidation of forces challenging tendencies towards undermining ethics in governance is also a testimony, on the other hand, to the articulation of an equally powerful voice which may not always be homogeneous, but remains united at least in terms of goal and spirit.

VII

Divided into six interrelated chapters, the book provides a long analytical statement on ethics in governance in India. By locating the possible reasons for the decline of ethics in public life, the book also links the wider social environment with the specific nature of ethics-deficit in governance. Exploratory in character, the exercise thus pursues the argument that social environment and ethics in governance are dialectically interconnected. While dealing with the foundational conceptual ideas regarding the citizen–administration interface, Chapter 1 provides an in-depth discussion of the issues that are critical in this respect. The importance of the chapter lies in the fact that, by situating the discussion in a theoretical perspective, it also creates a conceptual edifice for the discussion that follows. Chapter 2 focuses on how democratically decentralized decision making is an antidote to ethics-deficit in governance, contrary to the importance of the state in generating forces supportive of ethics in governance. By analysing critically the role of the two forms of democratic decentralization in India – *Bhagidari* in Delhi and *Panchayati Raj* in West Bengal – the chapter provides significant inputs to understand how they worked towards building an ethics-sensitive governance in Delhi and West Bengal respectively. By dwelling on the specific institutional efforts in India that led to the strengthening of governmental agencies responsible for the containment of corruption and malpractices, Chapter 3 seeks to capture how 'the official mindset' worked to weed out corruption. Two Administrative Reforms Commissions, appointed in 1964 and 2005 respectively, will stand in India's administrative history as examples of most powerful interventions striving to create ethically conscious governance. As is always believed, a key to corruption-free governance is an efficient civil service that is also sensitive to the fundamental canons of ethics. This is what is pursued in Chapter 4 which has not only assessed the role of the civil service in a historical perspective, but also dwells on the recommendations of the 1997 Fifth and 2006 Sixth Pay Commissions to show how important the concern for ethics was while suggesting measures to purge public governance of corruption and malpractices. Divided into two parts, Chapter 5 is a lengthy chapter. Part A is about two major institutional efforts that were undertaken in the era of India's plan-led development. Primarily state-driven exercises, the two attempts – the 1964 Santhanam Committee and the 1977 Shah Commission – are historically significant because, for the first time in independent India, corruption had attracted the attention of the policy makers, because of its pernicious impact on the country's socio-economic growth. Part B is a critical analysis of the Second Administrative Reforms Commission's recommendations for ethics in governance. That a full report was devoted to ethics in governance confirms the fact that the concern continues to remain critical to those in public authority. Besides the Commission's recommendations, the chapter also dwells on the role of two important committees of parliament – the *Rajya Sabha* ethics Committee and the *Lok Sabha* Committee – which are also significant in creating and nurturing the concern for ethics among parliamentarians. As history has shown, the growing incidence of corruption also provokes mass consternation, which is usually translated into movements against the sources and perpetrators of the corruption. Challenging those charged with abuse of authority, two important national campaigns – the 1974–5 movement, led by Jayaprakash Narayan and the 2011 Anna Hazare campaign – largely spontaneous at the outset, rocked India in an unprecedented way. Seeking to capture the dynamics of these two movements, Chapter 6 is a response to the complexities of events that was reflective of not only a proactive but also a vigilant citizenry. The participants may have been disappointed because the goal was not achieved; nonetheless, by making citizens alert and sensitive to their role in governance, these two movements are watershed events in contemporary India.

VIII

With six chapters, the book thus pursues a narrative on a theme – ethics in governance – in an analytical format that is theoretically informed and conceptually refreshing. By raising newer issues that are not merely administrative, but politically contrived, the book sets in motion specific intellectual queries. These need to be addressed by keeping in view the possible impact of the wider socio-political processes on ethics in public authority, because the narrow Weberian notion of internal administrative accountability is now simply inadequate. The basic contribution that the book claims to have made is two-fold: besides providing a brief contextual account of the decline of ethics in governance in India, it has, with appropriate academic depth, also dealt with the phenomenon in a historical perspective. Seeking also to unravel the conceptual intricacies of ethics in governance, the book thus creates a space for a debate on a theme that is being constantly reinvented in the light of the changing priorities of governance both globally and nationally following the dismantling of the erstwhile Soviet Union, representing an alternative ideological discourse.

Notes

1 Fritz Morstein Marx, 'Administrative ethics and the rule of law', *The American Political Science Review*, 43, 1949, pp. 1127–8.
2 Carl J Friedrich, 'Corruption concepts in historical perspective', in Arnold J Heidenheimer, Michael Johnston and Victor T LeVine (eds), *Political Corruption: a handbook*, Transaction Publishers, New Bruswick, 1989, p. 15.
3 Mark Philip, 'The definition of political corruption' in Paul Heywood (ed.), *Routledge Handbook of Political Corruption*, Routledge, Oxford, 2015, p. 22.
4 *'Deterring corruption and improving governance in the electricity sector'*, World Bank, April 2009, p. 118.
5 Human Development Centre, *Human Development in South Asia: the crisis of governance*, Oxford University Press, Oxford, 1999, p. 96.
6 Ibid., p. 105.
7 Ibid., p. 112.
8 Ibid,, p. 105.
9 Ibid,, p. 106.
10 R P Kangle, *The Kautilya Arthasastra*, Part II, University of Bombay, Bombay, 1972, p. 91.
11 Carl J Fredrich, 'Corruption concepts in historical perspective' in Arnold J Heidenheimer, Michael Johnston and Victor T LeVine (eds), *Political Corruption: a handbook*, Transaction Publishers, New Brunswick, 1989, p. 15.
12 Transparency International India, *India Corruption Study 2005: To Improve Governance: Volume I – Key Highlights New Delhi*. 30 June 2005. pp. 1–3.
13 Kamala Prasad, *Indian Administration: politics, policies and prospects*, Pearson-Longman, New Delhi, 2006, pp. 324–26.
14 Ashutosh Varshney, 'A Republic of Greed: why Narendra Modi must crack the whip on India's snowballing corruption'. *The Times of India*, New Delhi, 17 July 2015.
15 Jayant Sinha and Ashutosh Varshney, 'It is time for India to rein in its robber barons', *Financial Times*, 6 January 2011.
16 Ibid.
17 Vivek H Dehejia, 'Escaping India's gilded age', *New York Times*, 15 April 2011.
18 Jayant Sinha and Ashutosh Varshney, 'It is time for India to rein in its robber barons', *Financial Times*, 6 January 2011.

1 Situating ethics in governance
Citizens and administration

In conventional public administration, citizens remain recipients and hence they hardly have a role to play in governance. Endorsed by the Weberian notion of hierarchical bureaucracy, public administration, in its earlier articulation, did not seem to pay adequate attention to the role that the citizens are expected to play in public governance. Public administration was hardly public in sum and substance. The idea was challenged off and on; and there were changes in the texture and functioning of public administration as history progressed. One of the fundamental changes that was brought about as a result of politico-ideological campaigns in various phases of history was about the nature of public governance in which the role of citizens began to be recognized as integral to its functioning. It was made possible in a changed environment where top-down administrative values no longer remained as attractive as before. Instead, the idea of the 'bottom-up' administration, entailing the critical importance of the public in decision making, seemed to have become theoretically far more acceptable. The idea that citizens are important in governance is not new; what is new now is the effort towards articulating this idea in practice. Citizens need to be taken into account seriously while formulating policy decisions: they do not remain mere cogs in a machine, but are actively involved in running the machine in accordance with their ideological priorities.

Citizens' involvement in decision making is critical to ethics in governance. In order to make administration transparent, the role of stakeholders can never be undermined because it was they who, being faced by the reality, know what is better for their well-being. Only then are administrative decisions likely to be based on an appropriate understanding of the reality, something usually sacrificed given the appreciation of the top-down strategy of public administration. The aim is to create and also sustain an administration that is responsive enough to arrive at effective decisions for public well-being. What is basic here is to evolve mechanisms whereby citizens' views are respected while making decisions pertinent to their well-being both individually as well as collectively. This is an important aspect of governance in India, in its new *avatar* that has attracted immense attention. By concentrating on these instruments of citizens' empowerment in the changed socio-ideological circumstances, the chapter provides an elaborate study not only of these mechanisms but also their contextual roots in

India's volatile political milieu. The fundamental argument that the chapter makes relates to the consolidation of newer devices for citizens empowerment that are being meaningfully utilized to make public governance sensitive to the demands and also requirements of the stakeholders. These instruments seems to have become effective, the argument further underlines, because of a favourable socio-political environment supporting proactive citizens as integral to democratic political processes.

Interactions between citizens and administration

Being a citizen is more than a status; it is about the entitlement to the rights and privileges of a person that ensures a quality life. So, citizenship is more than a set of rights and obligations; it is an innate orientation for the well-being of state and society. The ancient Greeks realized that, and the polity of Athens institutionalized citizenship through its diverse associations, councils and authorities within the urban framework had evolved. In that environment, citizenship, in principle, meant participation in the co-production of policies. At the basis of this participation stood a belief in the 'happy veracity' of man. However, in modern times the status aspects of citizenship are stressed heavily and the qualitative aspects of citizenship appear to be grossly underestimated. In their wake, public administration as a discipline, was, until recently, more focused on the improvement of state apparatuses than on the development of citizenship and the involvement of citizenship in the making of governmental policies.[1] This dominant trend is responsible for the alienation of citizens and thus there is an increase in citizens' grievances against administration. Against this background, the present chapter deals with some significant dimensions of interaction between citizens and administration, namely citizens' perception about administration, pre-conditions for citizens' centric administration, people's participation in administration, forms of public accountability and the role of public grievance redress machinery in India.

In a democracy, the administration–citizen relations are significant because the support and consent of the governed is a prerequisite for the sustenance of representative government. The state and in actual terms the administration has the major responsibility of providing the major amenities of life – education, health, employment opportunities, improved means of transport and infrastructure, etc. All this affects the individual and collective life of a very large number of people concerned. In public administration, two noticeable trends have emerged in recent times. First, there has been a large growth in the size of governmental administration as well as a vast expansion in its powers and activities. Second, in the wake of the spread of general education, and political and social awakening, there has been a rise in the expectations of people of the administration. The relationship between law and public opinion in a democracy was discussed by A V Dicey at about the end of the last century.[2] The importance of the subject grew sharply after the Second World War, thanks to the growth of welfare as well as socialist ideologies in the new states. People in affluent societies are growing less concerned about the old concept of liberty than about a love of material comfort and pleasure. The focus of the relationship between state and society has shifted from political liberty to economic prosperity and social justice. The state has expanded its political base through universal adult franchise. Administration has, therefore, of necessity penetrated into every aspect of civic life. The bulk of the citizens who are voters and beneficiaries of state services are more keen to get services supplied than on the subtle aspects of how they get them.[3] The position of the citizens from being mere recipients of administrative help and services has now shifted to their being the prime movers in the affairs of governance.

There are different ways in which citizens interact with the administrative agencies in day to day life. Mohit Bhattacharya illustrates five categories[4] of such interactions. These could be in the form of:

- *Clients*: In this form, citizens seek to obtain benefits or services from governmental agencies. For example, a patient visits a governmental hospital for a medical check or treatment.
- *Regulatees*: As a regulatee, the public interacts with many government agencies such as the police, income tax authorities, licensing authorities etc.
- *Litigants*: As litigants, the public moves the court against 'unjust' actions of public agencies. For example, people seek redress from the court when the motor vehicles authority may be delaying issuance of car licenses.
- *Participants*: In this form people become direct participants in decision making in public agencies at different levels. For example, parents become members of a school's guardians' committee or an irrigation project associates the farmers with the different decision-making processes of the project.
- *Cutting edge encounters*: In this form people approach agencies that are responsible for day today primary services and facilities to the public. For example, people approach the municipal employees for water, electricity, and sanitation facilities.
- *Protesters*: besides the above five, there could be another form of interaction – people as protesters. People often interact with government agencies on public policy as protesters, opposing the injustice in government policy and action. For example, people oppose the construction of a dam in their locality.

Thus, the citizens in day-to-day life constantly interact with the administration. The contact may be for varied purposes; for example, it may be for getting basic services such as water, electricity and health services or it may be for getting a driving license or income tax return from the income tax department. Sometimes people get an opportunity to directly participate in policy-making and implementation of a governmental agency or project. When people do not get services in time or are harassed by public authorities, they seek redress of their grievances from the court and when they do not see justice coming from any side they resort to protesting or criticizing the unjust policy and action of the government. Through these happy or unhappy interactions, citizens form opinions about public administration.

Citizens' perception about administration

Though, ideally speaking, the interaction between citizens and administration is supposed to be trustworthy and purposeful, in reality, it is observed that this is always plagued by conflicts, stresses and strains. Discontent among the citizens, which is due to the result of a wide disparity between the performance of administration and popular expectations, has become a normal feature. The general feeling that persists among the people is that the policies are cumbersome, or the processes of administration are found to be unjust. Yet another important problem is the deterioration in the standards of honesty and integrity in both politics and administration due to corruption. Rigid observance of rules and regulations, non-acknowledgement of complaints and the inordinate delay in the disposal of various matters account for the lack of faith of the public in administration.

Research findings on citizen–administration relations in India reveal interesting data, and information studies on 'Police Administration' by Davis H Bayley (1969), 'Rural Development' by Rakesh Hooja (1978) and 'Urban Government' by V Jagannadhan (1978) reveal citizens' perceptions about public administration in India. According to Mohit Bhattacharya, the general perceptions of the people about administration that emerge out of these studies include:

- unhelpful attitude of officials especially lower level functionaries
- inordinate delay and waiting period
- favouritism in administration
- need for middlemen (brokers) to get things done
- citizens' ignorance about procedures involved in getting things done
- rich–poor discrimination in administration: the rich having access to administration and the general tendency of officials to avoid the poor and underplay their needs and interests.[5]

A recent study by the Centre for Media Studies shows that a majority of citizens are not satisfied with the delivery of public services. In seven out of the eleven departments covered by the study, less than one-third of the citizens are satisfied with the services delivered. In fact, in most needs-based services, such as the police, judiciary and municipalities, (which enjoy a greater discretion and power), not even 20 per cent of the households are satisfied with the services. Even in essential services such as the PDS (food distribution system), hospitals, and electricity and water supplies, a mere 30–40 per cent of the households are happy with the services.[6]

Thus, administration in India is generally perceived to be unresponsive, insensitive and corrupt. W A Robson observes that

In mind of average citizen, bureaucracy still suffers from traditional defects associated with it. These are an excessive sense of self-importance on the part of officials or an undue idea of the importance of their office, an indifference towards the feelings of the convenience of the individual citizens, mania for regulations, formal procedures and a failure to recognize relations between the governors and the governed as an essential part of democratic process.[7]

The sixth central pay commission's (2008) comments in this connection are worth noting:

For the common man, bureaucracy denotes routine and repetitive procedures, paper work and delays. This, despite the fact that the Government and bureaucracy exist to facilitate the citizens in the rightful pursuit of their legal activities. Rigidities of the system over centralization of powers, highly hierarchical and top down method of functioning with a large number of intermediary levels delaying finalization of any decision, divorce of authority from accountability and the tendency towards micromanagement, have led to a structure in which form is more important than substance and procedures are valued over end results and outcomes. Non-performance of the administrative structures, poor service quality and lack of responsiveness, and the subjective and negative abuse of authority have eroded trust in governance systems which needs to be restored urgently.[8]

In its visits to the states, the second Administrative Reforms Commission (2009) had several occasions to meet and hear from the public and most of the observations by citizens were about the poor quality of services provided by the government, the indifferent attitude of government servants, corruption and abuse of authority and lack of accountability. A common complaint pertained to excessive red tape-ism and the long time taken to get even routine work done. The Commission, in its twelfth report, identifies the following five barriers to citizen-centric administration in India:

- wooden, inflexible, self-perpetuating and inward looking attitude of the civil servants
- lack of accountability of civil servants
- red tape-ism
- ineffective implementation of laws and rules
- low levels of awareness of the rights and duties of citizens.[9]

The reason for administration not being citizen-centric can be attributed to the attitude and work of some government servants, the deficiencies in existing institutional structures and also to the lack of awareness about rights and duties on the part of the citizens.

Pre-conditions for citizen-centric administration

The poor image of government in the minds of large sections points towards inefficient and ineffective administration. This highlights the need for substantially reforming our governance systems. The former Prime Minister Manmohan Singh in his civil services day speech (2007) observed:

> It is in this context that 'reform of government' becomes relevant. 'Administrative Reforms' is a phrase that has been used widely to mean many things. It is used by some to mean change of any kind to deal with government problems of any description. Some regard 'administrative reform' merely as a means of 'making the government work' better. Others in fact see 'reform' as 'less government'. I view the reform of government as a means of making citizens central to all government activities and concerns and reorganizing government to effectively address the concerns of the common people.[10]

An analysis of the barriers to citizen-centric administration reveals that there are several pre-conditions that must be fulfilled in order to make administration citizen-centric. Some of the preconditions are discussed below.

Accountability

Accountability is defined as the state of being accountable, liable or answerable. To be accountable means to be obliged to report, explain or justify something. It ensures that something is carried out as expected. Accountability is a key requirement of good administration. It means public servants must be accountable to the public. They are not only accountable to the questions asked by the people but also they have to respond to demands and provide services to the people.

Accessibility

A good administration has to be accessible to the people. If people have any problem, administrative officials should be ready to listen to them and accordingly respond to their problems. There has to be no fear in the mind of the people regarding the status and rigidity of the bureaucracy. It also requires that there should be no discrimination and the poor have easy access to the administration.

Transparency

Transparency is an essential pre-condition for good administration. It is the antonym of secrecy, which is the traditional hallmark of public administration. It implies that the governmental policies and functioning are known to the larger society. Transparency means that information is freely available to and directly accessible by those who will be affected by such decisions and their enforcement. It also means that enough information is in easily understandable forms. Transparency enables citizens to keep themselves informed about the policies of the government, the rights that they have and what they should expect as service from the government. Right to information and citizens' charters are means of ensuring transparency in administration.

Participatory

Promoting citizen-centric administration also implies giving a voice to citizens in the governance process. It means involvement of people in administrative activities, particularly the participation of the beneficiaries of the developmental activities, both at the formulation and implementation stages, for the success of programmes. People's participation is also an important safeguard against the abuse of administrative authority. It is a method of tapping human and material resources for development. Meaningful participation by citizens in governance can be promoted through *Panchayati Raj* institutions, *Bhagidari* programmes and involving citizen groups in certain aspects of governance.

Responsiveness

Responsive administration is an apparently moral concept in public administration in as much as it calls for the accountability of public functionaries directly to the people. It is a micro-level concept, deriving its credibility and validity from the delivery system of a country's public administration. By being responsive, governmental institutions gain 'legitimacy' in the public realm, which will automatically ensure their wider acceptance and, thus, effectiveness in governance. Responsive administration also entails a mechanism for redress of grievances.

Effectiveness and efficiency

Success of an administrative system also depends on the effective and efficient delivery of services to the people. Effectiveness is the extent to which an objective or goal is achieved. If an organization has successfully achieved its objectives, it is considered effective. Effectiveness is thus a matter of comparing results with intentions. Efficiency on the other hand refers to the process by which the organization maximizes its objectives with the minimum use of resources.

In addition to the above-mentioned necessary pre-conditions of citizen-centric administration, decentralization and delegation of policies, adoption of modern technology, process simplification and integrity of the civil service are other features and norms of successful administration. In this connection, the words of Dr S Radhakrishnan, the then Vice-President of India, are worth noting, on the occasion of the First Annual Day of the Indian Institute of Public Administration on 20 November 1959. He wanted administration to be fair to all manners of people and that the administrators must feel that they were not there merely to lord it over the people but 'they are essentially servants of the people'. He also stated that 'administrators are not to regard themselves as a privileged class. They are not to grow into a bureaucracy'. The higher civil servants, Dr Radhakrishnan said, 'must understand the needs and aspirations of the common man and woman and try to protect them from the petty officials who are inclined to harass them and show their authority'. Above all he said, 'it is my great anxiety that in this country we "should have administrative integrity first, efficiency next, economy third" – with these conditions we will be able to build a happier Indian Society'. He thus placed integrity in administration above all other requirements for better governance.[11]

People's participation in administration

People's participation in the administrative process is very basic to its success. It means the direct involvement of citizens in the process of administrative decision making, policy formulation and implementation. People's participation also means collective and continuous efforts by the people themselves in setting goals, pooling resources and taking action that aims at improving their living conditions. To William Morrow, the term 'citizen participation' means the direct participation of ordinary men and women, in contrast to public and private elites, in policy making. Furthermore, it is employed to focus on the direct participation of the underprivileged and unfranchised in decisions that affect their lives.[12]

Citizens' participation in governance embodies a shift in the development paradigm from citizens as the recipients of development to one that views them as active participants in the development process. Equally, it involves a shift from a 'top-down' to a 'bottom-up' approach to development, involving increasing decentralization of power away from the Union Government and closer to grassroots levels. The concept of citizens' participation in governance is essentially based on the premise that citizens have a legitimate role in influencing decision-making processes that affect their lives, their businesses and their communities. In other words, citizens' participation refers to the mechanism and modalities by which citizens can influence and take control over resources and decision making that directly impacts their lives. At the ideological level, direct citizens' participation in governance is seen as contributing to a healthy democracy, because it enhances and improves upon the traditional form of representative democracy to transform it into a more responsive and thus a more participative grassroots democracy. It is now widely accepted that active citizens' participation can contribute to good governance in the following ways:

- It enables citizens to make government accountable, more responsive, efficient and effective.
- It helps to make government programmes and services more effective and sustainable.

- It enables the poor and marginalized to influence public policy and service delivery to improve their lives.
- It helps the individual develop a sense of civic maturity; they become more educated, tolerant and compassionate, which finally helps in improving the quality of policy.
- It helps in recognizing that citizens have vital contributors to make to the betterment of public policy.
- It helps to promote healthy grassroots democracy.
- It promotes better understanding between government and the people.
- It keeps the governance transparent and thus deepens its propensity towards obedience.

Peoples' participation in administration is not free from barriers, one of them being the existence of widespread inertia in the larger society resulting in apathy and passivity. In addition, under the name of people's participation, what may happen is a situation which William Morrow calls 'abdication', 'pacification', 'co-operation' and 'client-building'. Citizens' participation does not necessarily lead to the leaders representing their constituencies. Rather, they strike a tie-up with the local bureaucracy, which may silence them. The representatives, when interfacing with the bureaucrats represent their individual interest, not their constituencies' cause. It has also been observed that citizens' participation, when not prudently directed, may add to unnecessary delay in decision making and implementation, and finally increase red tape.[13]

The fact that participatory efforts are occasionally perverted does not mean that the perversions make the participatory movement meaningless to its original purposes. Citizens' participation demands certain preconditions, which have been laid with a view to making citizens' participation more effective. These are: enlightened political leader; citizens should be knowledgeable and competent; conscientious civil servants; informed and co-operative general public; information required for taking decisions should be clear and precise; well-organized communication network; both authority and citizens must demonstrate willingness to take responsibility; a practical survey of the environment should be made; and participation at all levels – both rural and urban – is necessary for public participation.[14]

Bhagidari and Panchayati Raj as instruments for ethics in governance

Participatory governance is a guarantee of less corruption in public administration; it creates conditions for the administration to become transparent in its true sense. As is shown in history, community-based governance is perhaps one of the best mechanisms to ensure ethics in public administration. In India, efforts have constantly been made to appreciate community involvement in decision making. Of all the nationalist activists who fought for participatory governance, Gandhi was the most prominent; his ideas and arguments were constitutionally endorsed with the acceptance of the Seventy-Third and Seventy-Fourth Amendment Acts in 1992. What is fundamental in these Acts is the insistence on localizing governance with the involvement of the communities. Instead of appreciating governance by a panoptical bureaucracy, the idea of localizing governance underlines the endeavour towards involving the stakeholders in deciding what is most appropriate for their quality survival in the area to which they belong.

Bhagidari and *Panchayati Raj* governance are illustrative of the shift of the locus of governance to the community that generally remains 'peripheral' in the traditional Weberian conceptualization of hierarchical public administration. One can thus safely argue that participatory governance is the outcome of the deepening of democracy in India that is being articulated by peoples' participation not only in the decision-making process, but also in building a meaningful channel of communication between the government and governed. The process may not be very smooth because it is not easy for traditional governmental authorities to willingly abdicate power. One of the factors that brought about a change in 'the rather status quoist mindset' is perhaps the growing strength of 'the community' in the context of movements for democratization all over the world – a trend that is visible in *Bhagidari* and *Panchayati Raj* governance in India. These two forms of local governance are thus powerful ideas of not only rewriting the history of governance, but also of reinventing the theoretical tools by meaningfully articulating the role of the community in public governance, overcoming all conceivable barriers.

In that sense, despite being localized, these instances have global repercussions in two significant ways: first, these examples are articulations of local experiences in which community and communicative dialogues become effective instruments of noticeable changes at the grassroots. Given the serious conceptual implications of such organically evolved forms of governance, it can be argued that community-driven governance is a powerful alternative, especially when the top-down model of public administration no longer remains as viable as it was in 'the age of hierarchy, when only those at the top of the pyramid had enough information to make informed decision'.[15] Second, this comparative study also confirms that the Gandhian notion of self-governing village republics is not at all utopian, but a practical design for participatory governance. Being self-reliant and capable of managing their own affairs, the village republics remain, as Gandhi endorsed, the nurseries of civic virtues and are important institutional resources for their continuity.

Conceptually, the idea of the village republic as a clear break with conventional hierarchical governance also has its resonance in the writings of classical liberals such as Rousseau, J S Mill and Henry Maine, among others. All of them converged on the point that the participatory governance that the village republic sought to execute was a powerful deterrent against authoritarianism. Along with obvious theoretical inputs which will help us understand comparable instances of organically linked forms of local governance, this comparative study provides an evidence-backed instance showing how organic participation creates an enabling environment within which social entrepreneurs can spark participatory innovations, the most effective of which can have important lessons for scaled-up interventions. Seeking to understand the critical interconnection between policies and institutions, this extensive comparative study provides meaningful cues to understand the processes of responsive governance as powerful incentives for collective involvement in activities for communal well-being. In other words, although the Indian example is distinctly textured, it has clear transcendental implications simply because it is rooted in a specific socio-economic and political context, the parallel of which is available elsewhere in the globe. In this sense, it is spatial but global in its theoretical implications.

Administrative accountability

Accountability is an essential feature of all forms of democratic governments. The concept of accountability refers to the liability of government servants to give a satisfactory account of the use of official power or discretionary authority to the people. This is considered as an effective safeguard against the misuse of power and abuse of public authority. The notion of accountability carries two basic connotations: answerability, which stands for the obligation of public officials to inform about and explain what they are doing, and enforcement, i.e., the capacity of accounting agencies to impose sanctions on power holders who have violated their public duties. The substance of accountability according to Mohit Bhattacharya places at least four requirements on public administrators.[16]

- make laws work as intended with a minimum of waste and delay
- exercise lawful and sensible administrative discretion
- recommend new policies and propose changes in existing policies and programs as needed, and
- enhance citizen confidence in the administrative institutions.

Administrative accountability in India

Administrative accountability in India is enforced by means of various controls. The purpose of control is to ensure that the public servants exercise their powers and discretion in accordance with laws and regulations. Broadly speaking, there are two types of administrative control; namely, internal and external control. The internal control operates from within the administrative machinery. The techniques of internal control are: budgetary system, hierarchical order, enquiries and investigations, pressure groups, press, and annual confidential reports. The external accountability over administration in India is maintained through legislative, executive and judicial control.

The administration is made responsible to elected representatives because in a democracy the people are supreme. Thus the legislature has been given certain powers through the constitution and through conventions so that it is able to keep an effective check upon malpractice and abuse of authority by the administration. The legislature applies a number of methods for controlling the administration, namely, asking questions during question hour, parliamentary discussions, parliamentary audit, no-confidence motions and complaints to the ombudsman. Executive control over the administration is another potent instrument in responsible government. The executive exercises control over the administration through a number of means and techniques, such as the power of appointment and removal, a rule making power, ordinances etc., civil service code, delegated legislation, budgetary system and making appeals to public opinion. Another important instrument through which administrative accountability is ensured is judicial control, which may take the shape of judicial review, statutory appeal to the courts and writs against the government. The primary objective of judicial control over the administration is the protection of the rights and liberties of citizens by ensuring the legality of administrative acts.[17]

Governance and the changing notion of accountability

The accountability question needs to be seen against the background of the paradigm shift that has taken place in public administration. In the practical world of public administration today, two closely competing but contemporary paradigms seem to hold sway: one is 'new public management' and the other is known as 'good governance'. Historically, as we have already discussed, the liberal democratic set-up evolved basic mechanisms of accountability such as ministerial control, parliamentary debate, legislative committees, and the ombudsman system. In recent times there have been some major changes – a sort of paradigmatic shift – in the mode of public governance under the rubric of 'new public management', and good governance.

In contemporary public administration, what is being advocated is a market-centred, neo-liberal approach to governance under which its objectives are shifted to economic growth and productivity and its normative standards are redirected toward efficiency, competition, profit and value for money. This is a radical departure from the traditional norms and objectives of governance enhancing human progress, removing poverty and unemployment, safeguarding citizens' rights and guaranteeing justice and fairness. There has thus emerged a unique set of challenges to the realization of accountability in the current phase of public administrative changes everywhere. According to Haque, the contemporary changes in governance – towards efficiency, outcome, competition, value for money, and customer orientation – pose formidable political, managerial and methodological challenges to accountability in terms of three specific dimensions:

- the standards of accountability (accountability for what)
- the agents of accountability (accountability to whom)
- the means of accountability (how is accountability ensured).[18]

So far as standards of accountability are concerned, these have, under the current mode of governance, become instrumental in nature, placing emphasis more on procedural and economic criteria such as efficiency and productivity than on substantive concerns like equality and representation. In other words, the accountability of public governance for market-based economic performance does not connote its accountability for welfare and justice. Second, under the new dispensation, public governance is accountable for the effective delivery of its services to customers who can pay, while it may remain indifferent towards low-income or poor citizens who are not in a position to use such services due to their financial incapacity. Accountability under this consumerist mode of governance is to the private affluent customer rather than to the collective public, and, as a consequence, the economically underprivileged citizens, who often depend on the state for basic services, do not qualify as customers since they are not able to afford user charges. So, the customer-view tends to diminish citizens' rights vis-à-vis the state and excludes common citizens from the equation of public accountability. The third dimension – the means of accountability – has been under challenge in the context of neo-liberal mode of governance. Recent policy to do away with the permanent tenure of civil servants and introduce contract-based appointments makes public servants more vulnerable to political executives exercising control over job contracts and careers; ministerial control as a means of accountability makes public servants extremely loyal to ministers, ignoring their accountability to the common people.

Thus, the issue of accountability in the context of the World Bank strategy of governance reveals the extent to which this idea is linked with the developed world. The primary concern here is to do away with 'dysfunctional and ineffective public institutions – broadly defined to include all institutions that shape the way public functions are carried out – (that) are seen to be at the heart of the economic developmental challenge'.[19] In a nutshell, accountability of administration has shifted from the common people to the customers who can afford user charges.

Machinery for redress of public grievances

According to the Chambers Dictionary, grievance means 'a ground of complaint, a condition felt to be oppressive or wrongful'. A grievance may arise out of non-fulfilment of certain demands and expectations. Demands may be related to policies of the government or to the performance of the administration in the implementation of policies framed by the government. A grievance is thus any sort of dissatisfaction that needs to be redressed. Some of the common grievances against the administration may be delineated in the following groups:

- corruption: demand and acceptance of bribery for doing or not doing things
- favouritism: doing or not doing things for obliging people in power or people who matter
- nepotism: helping the people of one's own kith or kin
- discourtesy: use of abusive language or other types of misbehaviour
- neglect of duty: not doing things that the law requires

- discrimination: ignoring poor and uninfluential citizens' genuine complaints
- delay: not doing things at the appropriate time
- maladministration: inefficiency in achieving the targets
- inadequate redress machinery: failure to attend to public complaints against administration.[20]

The basic principle of a grievance redress system is that, if the promised level of service delivery is not achieved, the citizen should have the right to recourse to a mechanism for redress. This mechanism should be well publicized, easy to use, and prompt and, above all, citizens must have faith that they will get justice from it.

Grievance redress mechanism in India

The Government of India, State governments as well as various organizations under them have set up grievance redress mechanisms to look into the complaints of citizens. At the national level, there are primarily two designated nodal agencies in the Union Government handling these grievances:

- Department of Administrative reforms and Public Grievances, Ministry of Personnel, Public Grievances and Pensions.
- Directorate of Public Grievances, Cabinet Secretariat.

Besides these nodal agencies, there are other institutional mechanisms, such as the central vigilance commission and the Lokayuktas, that have the mandate to look into complaints of corruption and abuse of office by public servants. Many organizations, for example, the Reserve Bank of India, have set up ombudsmen to look into grievances. Institutions such as the National and State Human Rights Commissions, National and State Women's Commission, the National Commission for Scheduled Castes and the National Commission for Scheduled Tribes also look into the complaints from the public in their prescribed areas. Today, with the increased awareness levels, the aspirations of citizen have gone up as have also the demand for prompt and effective resolution of their grievances. The role of some of the important institutions and other initiatives for redress of public grievance in India are discussed below.

The Central Vigilance Commission

On the basis of recommendations made by the Committee on Prevention of Corruption, popularly known as the Santhanam Committee, the Central Vigilance Commission was set up by the Government of India in 1964. The Commission advises the Union Government on all matters pertaining to the maintenance of integrity in administration. It exercises superintendence over the working of the Central Bureau of Investigation – the principal investigating agency of the Union Government in anti-corruption matters – and also over the vigilance administration of various ministries and other organizations of the Union Government.

Lokpal and Lokayukta

The first Administrative Reforms Commission had recommended the setting up of the *Lokpal*. The *Lokpal* Bill has been introduced several times in Parliament, but due to various reasons it has not been enacted into law. The *Lokpal* is supposed to be a watchdog over the integrity of ministers and members of parliament. The *Lokpal* Bill provides for the constitution of the *Lokpal* as an independent body to enquire into cases of corruption against public functionaries, with a mechanism for filing complaints and conducting enquiries, etc.

After the recommendations of the first Administrative Reforms Commission, many States have constituted '*Lokayuktas*' to investigate allegations or grievances arising out of the conduct of public servants, including political executives, legislators, officers of the State government, local bodies, public enterprises and other instruments of government. A member of the public can file specific allegations with the *Lokayukta* against any public servant for enquiry. The *Lokayukta* can also initiate *suo-moto* enquiry into the conduct of public servants.

E-governance

In the context of globalization, the recent conceptualization of E-governance or digital governance is of significance in public administration. Drawing on the latest information and communication technology (ICT), the aim of e-governance is to open up government processes and enable greater public access to information. Both digital and e-governance are of recent origin and there is not yet a universally acceptable definition. Digital/e-governance refers to the use of emerging ICT, such as the internet, web pages and mobile phones, to deliver information and services to citizens. It can include publication of information about government services on websites and citizens downloading application forms for these services. It can also deliver services digitally, such as the filling out of a tax form, renewal of licenses and processing of on-line payments. The purpose of digital government is to create 'super counters in [the government departments] and eliminate the endless maze citizens have to negotiate in going from door to door, floor to floor to obtain services'.[21] Appropriate use of various means of ICT will usher in a new era in public administration by seeking to make governmental functioning more transparent and accessible. Thus, e-governance through a technological innovation has 'changed the basic character of governance – its operational methodology, functional style, ideological orientation, even the spirit, heart and soul'.[22]

E-revolution in ICT has the potential to elevate the governance process to new levels. ICT facilitates efficient storing and retrieval of data, instantaneous transmission of information, processing information and data faster than the earlier manual systems, speeding up governmental processes, taking decisions expeditiously and judiciously, increasing transparency and enforcing accountability. It also helps in increasing the reach of government – both geographically and demographically. Recognizing the increasing importance of electronics, the Government of India established the Department of Electronics in 1970. In India, digital governance was legalized by the *Information Techno-logy Act* of 2000. The Act provides legal recognition for transactions carried out by means of electronic data interchange and other means of electronic communication, commonly referred to as 'electronic commerce which involves use of alternatives to paper-based methods of communication and storage of information to facilitate electronic filing of documents with the government agencies'.[23] Defining electronic form as 'any information generated, sent, received or stored in media, magnetic, optical, computer memory, microfilm, computer-generated micro-fiche or similar device', the Act accords legal sanction to devices which involve:

> (a) the filing of any form, application or any other document with any office, authority, body or agency, owned or controlled by appropriate government in a particular manner; (b) the issue or grant of any license, permit, sanction or approval by whatever name called in a particular manner, and (c) the receipt or payment of money in a particular manner.[24]

Legally endorsed, this Act is a powerful aid to ascertain ethics in governance because e-governance is certainly an attack on bureaucratic red tape-ism that causes unnecessary delay and corruption. It is a tool for achieving transparent governance that will also be user-friendly. The ultimate goal is to bring about better governance, termed as simple, moral, accountable, responsive and transparent (SMART),[25] and to create space for the regular involvement of citizens who, as customers of public services, have no direct access to governmental activities through ICT. With this aid, the citizens can not only view on-line governmental acts, they can also provide significant inputs through emails and other electronic devices. Technology is, thus, an important tool for integrating citizens' inputs and transparency into one model. The ICT-based e-governance has ushered in a new era in government innovations with capacities to (a) reduce the cost of government, (b) increase citizens' input into government, (c) improve public decision making by receiving inputs from the wider sections of the population, and (d) increase the transparency of government transactions. The object of e-governance is 'to arm the citizens to act as watchdogs of the government'.[26] In view of these useful (and also well-defined) functional characteristics, e-governance is also a very meaningful step towards combating corruption. By reducing discretionary powers, it curbs opportunities for arbitrary action. E-governance also empowers citizens by making their intervention in the transactions of government business regular through ICT.[27] The project – e-Sewa – that began in West Godavari district in former Andhra Pradesh, India, is illustrative here. The project is a tool to 'bridge the digital divide in the rural areas', through extensive use of information technology 'for providing access to various citizen to citizen (C2C) and citizen to government (C2G) services to people in rural areas'. Managed by women's self-help groups, the project is a class by itself as it enables 'the local women-participants' to emerge as 'information leaders' who remain critical in realizing the goal of e-Sewa.[28]

Computerized grievance redress mechanisms

A computerized public grievances redress and monitoring system developed by the Department of Administrative Reforms and Public Grievances in collaboration with the National Informatics Centre was installed in the Department on 5 September 2001. All the grievances received are entered in this system and processed. The internet version of this software was launched on 31 May 2002. It allows the citizen to lodge and monitor the progress of his/her grievance on the internet. A comprehensive website of citizens' charters in the Government of India was also launched on the same day.

Citizens' charters

The citizens' charter is an instrument that seeks to make an organization transparent, accountable and citizen friendly. The citizens' charter scheme in its present form was first launched in 1991 in the UK. The aim was to ensure that public servants were made responsive to the citizens they serve. A citizens' charter is basically a set of commitments made by an organization regarding the standards of service that it delivers. A citizens' charter is a public statement that defines the entitlements of citizens to a specific service, the standards of the service, the conditions to be met by users, and the remedies available to the latter in case of non-compliance with the standards. The charter empowers the citizens to demand the standards of service that were committed to. Thus, the basic thrust of citizens' charters is to make public services citizen-centric by ensuring that these services are demand driven rather than supply driven. In this context, the six principles of the citizens' charter movement as originally framed were:

- quality – improving the quality of services
- choice – for the users wherever possible
- standards – specifying what to expect within a time frame
- value – for the taxpayers' money
- accountability – of the service provider (individual as well as Organization)
- transparency – in rules, procedures, schemes and grievance redress.[29]

The citizens' charter, when introduced in the early 1990s, represented a landmark shift in the delivery of public services. The emphasis of the citizens' charter is on citizens as customers of public services. So far 111 central ministries/departments/organizations have formulated charters in India.

Right to information

Right to Information means the freedom of people to have access to government information. It implies that the citizens should have free access to all files and documents pertaining to the government's working process. Right to information has been seen as the key to strengthening participatory democracy and ushering in people-centred governance, as access to information can empower the citizens to demand and get information about public policies and actions, thereby leading to their welfare. Transparency in government organizations makes them function more objectively, predictably and also enables citizens to participate in the governance process effectively. In a fundamental sense, right to information is a basic aid to ascertain ethics in governance.

The story of the campaign for transparency in governance cannot begin without the role that the Rajasthan-based Mazdoor Kisan Shakti Sangathan (MKSS) played in its fruition. They, with their relentless drive for the cause, 'raised the [demand for right to information] in such a compelling manner that it changed the course on what had been seen for many years largely as an academic issue'.[30] What had begun in Rajasthan soon developed into a national movement for transparency with the formation of the National Campaign for People's Right to Information in 1996, which was instrumental in spreading the campaign throughout the country. The result was the adoption of the *Right to Information Act* (RTI) in 2005 which, as its preamble suggests, provides for 'setting out the practical regime of right to information for citizens to secure access to information under the control of public authorities, in order to promote transparency and accountability in the working of every public authority'.[31] It is also believed that the Right to Information is complementary to democracy that 'requires an informed citizenry and transparency of information which are vital to its functioning and also to contain corruption and to hold Governments and their instrumentalities accountable to the governed'.[32] This was reiterated by the Prime Minister of India who, while piloting the bill, forcefully argued that:

> the Bill will see the dawn of a new era in our processes of governance, an era of performance and efficiency, an era which will ensure that benefits of growth flow to all sections of our people, an era which will eliminate the scourge of corruption, an era which will bring the common man's concern to the heart of all processes of governance, an era which will truly fulfill the hopes of the founding fathers of our Republic.[33]

As articulated in the Act, the main objectives are: (a) greater transparency in functioning of public authorities, (b) improvement in accountability and performance of the government, (c) promotion of partnership between citizens and government in decision-making processes, and (d) reduction of corruption in government departments. In an environment of declining ethics in public life, the aim and mission of the RTI Act remain most revolutionary.

The Act provides for the proactive disclosure of information, the establishment of the Information Commission, the appointment of public information officers, procedures for getting information, etc. It is groundbreaking legislation empowering people and promoting transparency.

Replacing the 1923 *Official Secrets Act*, the RTI Act is also an enabling provision for citizens to challenge the culture of secrecy in public administration. As an expert laments,

> the culture of secrecy beginning from the colonial rule till the first six decades of independence fueled rampant corruption, in which large amount of public money was diverted from development projects and welfare schemes to private use through misuse of power by authorities. Lack of openness in the functioning of the government, provided a fertile ground for breeding inefficiency and lack of accountability in the working of the public authorities.[34]

In the light of the secrecy that had shrouded public governance in the past, the RTI Act is not only a refreshing mechanism, but also 'a potent weapon to fight against corruption, arbitrariness and misuse of power'.[35] What is basic to the Act is the institutional guarantee of openness in the functioning of the government. As proactive citizens, people can now maintain a constant vigil over what is being undertaken as public governance; by being participants in governance, they also perform their role in such a way as to make democracy not merely a structure of governance but integrally connected with their being. So, the RTI Act sets in motion processes whereby the core values of democracy are also realized. In that respect, the scope of this groundbreaking legislation is much wider, compared with other laws which are meant to articulate government functioning in accordance with specific ideological inclinations, since it also contributes to the creation of an environment in which citizens remain active partners in shaping governance, following what they consider appropriate for their well-being. Hence the RTI Act was hailed as perhaps one of the most revolutionary pieces of legislation in independent India. It was reiterated by the Second Administrative Reforms Commission, which, while underlining the seminal contribution of the RTI Act in strengthening the ethical roots of governance in India, emphatically declared that:

> the Right to Information law of 2005 signals a radical shift in our governance culture and permanently impacts all agencies of state. The effective implementation of this law depends on three fundamental shifts: from the prevailing culture of secrecy to a new culture of openness; from personalized despotism to authority coupled with accountability; and from unilateral decision making to participative governance.[36]

In two interrelated ways, the RTI Act seems to have unleashed significant processes curbing tendencies towards demeaning the institutional sanctity of governance. It has, on the one hand, reinforced the importance of the institutions holding public authority, which appeared to have been appropriated and unchallenged in the past by strong and well-entrenched vested interests. This has become possible, on the other hand, because of the consolidation of a proactive citizenry that holds their democratic rights not for mere seasonal exercises in elections, but as instruments for improvement in their daily struggle for existence. The scene has undoubtedly undergone a sea change: ethics in governance is no longer a mere descriptive category, but one that is inspirational and rejuvenating for those seeking to reinvent governance as an empowering design regardless of one's social and economic location and political views and predilections. Change is visible and governance seems to have become a level playing field, unlike in the past when it was appropriated for personal gain. The task is far from complete, as the Second Administrative Reforms Commission warns, despite the fact that this law

> provides us [with] a priceless opportunity to redesign the processes of governance, particularly at the grassroots level where the citizens' interface is maximum,… a lot more needs to be done to usher in accountability in governance, including protection of whistle blowers, decentralization of power and fusion of authority at all levels.[37]

It is common knowledge that there is hardly a magic wand to make an administration ethical by eradicating corruption overnight. And thus, a mere institutional guarantee can never be adequate to instil ethics in governance, which is the outcome of long-drawn-out processes. Nonetheless, the 2005 RTI Act is both a powerful legislative design and an effective legal means to support citizens' efforts towards seeking to build a system of governance that is averse to being used for private gains.

Role of voluntary agencies

Voluntary agencies are critical in India's development, primarily since their role rests in translating citizens' initiatives into achievable goals. By forcing the state to be sensitive to its obligations to the community, they also become an important instrument for ethics in governance. In brief, voluntary agencies have the twin goals of laying out and also fulfilling community-specific developmental plans and programmes, and, in so doing, they also contribute to the creation of an environment in which the state cannot but be attentive to what citizens demand for their well-being. In India, they became integral to the planning processes from the adoption of the First Five Year Plan in 1951, although their role was formally recognized only in the Third Five Year Plan (1961–6). This categorically stated that voluntary agencies are immensely important since

> properly organized voluntary efforts may go a long way towards augmenting the facilities available to the community or helping the weakest and the most needy to a somewhat better life. The wherewithal for this has to come from the time, energy and other sources of millions of people for whom

voluntary organizations can find constructive channels suited through varying conditions in the country.[38]

What was unique in the above assumption was the shift in the policy direction. Not only is the importance of voluntary organizations highlighted but that they are crucial in helping those at the periphery has also been underlined. This was further reiterated by the 1966 Rural–Urban Relationship Committee that laid emphasis on the role of voluntary agencies in mobilizing community support for local developmental activities. As its report unequivocally suggests,

> local voluntary organizations can be very helpful in mobilizing popular support and assistance of the people in the activities of local body. It is possible to maintain constant and close contact with the people through these organizations. The formation of a network of local organizations, like neighbourhood and *Mohalla* (localities) committees and citizens' forums, would be useful in mobilizing public participation.[39]

As the above report reiterates, their contribution was recognized in attaining the developmental goals of the Indian state, especially in rural areas where it had clearly failed to emerge as an agency for inclusive development. What was just an idea was amply illustrated in the Seventh Plan (1985–90) by stating that voluntary associations constituted an important source for development planning in India. The Seventh Plan took a major initiative in articulating an idea that was mooted in the Third Plan. Hence it has been argued that it took three decades 'to legitimize this role of voluntary agencies ... [in] making people aware of the alternatives means – other than the monopolistic delivery system of the government – of fulfilling their aspiration-driven goals and missions'.[40]

By formally recognizing the role of voluntary agencies in the development process, the Seventh Plan upheld the view that there were alternative ways of development, hitherto untapped, in which people's participation was crucial. Conceptually, this was a radical change: the state was just an actor in the gigantic processes of development and its success was contingent on the cooperation rendered by other actors involved in fulfilling the developmental aims of the state. What was most refreshing in this endeavour was to tap the indigenous initiatives and to translate them into concrete plans and programmes that were tuned to the villagers' needs.

A brief scan of the role of voluntary agencies reveals that their contribution is significant in identifying the limitations of the state-centric development that tends to ignore India's diversity as a socio-economic unit. Not only do they assist the state in realizing its developmental goals, they also contribute to their planning and implementation by devising ways and means that are appropriate for those at the receiving end. Their role is increasingly being recognized, because voluntary agencies have the special advantage of knowing the local conditions, which will help them, plan better. Their contribution in making people aware of what the state has devised for them has also been appreciated.[41] This is a clear shift in policy perspective. That both the state and voluntary agencies draw on each other strikes a new balance in contemporary development strategies. The past patron–client network seems to have been replaced by a new design of development in which the role of proactive citizens has become far more critical than the government bureaucracy in framing and also executing developmental schemes.

By being proactive partners in the processes of development, voluntary agencies are also important agents of ethics in governance in three interrelated ways: first, given the failure of the panoptical state to capture public interest at the grassroots, especially in a diverse socio-economic context, voluntary agencies provide powerful inputs while framing situation-specific and needs-based policy options. With their growing involvement in grassroots socio-political activities, they truly represent public interests, which would have been less significant to those making decisions had their input been absent. Second, the role of voluntary agencies remains critical in forcing the Indian state to fulfil its constitutional obligations to the citizen. That the state cannot be discriminatory would have remained an elusive constitutional principles if the voluntary agencies had not played their role effectively to highlight the cardinal principle of equality, regardless of one's socio-economic location and ideological predilections; they further provide a voice to those at the periphery of the processes of development if their constitutional rights are infringed. By making the hapless majority especially in rural India aware of their constitutional entitlements as citizens of the country, they helped translate the intent of the founding fathers into concrete designs fulfilling their aspirations. Third, despite being integrally connected with governance, voluntary agencies unleash processes whereby people get connected with endeavours seeking to realize their aspired goal; they, in other words, act as a bridge between citizens and public administration while discharging their role as a conscience keeper. This is a critical role, especially in the context of the emergence of the devastating democratic deficit all over the globe. It is alarming that, in many democratic systems, the form seems to have prevailed over the substance of democracy and the meaningful interface between citizens and the elected representatives holding political authority is minimal between elections. The very presence of voluntary agencies in governance, more particularly in rural areas, has made a critical difference: democracy is thus now translated not merely as an occasional participation in the electoral processes, but as a tool of empowerment and an avenue of translating one's heart-felt desires into reality. By directing popular zeal for participatory governance, voluntary agencies thus not only reinvent public administration by making citizens its core, but also re-establish the importance of ethical values in public life by challenging the tendencies responsible for creating democratic deficits.

Concluding observations

It may be concluded that the position of the citizens, from being mere recipients of administrative help and services, has now shifted to their being the prime movers in the affairs of governance; there has taken place a change from local beneficiary status to active 'participant status'. This is most critical in governance in a democracy. The aim is to create an accountable, accessible, transparent, participative and responsive administration for citizens' well-being. By being sensitive to what the citizens demand for the fulfilment of their democratic rights, contemporary governance seems to have reinvented its core principles which no longer remained glued exclusively to the Weberian notion of hierarchical administration leaving, at least conceptually, no space for external accountability. Governance is thus not merely instrumental, but has evolved as an effective mechanism to create an environment in which citizens are not merely recipients, but instigators of change. Instead of being reactive, public administration has become proactive, with citizens remaining perhaps the most important component. In two fundamental ways, such a conceptualization of governance is innovative: on the one hand, governance does not merely mean execution of policy decisions, which was the case in the past; it also refers, on the other hand, to processes whereby citizens' responses are translated into policy decisions. What is fundamental here is the idea of the citizen being preeminent in public administration.

In a similar vein, the idea of ethics in governance is re-conceptualized differently. In the past conceptualization of public governance, ethics in governance is usually articulated as being grounded within the conceptual boundaries of public administration and the institutions were considered to be most critical. What was unethical was always couched in institutional terms, which were always respected and zealously nurtured as sacrosanct. The primacy of institutional control was never questioned. Drawing on the Weberian notion of internal accountability, that remained most critical in so far as India's administration was concerned. It was a perfect mechanism, since Indian administration had hardly changed, at least in the structural–functional sense, from its colonial counterpart, except perhaps the fact that, instead of serving the colonial masters, it became an instrument for serving the Indian. Nonetheless, when it concerned ethics in governance, it remained committed to the Weberian conceptualization of internal accountability that was so assiduously upheld by the erstwhile colonial rulers.

In contrast with the past, there have been changes in the conceptualization of ethics in public administration. Administrative accountability is being reinvented in the light of the changing texture of governance, in which the role of citizens is as significant as those running the machine in accordance with well-defined rules and regulations governing its functioning. Citizens no longer remain mere recipients; they become active partners in framing policies for their well-being. For them, participatory democracy is not a mere descriptive category, but an empowering idea of connecting them with the actual articulation of public administration. Ethics has gained a wider connotation: an administrative action shall cease to be ethical if it violates citizens' constitutionally guaranteed rights. What is ethical is now determined by criteria that may not have been devised internally, but by those who are affected by specific administrative act.

Public administration is now a changed entity. In order to ascertain ethics in governance, the pyramidal structure of administration that is clearly top-down in character has undergone a sea change, because citizens have become active partners; it has become citizen-centric. There are two specific ways, as shown above, in which public administration is now less Weberian. On the one hand, changes in governance are attributed to civil society activism, which is essentially an outside influence. This has not been new, since politico-ideological movements were always an important source of change in Indian administration. As is evident, the British administration was forced to change some of its draconian laws, which were definitely unethical, in response to the campaign that the nationalists had launched. The trend continued in independent India. One of the important interventions happens to be the adoption of the RTI Act in 2005 following the decades-long ideological campaign for transparency in administration. The change is also visible within the administration. For instance, citizens' charters identifying the administrative obligations to the citizens are a powerful internal mechanism to translate ethics in governance into an achievable goal. Likewise, e-governance is another powerful aid to complement the endeavour towards making public governance transparent, ethical and really public in substance and spirit.

Citizens' involvement in governance is a powerful aid for administrative transparency. This is being encouraged both globally and nationally. With the consolidation of a proactive citizenry in India reflecting perhaps concern for transparency in administration, the Weberian rigid and hierarchical conceptualization of bureaucracy does not seem to be a useful analytical tool to comprehend the changed texture of public authority, especially in democratic systems. The impact is too commanding to be ignored so easily. Change is visible, and Weberian rigidity does not seem to be useful. It is, in fact, being described as an impediment to making public administration a citizen-centric endeavour. In that respect, the idea that citizens are immensely significant in conceptualizing public administration remains most critical in reformulating the fundamental theoretical premises in the discipline. So, this chapter, by highlighting the importance of citizens in governance, is thus illustrative of the changes in the texture of administration that needs to be understood against a different theoretical backdrop in which citizens remain the core of public administration. What is significant here, in other words, is the assumption that, by being proactive, citizens have become integral to the decision-making processes that now cannot be hijacked so easily since a transparent and ethically tuned administration makes public administration truly public in the true sense of the term.

Notes

1 Luc Rouban (ed.), *Citizens and The New Governance*, IOS Press, Amsterdam, 1999.
2 A V Dicey, *Lectures on Relation between Law and Public Opinion in England during the Nineteenth Century*, London, Macmillan, 1948 (2nd edition).
3 U C Agarwal (ed.), *Public Administration: visions and reality*, Indian Institute of Public Administration, New Delhi, 2004, p. 270.

4 Mohit Bhattacharya, *New Horizons of Public Administration*, Jawahar publishers and distributors, New Delhi, 2008, pp. 248–9.
5 Ibid., p. 257.
6 Second Administrative Reforms Commission, *Twelfth Report on Citizen Centric Administration: the heart of governance*, Government of India, February 2009, p. 12.
7 W A Robson, *The Governors and the Governed*, George Allen and Unwin, London, 1964, p. 18.
8 *Report of the Sixth Central Pay Commission*, Government of India, New Delhi, March 2008, p. 365.
9 Second Administrative Reforms Commission, *Twelfth Report on Citizen Centric Administration: the heart of governance*, Government of India, February 2009, pp. 14–16.
10 Ibid., p. 17.
11 U C Agarwal (ed.), *Public Administration: visions and reality*, Indian Institute of Public Administration, New Delhi, pp. III–IV.
12 William L. Morrow, *Public Administration: politics and the political system*, Random House, New York, 1980, p. 190.
13 *State, Society and Public Administration* (MPA-011), IGNOU, New Delhi, 2005, p. 136.
14 A Avasthi and S Maheswari, *Public Administration*, Lakshmi Narain Agarwal, Agra, 2010, p. 643.
15 David Osborne and Ted Gaebler, Reinventing Government: how the entrepreneurial spirit is transforming the public sector, Prentice Hall of India, New Delhi, 1992, p. 15.
16 Mohit Bhattacharya, *New Horizons of Public Administration*, Jawahar publishers and distributors, New Delhi, 2008.
17 Amita Singh, *Public Administration: roots and wings*, Galgotia Publishing, New Delhi, 2002, pp. 216–17.
18 M. Shamsul Haque, 'Significance of accountability under the new approach to public governance', quoted in in Bidyut Chakrabarty, *Reinventing Public Administration: the Indians experience*, Orient Longman, New Delhi, 2007, p. 131.
19 'Reforming public institutions and strengthening governance: main strategy, a World Bank Strategy' quoted in Bidyut Chakrabarty, *Reinventing Public Administration: the Indians Experience*, Orient Longman, New Delhi, 2007, pp. 133–4.
20 *Citizen and Administration*, EPA-02, Indian Administration, IGNOU, p. 13.
21 Jagdish C Kapoor, 'IT and good governance', *Indian Journal of Public Administration*, XLVI (3), July–September 2000, p. 394.
22 Bata K Dey, 'E-governance in India: problems, challenges and opportunities – a future vision', *Indian Journal of Public Administration*, XLVI (3), July–September 2000, p. 306.
23 Government of India, *The Information Technology Act, 2000*, Government of India, New Delhi, 2000, chapters I, p. 2. The Act is reproduced in the *Indian Journal of Public Administration*, XLVI (3), July–September 2000, pp. 417–55.
24 Ibid., p. 10.
25 Government of India, *The Tenth Five Year Plan*, approach paper, Government of India, New Delhi, 2000, p. 187.
26 Sameer Sachdeva, 'White paper on e-governance strategy in India', World Bank, Washington DC, December 2003 (unpublished), p. 5.
27 Subhas Bhatnagar pursues this argument in detail in his 'Administrative corruption: how does e-government help?' *Global Corruption Report*, 2003, Transparency International, New York, 2003, pp. 8–9.
28 I owe this point to Mr Sanjay Jaju, an Indian Administrative Service officer working as Vice Chairman and Managing Director, Infrastructure Corporation of former Andhra Pradesh.
29 Second Administrative Reforms Commission, *Twelfth Report on Citizen Centric Administration: the heart of governance*, Government of India, February 2009, p. 34.

30 Chetan Agrawal, 'Right to information: a tool for combatting corruption in India', *Journal of Management & Public Policy*, 3 (2), June 2012, p. 26.
31 *Right to Information Act*, 2005: Act no. 22 of 2005, p. 1.
32 Ibid.
33 The 11 May (2005) statement of the Prime Minister of India on the floor of the Parliament – quoted in M M Ansari, 'Impact of Right to Information on development: a perspective on India's recent experiences', an address, delivered at UNESCO, Paris on 15 May 2008 (TSS), p. 12.
34 M M Ansari, 'Impact of Right to Information on development: a perspective on India's recent experiences', an address, delivered at UNESCO, Paris on 15 May 2008 (TSS), p. 4.
35 Shilpa, '*Right to Information Act*: a tool to strengthen good governance and tackle corruption', *International Journal of Humanities and Social Science Invention* (online), 2 (2), February 2013, p. 50.
36 The Second Administrative Reforms Commission: first report, *Right to Information: Master key to good governance*, Government of India, New Delhi, June 2006, p. 56.
37 Ibid.
38 *Report of the Third Five Year Plan*, Planning Commission, Government of India, New Delhi, 1966, pp. 292–3.
39 Report of the Rural–Urban Relationship Committee, Ministry of Health, Government of India, New Delhi, 1966, p. 113 – quoted in Mohit Bhattacharya, 'Voluntary associations, development and the state', *The Indian Journal of Public Administration*, July–September 1987, p. 386.
40 Sanjit (Bunker) Roy, 'Voluntary agencies in development – their role, policy and programmes', *Indian Journal of Public Administration*, July–September 1987, p. 457.
41 Arjun Sengupta, 'Delivering the right to the development: ESCR (economic, social and cultural rights) and NGOs', *Economic and Political Weekly*, 9 October 1999, p. 2922.

2 Democratic decentralization and ethics in governance

As early as 1887, Lord Acton had warned that 'power tends to corrupt and absolute power corrupts absolutely'. This is a historically tested hypothesis and is usually referred to while explaining the rise and consolidation of undemocratic and authoritarian politico-ideological authorities. What is unique about the assumption is that it has also led to alternative conceptualizations of power and authority by drawing on powerful endeavours challenging concentration of power and centralization of authority. The idea is couched in a popular theoretical model of democratic decentralization that also encourages participatory governance involving the stakeholders. Implicit in this theoretical assumption is the idea that democracy, being complementary to decentralization, is a powerful instrument for effective governance since it allows the stakeholders to guide governance in accordance with their ideological priorities, with the panoptical state hardly having a role to play. Conceptually speaking, this speaks of a design of governance in which stakeholders remain integral to the entire administrative process. The outcome is two-fold: on the one hand, it creates an environment in which governance never becomes a distant object, but is part and parcel of the being of stakeholders. Given their involvement in administrative decision making, it also sets in motion, on the other hand, processes of accountability which cannot be ascertained so easily in the Weberian hierarchical form of bureaucracy, because of its lack of appreciation for external accountability.

As the following discussion will show, democratic decentralization is definitely a powerful device to ensure ethics in governance; not only is this an arrangement to challenge the bureaucratic grip over governance, it is also an effective and easily conceivable ideological design that draws on popular aspirations for governance as per their socio-ideological and economic priorities. Based on global experiences, it is also believed that democratic decentralization is not merely a refreshing conceptual category, but a doable mechanism to address the issues of lack of ethics in governance particularly in most of the developing countries. What is most striking is the fact that, despite being theoretically well structured and conceptually rich, democratic decentralization did not seem to have received adequate academic attention, perhaps for historical reasons. Persuaded by the effective role of panoptical bureaucracy, most of the leaders of the decolonized world did not seem to bother to explore whether it was adequately equipped to address their context-specific problems. Soon it was evident to the policy makers that typical bureaucratic governance was not at all appropriate for what had been conceptualized as their ideological mission. Countries that had won independence after prolonged colonial rule were almost crippled due to the lack of ethics in governance and consequently the rising importance of corruption in public life. So efforts were made to explore alternatives to arrest the rapid deterioration of ethics, morality and fair play in the public arena: one of the endeavours was to institute and also to strengthen local government because it was believed that 'only in an effective and empowered local government can the positive power to promote public good be reinforced and the negative impulse to abuse authority curbed'.[1] Besides the obvious institutional advantages of such an arrangement, an empowered local government was likely to create circumstances in which 'ordinary citizens can hold public servants accountable in the face of asymmetry of power exercised by the bureaucracy, [and] citizens who are directly affected by their action are empowered to exercise oversight functions'.[2] An alert local government is necessary to create an engaged citizenry that, by being involved in both policy making and its implementation, is a shield for protecting the moral fabric of governance. The outcome may not be visible instantaneously; what it will lead to is the unleashing of processes whereby citizens become integrally connected with the drive towards creating a system of governance that is ethics-driven and morally sensitive.

In view of the growing acceptability of democratic decentralization as a design for governance in India since she became politically free in 1947, this chapter seeks first to identify the theoretical sources of this conceptualization and later to show how it was sought to be applied as an effective means to address governmental deficits arising from the growing incidence of corruption and other malpractices in governance. It is true that the issue of lack of ethics in public life cannot solely be addressed by administrative means, although it will be a meaningful step towards creating an environment in which debasing tendencies in public administration are severely challenged to build ethically tuned and morally defensible systems of public governance. This is easier said than done, although the idea of democratic decentralization is a powerful theoretical formulation with adequate empirical depth to unsettle the well-established arguments that support bureaucratic hegemony in administration. Besides providing the fundamental theoretical ideas of democratic decentralization, which are universal in character, the aim of the chapter is also to show the historical trajectory of the idea in different phases of India's recent political history. Concerted efforts were made in the past through the two 1992 amendments to the constitution of India – the Seventy-Third and Seventy-Fourth – which seem to have radically changed the texture of the arrangement that came into being in the wake of the common urge for democratic decentralization in governance.

It is difficult to survey the experiences of each and every province in democratic India. Hence the chapter has selectively delved into two case studies of *Bhagidari* in Delhi and *Panchayati Raj* in West Bengal since they represent unique instances of the successful application of democratic decentralization in governance in both urban and rural settings respectively. On the basis of a detailed discussion of these two experiments, the chapter substantiates the argument that, in so far as means for ensuring ethics in governance are concerned, democratic decentralization is too persuasive to be ignored so easily. With the growing consolidation of the urge for ethics in public life which is held as a major reason for social, economic and political decadence, the drive for involving the stakeholders in public governance is a politically rewarding and ideologically fulfilling endeavour towards meaningfully addressing the sources of distortion and demeaning influences in governance.

Conceptual endorsement

Localizing development through participation is a powerful socio-political design in the discourses for empowerment. Thinkers in different phases of human history contributed to the participatory discourses, which were relative to the prevalent socio-economic and political circumstances. For Rousseau and the English Pluralists, the idea of civic engagement was to be instilled to avoid further social decay. This is an idea which also reverberated in the writings of the Federalists and Tocqueville: while the Federalists valued dialogue as perhaps the most effective means for the coming together of people with diverse social roots towards a common goal, Tocqueville attributed civic engagement in its applied sense to the success of democracy in America. By accepting participation as a vehicle for localizing development, as promoted by the activist–theoreticians, Gandhi had always strongly argued for dispersal of authority; de-concentration of authority is, in other words, a conceptually persuasive and empirically sound means of governance, especially in a democratic set-up where an alert citizenry always keeps the pubic authority on its toes. There are two important features of this thinking that immediately attract attention: first, participation involves self-initiated action, reflecting a specific voice and choice that results in an empowerment of the hitherto peripheral stakeholders at the grassroots; second, by decentralizing authority and creating space for the involvement of communities, this genre provides for a new and also contrasting mode of thinking in conceptualizing governance.

As is argued, key to success in governance is participation by the citizenry, which remains the core of democracy. Politically viable and ideologically meaningful, participatory governance is always referred to as an effective instrument for ensuring ethics in public life: the idea is that the greater the participation, the less the chances for corruption in governance. Perhaps the best exposition of this perspective happens to be one that Alexis de Tocqueville articulated in his *Democracy in America* by saying that:

> the nation participates in the making of its laws by the choice of its legislators, and in the execution of them by the choice of the agents of the executive government; it may almost be said to govern itself, so feeble and so restricted is the share left to the administration, so little do the authorities

forget their popular origin and the power from which they emanate. *The people reign in the American political world as the Deity lives in the universe. They are the cause and the aim of all change; everything comes from them and everything is absorbed in them* (emphasis added).[3]

Thus democracy was, to this French aristocrat, not merely a political form of governance, but also a site in which participation in the political processes was articulated and executed. The aim is to create a system of governance that, being sensitive to the needs of the citizens, never allows appropriation by vested interests for partisan gain. This is most fundamental to democratic governance, which, besides seeking to install a unique politico-ideological structure of authority on the basis of collective bonhomie, also creates a spirit to evolve a system of governance which is free from distortions and tuned to the universally accepted constitutional principles protective of human life, regardless of one's socio-economic location and ideological predispositions.

This was reiterated by Gandhi who, while justifying participatory governance as a key to the success of democracy in its truest spirit, expressed his ideas largely in typical Tocquevillian language. According to him, 'true democracy cannot be worked by twenty men sitting at the centre; it has to be worked from below, by the people of every village'.[4] What was unique in Gandhi's conceptualization of civic engagement in public affairs was his notion of the 'oceanic circle' that he developed while defending village *swaraj* by saying that

> Life will not be a pyramid with the apex sustained by the bottom. But it will be an oceanic circle whose centre will be the individuals always ready for the village, the latter ready to perish for the circle of villages, till at last the whole becomes one life composed of individuals, never aggressive in their arrogance but even humble, sharing the majesty of the oceanic circle of which they are integral units.[5]

Two ideas are pre-eminent here: first, for him, a circle of interdependent villages remained perhaps the most viable unit for sustained and equitable economic growth for any society; second, and perhaps more importantly, systematic economic well-being would certainly make the individuals within the circle self-reliant and thus confident. Hence he was very critical of the doctrine of 'the greatest good of the greatest number, [which] is a heartless doctrine and has done harm to humanity. [The only] real and dignified human doctrine is', according to Gandhi, 'the greatest good of all, and this can only be achieved by utmost self-sacrifice'.[6]

It is evident that Gandhi was deeply uneasy with the modern state. For him, a society based on *swaraj* – 'true democracy' or non-violence – was the only morally acceptable alternative to the modern state. According to him, the *swaraj*-based polity would be composed of small, cultured, well organized, thoroughly regenerated and self-governing village communities; elected by these communities, a small body of people would administer justice, maintain order, and take important economic decisions through interactive dialogues with the community as a whole. These units would thus not be merely administrative but also powerful economically and politically, fulfilling their role by seeking to articulate *swaraj* in its true form. As such, they would thus have a strong sense of solidarity, provide a genuine sense of community and act as nurseries of civic virtues. In conceptualizing the village *swaraj* that would finally lead to *Sarvadaya* (welfare for all), Gandhi was drawn to *dharma*, which, in his view, consisted of sensitivity and responsiveness. After having theoretically justified *swaraj* as an efficient form of civic engagement that emphasized the importance of both individuals and communities, the Mahatma evolved his model by identifying twelve basic principles for what he conceptualized as an authentic form of participatory democracy. These principles were:

(1) involving men in productive employment, (2) a man who does not do bodily labour does not have the right to eat, (3) equitable distribution of resources, (4) trusteeship by the wealthy of the superfluous wealth possessed by them, (5) decentralization of power and authorities, (6) inculcating the *swadeshi* (self-reliance) spirit in the community, (7) making the villages independent and interdependent in terms of need in the circle of villages, (8) cooperation provides fundamental resources for healthy communal existence, (9) *satyagraha* (non-violent means of protest) is an obvious choice in cases in which village authorities deviate from the common good, (10) secularism (equal respect to all religions) is critical to cement a stable bond among the members of the community, (11) regular annual elections to constitute *Panchayati Raj* (rural government) and (12) *Nai Talim* (new education), insisting on vocational training in handicrafts, is a sure step towards making individuals self-reliant and also appreciative of the dignity of labor.[7]

What was fundamental in Gandhi's conceptualization of village *swaraj* was the idea of self-reliance through a meaningful articulation of the decentralization of power and authority. He always used a moral argument to persuasively pursue his point of view. Hence he always felt that, without devotion to the cause, nothing substantial could be achieved. In his words,

devotion means faith – faith in God and in one's self [which] will lead one to make all sacrifices … and if sacrifice is made in the service of others, it is easy … [because] no mother would want to sleep in the wet for her own sake, but she would gladly do so if she can thereby find for her child a dry place to sleep.[8]

On another occasion, he defended care for others in distress as unavoidable in a human being. 'One ceases to be a human being', argued Gandhi, 'unless one makes the distress of others as his (*sic*) own and tries to relieve it'.[9] On the basis of the above brief exposition of Gandhi's model of participatory rural governance, it can fairly be said that his approach to civic engagement was based on high moral values, which may not have always been realistic in the prevalent world of capitalistic expansion through cut-throat competition, although its conceptual validity is beyond question. What is distinctive about Gandhi's argument for civic engagement in public affairs was his unalloyed faith in the indigenous traditions that seemed to have been submerged in the avalanche of industrial civilization of the Western variety that came to India, piggybacking on colonialism. Gandhi's idea of village *swaraj* is a unique conceptualization because, besides drawing upon India's indigenous tradition of governance, he also based it on what he learned from Western sources while crafting a context-sensitive model of civic involvement in public affairs.

As is evident, according to the classical thinkers, the key to the success of democracy in its actual spirit is a participatory governance that ensures meaningful civic engagement. This, they strongly felt, would act as a deterrent against attempts at appropriating institutions of authority for private gain. Their primary concern was to found a system of governance that was neither discriminatory nor prejudiced, but fair and well equipped to translate into reality the true spirit of democracy. For them, since governance was contingent on the prevalent socio-economic and ideological milieu, it would be wrong to comment on its nature without reference to the contextual constraints. Mere tweaking of the structure was not going to work; what was thus necessary was to create an environment in which the basic values of ethical governance were uncritically appreciated. This was a systemic solution which needed to be supplemented by the strengthening of society's moral fabric; it was a solution which called for reinventing one's self in accordance with the desire to work for the collective well-being because, with a contended collectivity, a society was bound to be free from prejudices that appreciate sectional partisan goals at the cost of the multitude.

What is unique here is the fact that, despite being rooted in diverse socio-economic and political circumstances, not only were these ideas reflective of a common concern, but they also conveyed an identical message to rescue governance from the quagmire of corruption and demeaning influences. To them, governance needed to be conceptualized at two interrelated levels. At one level, it was characterized clearly in an instrumental sense as a goal-driven exercise. At another, by arguing that the nature of governance was context dependent, the classical thinkers seem to have highlighted its wider connotations, which remained elusively independent of the existent socio-economic and ideological milieu.

The efforts are being continued. What the classical thinkers so strongly felt seems to have found an echo in the endeavours that the World Bank has recently undertaken to defend democratic decentralization as a key to common well-being. While arguing for the dispersal of public authority and the expansion of its base by involving stakeholders, the World Bank identifies four major structural concerns – transparency, openness, accountability and probity – which are critical in articulating governance in its unalloyed sense. First, transparency is the hallmark of democratic decentralization which 'can make government processes more visible and intelligible to ordinary people [because] ... when decisions are made at or near the local level,... it is far easier for ordinary citizens to find out about them'.[10] Second, one of the primary factors for the growing acceptance of democratic decentralization is the fact that it creates systems that are 'more transparent and easier for individuals and groups at local and supralocal levels to access and influence'.[11] This openness is a major characteristic of local governance which not only encourages participation, but also creates an environment in which government is no longer something captured by the elites. Third, democratic decentralization stands out as an arrangement because it 'tends strongly to foster more accountable government'[12] by making those in decision making accountable not only to the stakeholders, but also to the fundamental constitutional values and ideological concerns of the polity in question. Accountability cannot be ascertained merely by administrative feats, but by an engaged citizenry that, by being vigilant, keeps a check on distortion in governance. Finally, despite the fact that democratic decentralization fails to completely rule out corruption in public life, it has, nonetheless, set in motion processes whereby the values of probity, integrity and honesty are being taken seriously by the decision makers and the governed alike. These are societal values which will have a better chance of survival and appreciation provided the society in question is favourably disposed towards this; otherwise, as a top-down dressing, probity cannot succeed as a determinant of a prejudice-free administration.[13]

The above discussion highlighting the conceptual underpinning of the arguments reveals two basic points which are relevant to comprehend ethics in governance: first, democratic decentralization contributes to an arrangement of governance in which the idea of ethics seems to have been naturally ingrained. An administrative feat cannot be adequate to address this concern; it requires a concerted effort by the citizens who always remain core to governance. Nonetheless, as a principle upholding a specific design for exercising public authority, the devolution of power, is a powerful alternative seeking to articulate public voice in governance. Second, the importance of democratic decentralization is being increasingly felt, because of the equally powerful drive towards 'state capture' for self-gratification. In view of the fact that moral values in public life are declining at an alarming rate, the global concern does not seem to be overstretched, but real. As shown above, the World Bank has its own solution, which may not have universal applicability despite being conceptually viable. What is thus critical is the fact that moral decadence is not peculiar to specific countries, but has affected nations across the globe. This means that it has societal roots that need to be probed far more seriously than is being attempted now. Nonetheless, specific administrative feats that have already been undertaken by political leaderships across nations remain significant ideological steps to at least initiate a debate on what is deemed to be most appropriate to rejuvenate governance, keeping in mind the centricity of the citizen.

The Indian case study

The enactment of the Seventy-Third and Seventy-Fourth constitutional amendments in December, 1992 was a legislative feat that formalized democratic decentralization as a form of governance. This is a unique piece of legislation, because it concerned democracy and representation, unlike the previous endeavours in which attempts at democratic decentralization had been initiated to fulfil developmental and administrative goals. Besides giving the stakeholders a voice in the decision making, these enactments were also reflective of a genuine concern from the political leadership, who seemed to have become mute observers of India's rapid moral decline, given the consolidation of tendencies for appropriating public authority for personal benefit. Corruption was not an anathema, but had become integral to public governance. The concern for ethics in governance figured prominently in public speeches delivered by those in power, but never seemed to become critical when it mattered. Arguing that the constitutional guarantee of democratic decentralization was necessary to re-build popular faith in governance, India's erstwhile Prime Minister exhorted that

> a wide chasm separates the largest body of the electorate from a small number of its elected representatives. This gap has been occupied by the power brokers, the middlemen and vested interests.... With the passage [of the bill which finally became the Seventy-Third and Seventy-Fourth Amendment Acts], the *panchayat*s would emerge as a firm building block of administration and development ... as an instrument in the consolidation of democracy at the grassroots.[14]

Despite the fact that it was a masterstroke on the part of the ruling Congress to take steam out of the opposition, the above statement is a testimony to the decadence that considerably plagued public authority in India. There was a trust deficit, and government failed to generate public confidence because of the alleged involvement of those in power in deeds that were clearly contrary to all established ethical norms. Nonetheless, in such gloomy circumstances, serious attempts were made to address the concern for rebuilding public trust, and the result was the enactment of those groundbreaking pieces of legislation which accorded a constitutional guarantee to local governance that, by virtue of being located in Part IV (Directive Principles of State Policy) of the Constitution of India, was never justiciable. A remarkable constitutional design, these amendment acts have both revolutionized our approach to local governance and also sought to evolve alternative methods of power sharing, which are ethically appropriate and also morally justified in the context of an apparent mass disillusionment with those in positions of governance. Besides being nurseries of civic virtues, these institutions of local governance help articulate a powerful public voice in development and overall administration that so far remains an exclusive bureaucratic domain. In order for democratic governance to flourish in its true spirit in India, these amendment acts seem to have become the most prominent legislative provisions in radically altering the texture of power. Elected representatives, rather than being solely the agents of power, have become a conduit for the aspirations of the people electing them to govern. Politically empowering, these pieces of legislation have again catapulted the stakeholders onto the centre stage of politics at the grassroots in rural India by further reinforcing the importance of ethics in governance, something which seems to have taken a backseat in India's recent past.

Two specific instances: Bhagidari and Panchayati Raj

Bhagidari in Delhi and *Panchayati Raj* in West Bengal are two successful examples of participatory governance in India. Seeking to translate into reality the idea of democratic decentralization of power, the former is an experiment in citizen–government partnership in a typical urban setting while the latter is about people's involvement in governance in an Indian province that was uninterruptedly ruled by a coalition of political parties of the left for more than three decades. Besides involving the stakeholders in the decision making, both of these forms seem to have followed a well entrenched tradition of decentralization of power in India. Conceptually, *Panchayati Raj* governance and *Bhagidari* represent efforts at community development through the decentralization of power: the former is a mechanism to bring villages, urban neighbourhoods or other household groupings into the process of managing development resources without being dependent on the institutionalized forms of government authority; decentralization fosters involvement of the stakeholders in the decision-making process, which is contrary to the Weberian top-down model of governance. Different from 'deconcentration' of power, which is clearly Weberian, decentralization opens up the foundation of administration with the institutional recognition of those who remain integrally linked with governance at the grassroots. This is always advantageous, since local participants enrich decisions by incorporating local knowledge and preferences in the institutionalized processes of decision making. So decentralization and community involvement seem to have translated 'participatory governance' into a distinct reality, which enhances 'pro-social thinking, strengthens citizenship, and enables more inclusive civic engagement [by making] the community decision making integral for building capacity for self-reliance and collective action'[15] or, social capital, as it is usually defined in contemporary social science literature. Contemporary public administration is not only about efficiency; it also upholds democratic participation, accountability and empowerment. There is thus a constant tension between (a) how to make the government efficient and (b) how to keep it accountable. This is a challenge that government confronts, especially when the conceptions of people are 'as consumers in the market-driven neo-liberal political set-up' and of people are 'as citizens in democratic governance'.[16] This reveals the increasing importance of participation in public affairs. The aim is 'to strengthen [the people's] voice in general – and the voice of the poor, in particular'. The strategy is 'to revamp the rules of the game that shape the incentives and actions of public actors – including the voice mechanism that promotes the rule of law and accountability of government to its citizens'.[17]

One cannot avoid looking at Gandhi's conceptual framework while assessing participatory decision making as a phenomenon, since it is intellectually rooted in such a conceptualization. One of the important sources which acted critically in articulating participatory governance in India happens to be Gandhi's notion of village *swaraj*, which he developed in a series of letters that he exchanged with his colleagues during India's nationalist movement and public speeches that he made to fulfil his political mission of India's independence. For Gandhi, Henry Maine seemed to have provided a very critical intellectual impetus in his conceptualization of participatory governance. It is thus not strange to find a clear imprint of Maine's description of autonomously governed and self-reliant Indian village communities, which he developed in his *Village Communities in the East and* West,[18] in Gandhi's argument of strongly defending the community's involvement in local administration. In Gandhi's well thought out views, participation in community life and self-accountability while discharging that role remain two important and also non-negotiable conceptual pillars of public governance. Drawn on his perception supporting participatory governance, he thus elaborated his argument by saying that:

> every village has to be self-reliant and capable of managing its affairs even to the extent of defending itself against the whole world. It will be trained and prepared to perish in the attempt to defend itself against any onslaught from without.... Such a society is necessarily highly cultured, in which every man and woman knows what he or she wants and, what is more, knows that no one should want anything that others cannot have with equal labour.[19]

Gandhi's main concern was to make villages self dependent not only in terms of resources, but also in terms of running the administration. By making discussion an integral part of local administration, he also created a distinct space for induced participation, through methods that are inculcated over a period of time. This usually works miracle, especially in a context in which civic engagement is organic to the human psyche. This is what explains the success of self-sustaining local governance in India. The growing involvement of the people in the *Panchayati Raj* institutions has made the concept of 'peoples' audit' meaningful. That serves as a powerful check on the aberrations in bureaucratic functioning in the development sphere, be they the misappropriation of funds, false reporting or wrongful identification of beneficiaries.

The systems of the *Panchayati Raj* and *Bhagidari* forms of governance are rooted in Gandhi's conceptualization of *swaraj*, which is a powerful theoretical construct of participatory governance at the grassroots. A mechanism of social inclusion, *swaraj* also creates an environment for inclusive governance whereby people regardless of caste, class and clan participate in the decision-making processes. As he argued,

> Swaraj is ... complete freedom ... because it is as much for the prince, as for the peasant, as much for the rich landowner as for the landless tiller of

the soil, as much for the Hindus as for the [Muslims], as much for the Parsis as for the Jains, Jews and Sikhs irrespective of any distinction of caste or creed or status in life.[20]

Apart from delineating the exact nature of *swaraj*, he also, in a Lockean way, allowed the governed to remain the actual custodians of administration by giving them the authority to dismiss the truant government at any time. Hence he was insistent that 'real Swaraj will come not by the acquisition of authority by a few but the acquisition of the capacity by all to resist authority when it is abused', and self-government in its true sense 'depends', he further argued, 'entirely upon our internal strength, upon our ability to fight against the heaviest odds'.[21] There are two important conceptual points which need to be highlighted, given their applicability to the Indian case. First, unlike the post-Gandhian theoretical discourse on local governance, the Gandhian formulation is most enlightening given its organic roots in Indian thinking. The idea of *Panchayati Raj* and *Bhagidari* seem to have been grounded in Indian psyche and Gandhi's articulation translates them into practice. This is where Gandhian conceptualization is far more effective in comprehending the reality than any other derivative theoretical parameter. Second, Gandhi's formulation is useful not only to understand the nature of local governance, but also to conceptualize how it is constituted, especially in a diverse society such as India, which represents a multiplicity of identities. In this sense, he has drawn our attention to that system of governance that derives its sustenance not from the institutions on which it is based, but from those who constitute it. What thus gains ground is the idea that the governed remain the most significant ingredient in governance.

Gandhi's conceptualization provides creative inputs in deciphering the distinct nature of participatory governance. What is fundamental in such a conceptualization is the idea of collaborative endeavour in addressing visible deficits in governance. In contemporary academic intervention, this is being dealt with at greater depth, given the rising complexities in public administration. Patsy Healey found planning as instrumental to organize disparate societies. By focusing on 'fragmented societies', Healey evolves what she calls a 'communicative approach to the design of governance systems and practices ... fostering collaborative [and] consensus-building practices'.[22] There is a clear Gandhian tone not only in Healey's formulation of a communicative approach, but also in its functional manifestations which is evident when she says that

the communicative approach both offers a way forward in the design of governance processes for a shared power world and takes as a normative position an ethical commitment to enabling all stakeholders to have a voice. It also offers a format for change through collective efforts by transforming ways of thinking [which remain at the heart] of participatory democracy in pluralist societies.

This is reinforced by Judith E Innes and David E Booher while conceptualizing collaborative planning in the context of a water crisis in the Sacramento region of California. Different from the traditional linear method relying primarily on formal expertise, they insist on 'collaborative dialogue' which draws on 'nonlinear socially constructed processes engaging both experts and stakeholders'.[23] Implicit in this formulation is the assumption that collaboration aims at creating 'a shared or collaborative rationality' which acts decisively in shaping a meaningful policy towards addressing problems of serious magnitudes. Clearly Gandhian in spirit, the idea of collaborative rationality draws fundamentally on the collective self that emerges out of intensive cooperation, which may be both instantaneous and institutionalized. In other words, by emphasizing the importance of the collective self in governance, these authors take into account the importance of deliberations involving multiple stakeholders in constructing 'a social response' contributing to what it is sought to be achieved for the common benefit. In conceptual terms, collaborative rationality leads to 'communicative planning', based on another powerful idea of 'dialogical incrementalism which draws its sustenance from dialogical communication involving stakeholders'.[24] There is a flip side as well, because communicative planning does not always reflect the true nature of deliberations due to 'the class bias' and 'unequal power relations' in the society in question. Here, planning acts as a control mechanism, whereby the will of the hegemonic class prevails over the rest, as Yiftachel persuasively argues while providing a Foucauldian perspective to the planning processes. As shown by the author in the context of Israel, planning is a class device, meant for protecting the prevalent class balances in such a way as not to disturb the vested interests.[25] So planning, despite its deliberative roots, continues to remain power-driven and its nature is thus pre-determined even before it is conceptualized in black and white.[26]

There are thus two complementary perspectives in conceptualizing local-participatory governance. First, community remains most significant in articulating needs, mobilizing resources and managing local affairs. Development is to proceed from the bottom up with the local unit normally taken as the basic unit of planning at the grassroots. Second, implicit in this assumption is the idea of social ownership, which implies that the productive resources in a community are communally owned and managed. The resources generated are meant to provide civic amenities to the community. In this most critical sense, local governance that is also participatory is a clear alternative to the hierarchical Weberian bureaucratic form of organization.

Within this broad theoretical format, as explained above, this chapter seeks to test whether the participatory mode of governance is an appropriate conceptual tool to understand *Bhagidari* in Delhi and *Panchayati Raj* in West Bengal as examples of participation-driven local self-government. The other important area of concern is to show how sustained civic engagement in local governance brings about a dramatic metamorphosis in local administration, which is not remote controlled, as in the Weberian theoretical mould, but partakes in issue solving on the basis of the stakeholders' inputs, drawing on what they feel appropriate for their localities.

Bhagidari in Delhi

Bhagidari is a citizen-dependent format of local self-government, based on 'citizens' partnership in governance'. In order to make administration responsive and participative, it seeks (a) to utilize the processes and principles of multi-stakeholder involvement by institutionalizing the role of citizen groups, non-governmental organizations and government in governance; (b) to develop 'joint-ownership by the citizens and government of the processes of change', and (c) to facilitate people's participation in governance.[27] Although *Bhagidari* is still in its formative stage, it has radically altered Delhi's public governance by charting out meaningful roles for the stakeholders. There is no doubt that the initiative came from the party in power, which gradually lost its grip over the programme due largely to the spontaneous involvement of the citizens in activities contributing to their well-being especially in areas of 'operation and management of civic services, capital investment in infrastructural projects, planning and participatory budgeting and maintenance of neighbourhood security'.[28] By creating partnership between government and citizens, organized through residents' welfare associations, market trader associations, industrial associations, village groups and non-governmental organizations, *Bhagidari* is an attempt 'to address the deadlock in governance by involving different stakeholders as partners'.[29] These new 'collective actors' take part in those programmes that may appear peripheral to the government. In this sense, they are also meaningful partners in public administration, which cannot remain indifferent to those issues which they raise, due to the obvious political consequences. *Bhagidari* has thus translated a true partnership between citizens and government into a reality in urban governance in Delhi.

A citizen-friendly format of governance, *Bhagidari*, which means participation, is also an attempt to translate some of the neo-liberal assumptions on administrative reform into reality. For instance, by formally recognizing the role of citizens in local governance, the participatory design of *Bhagidari* is clearly a break with the past when the government remained the only agency in public administration. In this respect, *Bhagidari*, despite initial hiccups, seems to have provided a clear solution to the administrative inadequacies of over-burdened government. With the articulation of *Bhagidari*, public administration is now pluralized, in the sense that the roles of other agencies are considered complementary in governance. By recognizing the importance of multiple agencies in societal problem-solving, this indigenous form of urban governance, which came into existence in 2000 in Delhi, also redefines the role of citizens in public governance. Instead of being passive, citizens are now drawn into the administrative process, which had so far remained the exclusive domain of the seasoned bureaucrats. *Bhagidari* is therefore a unique experiment in public governance that has simultaneously shrunk the government and expanded its reach: while *Bhagidari* has taken away some of the critical responsibilities from the government, it has, at the same time, stretched its domain by involving the stakeholders who so far remained peripheral in governance. By 'de-centring' administration,

Bhagidari is a powerful theoretical intervention in re-conceptualizing some of the major hypotheses of decentralized public administration. Not only is *Bhagidari* a persuasive critique of the Weberian hierarchical form of government, it also seeks to provide an alternative conceptualization of public administration by demarcating the role of non-governmental actors in governance. *Bhagidari* seems to have 'realigned the channels by which citizens can access the state as partners. [It has thus effectively] gentrified the channels of political participation, respatializing the state by binding the unpropertied poor to the local state'.[30] What is striking about *Bhagidari* is its role in re-invigorating the urban administration in India's capital city of Delhi, where government is supposedly overactive for obvious reasons. Can one attribute the growing importance of *Bhagidari* to the cosmopolitan character of Delhi that, besides being the capital city, can also be described metaphorically as 'a salad bowl', given its multicultural character? *Bhagidari* is thus a well articulated and context-sensitive response, seeking to redefine urban governance by charting out meaningful roles for the stakeholders.

Panchayati Raj in West Bengal

Much of the economic change in rural West Bengal since 1977 is made possible because of a significant political process, initiated and carried forward by the Left Front government. The devolution of power– including considerable financial powers – to the elected rural political authority, known as *Panchayats*, has been important here. This step, together with a strong political commitment to implementing land reforms, has ensured a process of genuine democratic participation by the rural poor in the remaking of their lives and their socio-economic environment. Although the enactment of the *Seventy-Third Amendment Act* in 1992 was a significant step towards revamping the *panchayati* institutions in the country, the Left Front initiated the process as early as 1977–80 by giving *Panchayats* substantial power for local development.

Contrasted with *Bhagidari*, the *Panchayat* system in West Bengal has a long history of three decades.[31] There is however one similarity: like *Bhagidari*, the West Bengal experiment of local governance was initiated by the Left Front government as soon as it came to power, for the first time, in 1977. But that is all. The programme that kicked off with government patronage is being nurtured by the constituents of the ruling Left Front. Undoubtedly, the *Panchayat* system of governance in West Bengal led to the involvement of the people at the grassroots in which the role of the party was most critical. Unlike *Bhagidari*, in which the stakeholders gradually became formidable, the *Panchayati* system of governance largely remained a stooge to the party in power.[32] As a result, besides the loyalists, the rest of the stakeholders were pushed to the periphery to avoid opposition. So the story of the Left Front's ascendancy can also be told in a different way. The *Panchayat* system has served the political purposes of the Left Front reasonably well. It has formed the basis of the political support of the party. Yet, the party does not allow the *Panchayats* to be independent of its control simply because it has a tradition of strong centralized party discipline. Accordingly, there is a tendency to use local *Panchayats* by the central committee at the state level as an instrument of political mobilization and cultivation of political clientelism. The fact that the ruling party candidates win unopposed in a large number of *Panchayat* constituencies is indicative of a dangerous political trend that hardly allows opposition to crystallize simply because they would not dare to provoke a situation in which they would face the combined wrath of the party cadres and police. The implications are disastrous, as a survey confirms by highlighting that

> the high-handed and violent ways of meeting any resistance on ground... galvanized the opposition in the ... State, in addition to causing disunity within the ruling coalition and eroding its general credibility as a defender of the interests of vulnerable rural population.[33]

Furthermore, contrary to the Left Front's claim, the downward devolution of power has given way to the rising middle sections of rural society who now control the *Panchayats*.[34] The local *Panchayats* have thus been appropriated to pursue partisan goals by those who reigned supreme by holding institutional responsibilities within the party. It is, therefore, not surprising that the *Panchayati Raj* institutions that had brought hope to the people at the grassroots eventually faced sharp criticism from those who had previously viewed the *Panchayati Raj* as the most effective form of rural governance and development. As a result, these bodies have become 'synonymous with the elected popular bureaucracy'. Governed by what is known as a 'political–organizational perspective', the leading partners of the government, the Communist Party of India (Marxist) (hereafter CPI (M)), for instance, justified the hegemonic control of the party in terms of the ideological goal of 'democratic centralism'. The party cannot simply be bypassed. In order to translate the party's perspective, the CPI (M) State Committee constituted at the level of the *Panchayats* a guiding cell (*Parichalan committee*) that was entrusted with the task of steering the *Panchayats* in accordance with the directives of the party high command.[35] The growing hegemony of the party provided, on the one hand, organizational strength to the *Panchayats*; it also, on the other hand, strengthened the party functionaries who, despite being 'outsiders', continued to remain significant in the *Panchayat* bodies simply because of their assigned role in the party directives. So, centralization of power actually struck at the very root of devolution of power. Yet, the Left Front had been continuously winning elections for more than three decades, which was attributed to its success in integrating the governmental pro-people policies with the strategies of political mobilization. By contextualizing Marxist ideology, the CPI (M)-led coalition shifted its social base from being a party of the industrial proletariat to one of marginal farmers, sharecroppers and the landless poor. This social base was consolidated further by uniting the socially marginalized groups, including *Dalits*, Tribals and Muslims, around the party's social-democratic ideology. The sustained viability of the Left Front for more than three decades can be attributed to 'this unique class–community coalition' that made the Left Front invincible in rural Bengal.

Changing nature of local governance

This comparative study of two different types of participatory governance in India has underlined two important features of public administration that are critical in conceptualizing its nature in the context of the rising importance of 'the global village'. First, by involving citizens in public governance, *Bhagidari*, which came into existence in 2000 in Delhi, is undoubtedly an innovative design seeking to articulate an alternative form of governance. An institutionalized mechanism of cooperation between civil society organizations and government, this is also a scheme in which stakeholders are expected to play a critical role in 'reinventing government' in India, where the government is over-burdened with responsibilities for historical reasons. A citizen-friendly form of governance, *Bhagidari* is also an attempt to translate some of the neo-liberal assumptions on administrative reforms into reality. For instance, by recognizing the role of civil society organizations in public administration, *Bhagidari* seems to have translated public–private partnership into a concrete and meaningful programme of action. Conceptually, public–private partnerships refer to contractual partnerships between public and private sector agencies, specifically targeted towards financing, designing, implementing and operating infrastructure facilities and services that were traditionally provided by the public sector. Such collaborative ventures are built around the expertise and capacity of the project partners and are based on a contractual agreement that ensures appropriate and mutually agreed allocation of resources, risks and returns. Furthermore, by upholding the role of citizens in local governance, *Bhagidari* provides a participatory design of governance that is clearly divorced from the Weberian notion of 'closeted' governance. In this respect, *Bhagidari*, despite initial hiccups, seems to have addressed meaningfully the administrative inadequacies resulting from over-burdened government.

Second, while *Bhagidari* is an extra-constitutional mechanism of governance, *Panchayati* Raj is a scheme that derives its sustenance from the Constitution of India. Reaffirming the constitutional commitment, the *Seventy-Third Amendment Act* further strengthens this form of rural governance that has evolved organically with the consolidation of India as the world's largest democracy. Dissatisfied with the functioning of municipalities in Delhi, citizens appear to have zealously supported the *Bhagidari* campaign, which also gained a fresh lease of life with the return to power of the Indian National Congress in 2008.[36]

The *Panchayati raj* system has a comparative advantage because of the constitutional sanction which *Bhagidari* lacks. The government in rural India has become truly people-centric in the sense that the local inhabitants remain integrally involved in the processes of governance through democratic means of deliberations and negotiations. The West Bengal example is illustrative here. As a system of governance, *Panchayats* have radically altered the structure of power in rural West Bengal where 70 per cent of the state's population lives. With the presence of Left Front activists in every key institution at the grassroots – ranging from the governing bodies of credit societies to the primary schools – the government has been able to build and sustain a well entrenched network among the rural population. This has led to the consolidation of what is identified as 'governmental locality', which signifies the presence of government in a locality as an institution and also the locality's presence in government as a process. Such governmetalization of rural localities has generated a new and innovative correspondence within and between village representative bodies and tied them to the state power. In such a symbiotic network between the villagers and the Front activists lies the explanation as to why the Left Front retains its grip in rural West Bengal without any substantial setbacks. Nonetheless, the hegemonic presence of the ruling parties has also gagged the voice opposing the government, which is contrary to the very spirit of participatory governance and the inculcation of democratic processes. It is true that, with the formation of *Panchayats* in villages as the centre of governance, villagers were drawn to rural governance. In course of time, however, the party activists seem to have appropriated roles that were meant for the people regardless of party affiliations. This is undoubtedly a serious distortion of the foundational values of participatory democracy that did not go unchallenged, as the outcome of the 2011 assembly election suggests. The ruling coalition, which played a critical role in empowering people by making them integral to governance through the institution of *Panchayats,* became a clear victim of what its constituents did to reverse the process. With its ignominious defeat in the 2011 assembly poll, the ruling coalition paid the price for their open complicity with anti-democratic forces challenging the people's voice of resentment, anger and disenchantment with the Left Front government.

The West Bengal situation is also illustrative of a historical paradox of a global nature that manifested first with the disintegration of the former Soviet Union and also the dramatic ideological shift in China. These examples are sharp comments, perhaps more on the application of a libertarian ideology, known as Marxism, and less on the nature of the ideology itself. Taken together, these examples also direct our attention to the critical role of 'the people', irrespective of ideological divide, in redrawing the contours of governance in various socio-political and economic contexts. There is no specific formula, though one can safely argue that the core values of participatory governance – diligence, cooperation and self-help – seem to have catapulted citizens onto the centre-stage of public governance and thus have provided a sure guarantee for people-centric democratic politics.

The story will, however, remain incomplete unless we address 'the problem areas' in otherwise successful efforts at involving the community in governance. *Bhagidari*, a very recent addition to the lexicon of public administration, may have translated into reality community participation in governance but it does not seem to have inspired the Delhi inhabitants to the extent it was expected to at the beginning. Presumably because of the complex socio-economic and political setting of Delhi, *Bhagidari*, a product of an executive intervention, has so far failed to evolve as a politico-administrative design in the city.[37] In this sense, it is unlike the *Panchayati Raj* governance in West Bengal that, because of its organic roots in villages, evolved at the outset in parallel to the processes of democratization at the grassroots. For the villagers, the *Panchayati Raj* is nothing but an extension of the larger family spreading across the villages, seeking to take care of their socio-economic and political needs. Nonetheless, it has faced rough weather, primarily because of the distortion that has crept into the system due to its growing politicization in recent years. The obvious outcome is the declining importance of 'the community' and 'the hegemonic grip' of the political bosses of the ruling coalition over the rural institutions of governance, ignoring the stakeholders to the extent of diluting the very spirit of participatory democracy for partisan gains.

The sustained popularity of the left in West Bengal is attributed to a well entrenched party machinery that manages 'conflict and also co-opts the aggrieved through its patronage network'.[38] This also suggests how populist policies of doling out patronages at the grassroots consolidated 'a clientelistic relationship' between the party and the electorate. The unusual political stability in rural West Bengal seems to be associated positively and significantly with the receipt of recurring benefits. Those drawing benefits tend to vote for the left because of the mutual benefit accrued. 'It is [therefore] not surprising', argued experts, 'that the land-less and socially and educationally backward sections' constitute a strong base for the Left.[39] The clientelistic relationship has its flip side as well. Because the winner has direct control over the substance of the village-level plan and the selection of the beneficiaries, the *Panchayat* system invariably indulges in politicization of the planning process and the implementation of the public projects. *Panchayats* failed, on occasion, and the party functionaries appropriated these grassroots institutions to fulfil their selfish goal, as the available literature confirms. People are disillusioned because the local *Panchayat* leaders squandered the government funds for development to buy liquor and build club houses for their own benefit.

It is not therefore odd to find that the *Panchayati Raj* institutions that brought hope to the people at the grassroots are now subject to trenchant criticism by those who found them a most effective form of rural governance when they were introduced in West Bengal. The reasons are not difficult to seek. A large sample survey carried out in 2006 confirms that the credibility of those at the helm has been waning. That most *Panchayat* members were corrupt was endorsed by the survey, which further indicates a pervasive distrust of the moral authority of those who claim to mediate, on political grounds, the contending claims of livelihood, fairness and dignity. It is this 'popular distrust' that accounts for the gradual decline of the left forces in rural West Bengal. While this distrust causes a clear dent in the left's support base, it has also alienated the poor, especially the *Dalit* and the tribal population, from the institutions of *Panchayat* governance. If these institutions cannot find innovative ways to accommodate the poor, the atrophy, as the survey suggests, may create space for various violent extremist movements that have little regard for the existing democratic norms. The growing consolidation of 'ultra-radical extremist forces' in various districts in West Bengal is illustrative of the growing disenchantment with the incumbent government, which appears to have been alienated, to a significant extent, from the people by being insensitive to, if not completely ignorant of, their demands and requirements. A piquant situation has emerged with the transformation of the *Panchayats* into 'mere tools' to realize partisan aims at the cost of the foundational principles of participatory governance. It is therefore no surprise that the ultra-radical extremist political outfits seem to have gained enormously in recent years by championing what the ruling left parties promised for the hitherto marginalized sections of the society at the beginning of the long reign of people-centric governance in 1977.

Similarly, *Bhagidari* is seriously handicapped, primarily because of Delhi's complex administrative structure in which it is located. Delhi is a state, but of a different kind due to the fact that it is also the capital of the Union of India. Accordingly, critical aspects of Delhi's government are in the hands of the Union Government of India. For instance, the Delhi Police, Delhi Development Authority, Municipal Corporation of Delhi, and New Delhi Municipal Corporation are accountable to the Union Government. Furthermore, unlike any other constituent state in India, the elected government of Delhi is not constitutionally authorized to legislate on all subjects in the State List in the seventh schedule of the Constitution of India. The state government is, for instance, debarred from legislating on important subjects relating to land, police and law and order, because these are areas of concern for the Union Government of India as well. This is a serious structural constraint that invariably impinges on the functioning of *Bhagidari*.[40] Due to overlapping jurisdictions and lack of adequate financial support, the government of Delhi has failed to execute a large number of developmental projects that have emerged from Large Group Interactive Sessions. For instance, matters falling within the jurisdiction of the Municipal Corporation and Delhi Development Authority may be shelved unless they are approved by the relevant departments within the Union Government of India. This is likely to cause tension between the two governments. The fact that the Congress Party, which held power in Delhi, was also a dominant partner in the ruling coalition at the national level allowed differences of opinion between the two levels of government to be resolved through political dialogue among Congress Party members. The situation would have been different if the party in power in Delhi had not been the one that wielded power at the Union level. The basic weakness of *Bhagidari* stems from the fact that the programme continues to remain an administrative mechanism without constitutional recognition. With the formation of the *Bhagidari* cell directly under the supervision of the chief minister, the government may have provided an administrative sanction that remains meaningful only so long as the government in power endorses it; there is, thus, an uncertainty that cannot be ruled out. Nonetheless, *Bhagidari* is one of the few successful government-sponsored schemes that have created an ambience in which citizens seem to have realized their potential as agents of change.

Concluding observations

In view of the clear evidence, it is now believed that institutions are not adequate shields to arrest the rapid deterioration of moral values in society, because it is rooted in the wider socio-economic and political circumstances, which appear to have created an atmosphere of helplessness and disillusionment. India has recently been rocked by the revelations of scam after scam in which ministers and top bureaucrats were reportedly involved, who besides being supportive, were also charged for having masterminded these nefarious acts. This is not new, because there are instances even in the past when governance was not absolutely free from degenerative practices; what is alarming is the increasing number of cases that have brought to public notice in recent years. It is true that there cannot be an explanation that is universally valid, given the specific nature of each of the scams that seems to have considerably dented administrative efficiency. Nonetheless, these instances are a testimony to the decline of ethics in public life, which is linked to the overall moral decadence confronting Indian society. Although society is to be blamed, because of its failure to strengthen its moral fabric, institutional responses should not be belittled since they also aim at reforming the structure of governance by introducing several schemes and designs which are potentially strong enough to radically alter the texture of its functioning. As shown in this chapter, some of the institutional steps, including the constitutional guarantee to democratic decentralization as a form of local governance that the Indian state has recently adopted, seem to have acted decisively in curbing malpractices in governance. Given its well entrenched roots in society, corruption cannot be removed so easily, although the importance of participatory governance such as *Bhagidari* and *Panchayati Raj* in arresting the decline of ethics in public authority cannot be easily undermined.

Participatory governance drawing on the spirit of democratic decentralization is an antidote to centralization in administration which, as per the Second Administrative Reforms Commission, 'delegitimizes democracy, alienates the citizen, perpetuates hierarchies, and often breeds corruption and inefficiency'.[41] Being aware that the 'propensity to abuse authority is intrinsic to all authorities', the Commission thus recommended certain specific mechanisms to measure citizens' satisfaction as the consumer of public services, which entail 'report cards, citizens' feedback at delivery and service counters, call centres and such for the citizens' voice to be heard and feedback to be counted ... and social audit through credible community based organizations'.[42] The aim is to ascertain citizen-centricity in administration which will, the Commission believed, contribute to the sustenance and consolidation of ethics in governance through an effective empowerment of stakeholders, accompanied by putting the appropriate institutional mechanisms in place. The Seventy Third and Seventy Fourth amendment acts seem to have initiated powerful processes towards fulfilling the constitutional aim of truly democratizing our administration in which ethics as much the concomitant institutional values remain the critical governing ethos.

the fact that the spirit in which these amendment acts were promulgated remains a distant one, there is no doubt that they are among the few pieces of legislation that, along with reinventing the nature of public authority in India, have also reinforced the centricity of the citizen in governance as perhaps one of the most effective means to contain tendencies towards crippling ethics in public life. They may not be adequate, in other words, to contain corruption completely, but the institutional changes that they have brought about in governance at the grassroots seem to have dramatically transformed the texture of local administration. They have done so by involving the stakeholders who, so far, remain peripheral in the top-down bureaucratic structure in post-independence India. What is fundamental here is the fact that *Bhagidari* and *Panchayat Raj*, despite not being full-proof mechanisms to combat corruption and ensure ethics in governance, are powerful alternative statements on how to make public authorities accountable and sensitive to the citizens' requirements of realizing democracy both in spirit and in substance.

What sustains the momentum for ethics in governance is the drive towards the opening up of political authority, which until now remained the captive of the dominant elites of the past. The enactment of the Seventy-Third and Seventy-Fourth amendment acts, however, radically altered the texture of local governance 'by bringing the locus of decision making closer to citizens, which increases the benefits of participation while reducing its costs'.[43] The more the citizens participate in governance as part of their being in a locality, the more democratic it will become and the less will be the tendencies towards appropriating public authorities for partisan gains, because the citizens will be vigilant in relation to governmental policy designs and acts. Participation has, as history shows, a snowball effect because 'when enough people are convinced of the value of participation [and] they sense a fundamental change in the nature of politics and power',[44] governance will become an empowering instrument to execute what is deemed to be useful for the people at large. With their involvement in governance, the engaged citizenry will not only become 'potent political forces, [they can also] move the actions of the local governments towards [their] interests by adding their voice to the mix of necessary accommodations'.[45] What is fundamental here is the fact that participatory governance is a powerful means to articulate democratic decentralization in its true form. By reaffirming the critical role of citizens in governance, India's empowered local government seems to have set in motion processes whereby governance has been reinvented in the light of the growing democratization that has already gripped India to a significant extent. This confirms the contention that institutional changes cannot completely arrest the moral decadence or large-scale decline of ethics in society, although they are strong enough to oppose those seeking to destroy the publicness of public authorities. Here perhaps lies the reason as to why changes in local governance were heartily welcomed, since they were powerful legislative steps to make local authorities completely citizen-centric and also conscious of those ethical codes of conduct that are most pertinent in fulfilling the fundamental ethos of democratic decentralization.

The narrative would not, however, be complete without commenting on the gradual deterioration of both *Bhagidari* and *Panchayati Raj* in recent years. *Bhagidari* seemed to be dead following the ignominious defeat of the Congress Party in 2015, though it has reappeared in the form of *Mohalla Sabhas* which the Aam Admi Party-led government meaningfully utilized during the election campaign and its aftermath to garner support in its favour. Instead of being genuinely representative of segments of society, these *Mohalla Sabhas* have become a constant source of distrust among those who had been integral to *Bhagidari* in the recent past. Notwithstanding their capability of bringing people together, these new institutions of local authorities do not seem to have realized their full potential so far, perhaps because of their failure to emerge as acceptable political platforms for the people regardless of ideological predilections. Nonetheless, given their strategic location in Delhi's governance, they can be optimistically expected, argues an analyst, 'to act as a torque through which both the state and citizenry bargain their respective axial positions'.[46] Similarly, *Panchayati Raj* institutions were also not free from criticism, given the degeneration that affected their functioning over the years. Like *Bhagidari*, they also became instruments for self-gratification, undermining significantly the values and principles that informed their formation and gradual consolidation in West Bengal. They were powerful tools for citizens' involvement in governance but gradually lost their relevance as the party-pampered elites captured the government machineries in the localities. So, the clamour for ethics in governance, which also entails respect for local voices when taking decisions meaningful to the stakeholders, no longer remained as pertinent in governance as before.[47] In course of time, the devolution of power in West Bengal through *Panchayati Raj* transformed 'the form of rent-seeking from outright theft and graft to other, more pernicious and ostensibly legal avenues of resource capture'[48] undermining considerably the ideological aim of ensuring equity and instilling efficiency in governance. Despite the criticisms, which are genuine, there is no doubt that *Panchayati Raj* has contributed to the creation of an alert citizenry that, by always being vigilant, never allows the government to remain indifferent to their demands and the issues that they raise for their well-being.

The stories of *Bhagidari* in Delhi and *Panchayati Raj* in West Bengal are thus not merely indicative of significant institutional changes, but also a testimony to the changing socio-economic and political fabric supportive of meaningful engagement of citizens in governance. By being proactive, citizens have also become instigators of change, and governance is a practical arena in which decisions arrive out of multiple processes of deliberations, challenges and negotiations and in which the citizen will always remain critical. In other words, contrary to the Weberian top-down administration, governance, which is moulded in the spirit of democratic decentralization, is a differently textured design of citizens' involvement in the decision-making processes. The key to the success of governance, especially in a nation as complex and diverse as India – spanning the seventeenth century to the twenty-first – is contingent on how efficiently these conflicting aims are reconciled. Democratic decentralization is perhaps that effective ideological arrangement which is both accommodative and also forward looking. Various instances of misuse of authority notwithstanding, *Bhagidari* and *Panchayati Raj* are undoubtedly effective designs of policy making, through which attempts were made to make governance sensitive to the basic ethical ethos of administration, which is both ideological in nature and politically construed. In three distinct ways, they can be said to have initiated processes for ensuring ethics in governance that cannot be easily belittled. First, they are primarily, at least in theory, designs for engaging citizens in governance; critical of bureaucratic hegemony, *Bhagidari* and *Panchayati Raj* are conceptually different forms of governance at the grassroots in which citizens remain the focal point. Second, governance is not only about institutions, but also about appropriate policy decisions seeking to contribute to the well-being of the stakeholders. For those holding authority, being ethically tuned entails being attentive to what satisfies the citizens most, for which they need to be both accessible and interactive; otherwise, the idea of meaningful civic engagement for effective governance will always remain elusive. Third, being offshoots of intensive democratic churning at the grassroots, both *Bhagidari* and *Panchayati Raj* represent popular urges for democratizing administration which, by ensuring the determining role of citizens, represent a powerful effort towards articulating one of the fundamental principles of the Constitution of India. Being ethical means being tuned to these principles, which also include powerful checks against the capturing of resources for partisan gain. What *Bhagidari* and *Panchayati Raj* have shown is how effective meaningful institutional changes can be for restoring ethics in governance, even in the midst of overall moral decadence, by catapulting the citizens onto the centre stage of politics. This constitutes a new parameter of politics, which gained an easy acceptance once *Bhagidari* and *Panchayati Raj*, as has been shown in this chapter, were conceptualized as alternative forms of governance through which issues of ethics, values and principles could become far more significant than before.

Notes

1 *Local Governance: an inspiring journey into the future*, Sixth Report, Second Administrative Reforms Commission, Government of India, New Delhi, October 2007, p. 16.
2 Ibid.
3 Alexis de Tocqueville, *Democracy in America*, Vol. 1, Vintage Classics, New York, 1990, pp. 57–8.
4 M K Gandhi, *The Village Swaraj*, Navajivan Publishing House, Ahmedabad, 1962, p. 41.
5 M K Gandhi's press interview, 28 July 1946, *Hindustan Times*, Delhi, 30 July 1946.
6 *The Diary of Mahadev Desai*, Navajivan Publishing House, Ahmedabad, 1953, p. 149.
7 M K Gandhi, *The Village Swaraj*, pp. 30–43.
8 Ibid., p. 477.
9 M K Gandhi's letter to the *Ashram* sisters, 7 January 1927, *The Selected Letters, 1921–1927*, Vol. 1, Navajivan Publishing House, Ahmedabad, 1953, p. 138.

10 Richard Crook and James Manor, *Democratic Decentralization*, OED Working Paper Series, No. 11, The World Bank, Washington DC, 2000, p. 11.

11 Ibid., p. 11.

12 Ibid., p. 12.

13 Ibid.

14 Rajiv Gandhi, India's former Prime Minister made this statement on the floor of parliament in 1989. This is quoted from Niraja Gopal, Amit Prakash and Pradeep K Sharma (eds), *Local Governance in India: decentralization and beyond*, Oxford University Press, New Delhi, 2006, p. 6.

15 Ghazala Mansuri and Vijayendra Rao, *Localizing Development: does participation work?* The World Bank, Washington DC, 2013, p. 16.

16 Martin Minogue, 'Changing the state: concepts and practice in the reform of the public sector' in Martin Minogue, C Polidano and D Hume (eds), *Beyond the NPM: changing ideas and practice in governance*, Edward Elgar, Cheltenham, 1998, p. 17.

17 *Reforming Public Institutions and strengthening governance: a World Bank strategy*, Public Sector Group, The World Bank, 2000, p. 2.

18 Henry S Maine, *Village Communities in the East and West*, Henry Elliot Company, New York, 1876.

19 M K Gandhi, 'Village *Panchayat*', *Harijan*, 28 July 1948, *The Selected Works of Mahatma Gandhi*, Vol. VI, Navjivan Publishing House, Ahmedabad, 1968, p. 451.

20 M K Gandhi, 'Self-government in practice', *Young India*, 5 March 1931, *Collected Works of Mahatma Gandhi*, Vol. 48, Ministry of Information, Government of India, 1968, p. 561.

21 M K Gandhi, '*Swaraj*', *Young India*, 5 March 1927, *Collected Works of Mahatma Gandhi*, Vol. 48, Ministry of Information, Government of India, 1968, p. 631.

22 Patsy Healey, *Collaborative Planning: shaping policies in fragmented societies*, UBC Press, Vancouver, 1997, p. 7.

23 Judith E Innes and David Booher, *Planning with Complexity: an introduction to collaborative rationality for public policy*, Routledge, Oxford, 2010, p. 5.

24 T Sagar, *Communicative Planning Theory*, Aldershot, Avery, 1994.

25 O Yiftachel, 'Planning as control: policy and resistance in deeply divided societies', *Progress in Planning Series*, Vol. 44, Pier Gammon Elsevier, Oxford, 1995, p. 17.

26 T Richardson, 'Foucauldian Discourse: power, truth in urban and regional policy making', *European Planning Studies*, 4 (3), 1995, pp. 279–92.

27 *Bhagidari – the Citizen–Government Partnership: some preliminary observations*, Department of Information and Publicity, Government of Delhi, Delhi 2012, p. 2.

28 Debolina Kundu, 'Elite capture in participatory governance', *Economic and Political Weekly*, 5 March 2011, p. 23.

29 *Bhagidari – the Citizen–Government Partnership*, p. 7.

30 Ghertner, 'Gentrifying the state, p. 504.

31 Atul Kohli, *The State and Poverty in India: politics of reform*, Cambridge University Press, Cambridge, 1989.

32 Abhirup Sarkar, 'Political economy of West Bengal', *Economic and Political Weekly*, 28 January 2006, pp. 31–4).

33 Pranab Bardhan, Sandip Mitra, Dilip Mookherjee and Abhirup Sarkar, 'Local democracy and clientelism: implications for political stability in West Bengal', *Economic and Political Weekly*, 28 February 2009. p. 58.

34 Dwaipayan Bhattacharya, 'Of control and factions: changing party–society in rural West Bengal', *Economic and Political Weekly*, 2009, p. 241.

35 *Political Organizational Report*, Communist Party of India (Marxist), 1982, pp. 19–22.

36 George Koreth and Kiron Wadhea, *Building a Citizens' Partnership in Democratic Governance: the Delhi Bhagidari process through large-scale group dynamics*, Sage, New Delhi, 2013, p. 114.

37 Debolina Kundu, 'Elite capture in participatory governance', *Economic and Political Weekly*, 5 March 2011, p. 25.
38 Rajarshi Dasgupta, 'The CPI (M) machinery in West Bengal: two village narratives from Koochbehar and Malda', *Economic and Political Weekly*, 28 February 2009, p. 81.
39 Pranab Bardhan, Sandip Mitra, Dilip Mookherjee and Abhirup Sarkar, 'Local democracy and clientelism: implications for political stability in West Bengal', *Economic and Political Weekly*, 28 February 2009. pp. 57–9.
40 Ghertner, 'Gentrifying the state' p. 511.
41 *Local Governance*, p. 21.
42 *Local Governance*, p. 20.
43 Ghazala Mansuri and Vijayendra Rao, *Localizing Development: does participation work?* The World Bank, Washington DC, 2013, p. 100.
44 Ibid., p. 111.
45 Ibid., p. 98.
46 Aditya Mohanty, 'From *Bhagidari* to Mohalla Sabhas in Delhi: when participation trumps governance', *Economic and Political Weekly*, 5 April 2014, p. 18.
47 Pranab Bardhan and Dilip Mookherjee have shown the gradual deterioration of the *Panchayati Raj* institutions of governance in their 'Political Clientelism and Capture: theory and evidence from West Bengal', Working Paper, Department of Economics, University of California, Berkeley, 2012.
48 Mansuri and Rao, *Localizing Development*, p. 122.

3 Ethics and administrative reforms in India

Historically speaking, there are two ways in which the issue of the decline of ethics in governance has been addressed. First, some hold the view that the decline of ethics in governance cannot be conclusively arrested through administrative acts, given its roots in the wider socio-economic and political milieu. What is therefore required is to create an environment in which values of integrity, honesty and the rule of law are uncritically appreciated and respected, notwithstanding provocations to the contrary. This is easier said than done since it involves an overhauling of the system, drawing its sustenance from the milieu in which it is located. To accomplish the goal, one needs to devise means that will have long-term effects on society. These means must be nurtured through socialization, beginning with one's childhood; they are not merely means in the conventional sense of the term, but are effective designs for fundamental socio-economic and political changes that are subtle and goal-driven. As history has shown, sustained endeavour in which these means remain critical results in transformations. These also create impulses for change, a change seen as being natural and integrally connected with efforts towards building a society free from retarding influences.

The second device that is resorted to quite often to arrest the deterioration in ethics in public authorities is taking steps towards reforming administration at regular intervals. Based on the belief that the key to the decline of ethics is the rising tide of corruption, some experts have sincerely pursued a line of thinking in which administrative reform is seen to be an effective mechanism. By suggesting various ways of tackling corruption and malpractices, which have an obvious debilitating effect on governance, they usually end up with a design of administration which, they think, is adequately equipped to take care of administrative decay. Logically persuasive and administratively feasible, these designs are usually aimed at putting in place a system whereby the fundamental objective of public administration – serving the public – is neither compromised nor bypassed. This seems to be relatively easier than the first option, because, drawing on its collective experience, the state is well equipped to suggest ways and means for improvement. Since designs for administrative reforms do not radically alter the ideological texture of the system, they are rather easily accepted. This suggests that administrative reforms provide a better and also far more effective means of arresting administrative decay. There are two assumptions which are critical here: on the one hand, it is assumed that the key to change in administration is consciously chosen designs for reforms which are both contextual and futuristic: contextual, because they are usually centred around those issues which seem to have bothered the decision makers; futuristic, since these designs are prepared keeping in view the possible changes in administration and the repercussions from the public and those involved in governance following the implementation of the measures. Seeking to address the new social, economic and politico-ideological concerns for which the prevalent administration appears to be inadequate, the second assumption underlines, on the other hand, the importance of stakeholders in shaping an appropriate administrative design for them. An administration's inner strength and capability is judged and assessed on whether it is an effective tool for fulfilling a goal. So, administrative reforms are also an attempt at adapting administration to the interests of those who are expected to be served; the failure here denotes distortions in administration that contribute to an environment in which tendencies towards undermining ethics in governance seem to have an edge.

There is, however, a cautionary note. Ethics in governance cannot be ensured by administrative acts alone; they also require societal changes, in which the values of ethics are respected. The significance of administrative reforms should not be underestimated: they provoke debates on the critical nature of ethics in public life. What is argued here is the importance of the dialectical interconnection between administrative reforms and societal changes, at the same time as seeking to understand and conceptualize the processes for establishing ethics in governance. The argument hinges on the point that administrative reforms will become far more effective if they are supplemented by a consolidated societal drive against the tendency to belittle ethics in governance. Keeping in view this fundamental observation, this chapter, by delineating the salience of administrative reforms for ethics in public life, concentrates on how they have contributed to transforming Indian administration over the years. It is also argued here that administrative reforms are definite measures that nurture and also protect the ethical basis of administration, as the history of administrative reforms in India has shown. Administrative reforms are both transformative and also designs reflecting a drive towards adapting the administration to context-specific societal demands. By providing a detailed study of the various schemes of administrative reform that India has undertaken, particularly since her political independence in 1947, this chapter, reconfirms the point that administrative decrees for reform, despite being context-dependent, always have a societal impact by arresting distortions in administration and consequently reaffirming the importance of ethics in governance.

What is administrative reform?

Administrative reform is basically related to the idea of a change in administration that is brought about through deliberate effort. It should, however, be borne in mind, as Machiavelli warns, that there is nothing more difficult to arrange, more doubtful of success and more dangerous to carry through than initiating changes in a state's constitution. The innovator makes enemies of all those who prospered under the old order, and only lukewarm support is forthcoming from those who would prosper under the new.[1]

Administrative reform is therefore 'a risk, a gamble in which the odds are heavily against success ... [and] it can take generations for administrative behaviour and values to change appreciably'.[2] There are, thus, hardly any magical keys to administrative reform. It is a long-term process that requires talent, zeal and commitment, scarce resources and, above all, time, whereas governments tend to look for short-term and quick solutions. Reform is, thus argues Gerald Caiden, 'tossed around like a boat in a storm [since] from conception to finality is a long, arduous and difficult journey beset with numerous obstacles, unforeseen perils and unexpected surprises'.[3] Underlining the criticality of the political ambience in which administrative reforms are attempted, Caiden further argues that they are 'an artificial instrument of administrative transformation against resistance'.[4] While elaborating on administrative reform as a conceptual category, he thus identifies three important characteristics: first, it entails a thorough reconstruction of the machinery of government which, in effect, means a complete or partial overhauling of the existing administrative structure that appears to have lost momentum in the changed circumstances; second, it aims at systematic transformation and not piecemeal change, permanent alterations and not cosmetic touches, in structure, territorial organization, budget management, planning processes and personnel practices to reduce corruption, incompetence and red tape; third, the different sectors and programmes must be rationalized and reorganized for more effective performance; and, finally, the machinery of government must be simplified and streamlined to eliminate unnecessary duplication, reduce inconvenience and minimize pluralism.[5] It is thus believed that administrative reform is a persuasive tool to bring about changes in public governance in accordance with what is deemed to be appropriate in a specific context. As a goal-driven initiative, administrative reform thus provides a way to arrest distortions in governance and also contributes to processes whereby the issue of ethics receives adequate attention in decision making. Difficulties notwithstanding, the drive towards administrative reform always remains, as history shows, integral to the socio-political churning that usually creates an environment for change. The political authority cannot easily escape this drive, given its organic roots in the wider social, economic and political milieu. The desire for ethics in governance is also based on the internal concern for streamlining governance to make it sensitive to the values of public service; this can be a determining source of administrative reform, although the importance of external stimuli cannot be neglected, because ethics in governance is usually the outcome of a contextual dialectical interconnection between internal necessity and external insistence. In the ultimate analysis, administrative reforms seeking to reinforce the fundamental ethos of administration are a deliberate mechanism for the administrative changes required to make governance attentive to the basic moral code of conduct while still fulfilling its goals.

Ethics and administrative reforms in India

Governance in a democratic polity cannot be absolutely aloof from ethics, since it is meant to serve the public; even in an authoritarian regime, despite its inherent tendency to pursue partisan goals, public administration cannot publicly declare its private goal because of the obvious adverse impact on the governed. There is therefore depth in the argument that public authorities, notwithstanding their context-dependent instrumental goals, cannot afford to ignore their publicness at any cost. Public administration is, in other words, devoid of its kernel if it is conceptualized without understanding its emphasis on public well-being as a fundamental goal. The section thus argues that governance is an act of articulating and also implementing ideology-driven socio-economic and political objectives in specific circumstances. The fundamental ethos of administration can be conveniently bypassed if the publicness of public administration is heavily compromised. In such circumstances, the considerations of ethics in public life do not appear to be as critical as expected. Ridden with distortions, governance thus becomes clearly instrumental, being utilized for fulfilling personalized goals and missions. This, however, does not happen overnight since governance-deficit is an offshoot of long-drawn-out processes which are also linked to overall social and political decadence in the society in question. Administrative reforms, as argued above, are about those devices that are considered to be effective in arresting decadence in public authority. These are both internally articulated and driven by external demands; they can thus be said usually to emerge out of a respect for justice and fair play, because this is what ethics in governance is all about. Ideologically charged and empirically designed, administrative reforms are thus not merely tools of change, but also thoughtful endeavours towards charting out a definite course of action which is, in principle, tuned to the ethical concern for public well-being.

Turning to the 'reforms' scenario in India, one has to run through a long period of bureaucratic ups and downs since the advent of colonial rule. During the imperial rule, the core purpose of administration was to bolster colonialism, with the people's interests being absolutely peripheral if not entirely absent. Hence administrative reforms had, for obvious reasons, the single priority of perpetuating British rule. This was suppressive and contrary to the values of the British Enlightenment, which highlighted social virtues such as benevolence, compassion and tolerance. Colonialism, assessed in such a perspective, was an aberration, since it struck at the very foundation of the Enlightenment principles. Nonetheless, the most significant change that the British administration initiated had been the gradual suppression of custom by law in the management of public services. It was also strongly felt that involvement of Indians in the administration was necessary to create strong roots in the society under British rule. The 1892 *Indian Council Act* thus stated that the aim of this Act was to widen and expand the functions of the Government of India, and to give further opportunities to the non-official and native elements in Indian society to take part in the work of the Government, and in that way, to lend official recognition to that remarkable development both of political interests and political capacity that had been visible among the higher classes of Indian society since the Government of India was taken over by the Crown in 1858.[6]

In conformity with the above claim to expand the foundation of governance in India by accommodating Indians in the administration, several legislative enactments were made, despite the fact that centralization of power and authority remained the preeminent goal of British administration, and one that was never compromised. Nonetheless, a change in governance was visible with the involvement of Indians in administration; though in a very limited way, the administration was receptive to the voice that came from the grassroots against tyrannical exercise of power. Perhaps the most (and last) significant constitutional measure in India during the British rule was the 1935 *Government of India Act,* which drew on inputs from the Indian Statutory Commission, the All Parties Conference, the Round Table Conferences and the Joint Parliamentary Committee of the British Parliament. Seeking to establish a federal form of government in which the constituent provinces had autonomous legislative and executive powers, the Act paved the way for a parliamentary form of government in which the executive was made accountable within certain bounds to the legislature. This radically altered public administration in India, including the civil service in the country. Although the well-espoused federation never came into being, the Act was nonetheless a powerful comment against an integrated administrative system of the colonial variety. A perusal of the Act draws our attention to the following features:

- a provincial autonomy was recognized by giving the provinces a separate legal identity and liberating them from central control except for certain specific purposes;
- a federation of India was established, demarcating domains between the provincial governments and the federal central government;
- dyarchy, discontinued in the provinces, was introduced at the centre. The responsibilities for foreign affairs and defence were 'reserved' to the control of the Governor-General; the other central responsibilities were transferred to ministers in the provinces, subject to 'safeguards';
- the federal principle was recognized in the formation of the lower house of the central legislature though the de facto ruler, remained the Governor-General;
- a separate electorate was retained following the distribution of seats among the minority communities, as devised by the 1932 Communal or MacDonald Award.

The *Government of India Act* redefined 'public' in public administration. The introduction of provincial autonomy enabled the Indian ministers to be directly involved in administration, although they had to function under the overall restriction of colonialism. Hence it was characterized as 'a gigantic constitutional façade without anything substantial within it'. The Act was also a sign of the determination of the British government to shift the Indian question towards electoral politics. By involving Indians in the administration, the Act had brought more players into the arena of public administration. There is no doubt that the Act introduced Indian politicians to the world of parliamentary politics and, as a result of the new arrangement stipulated by the Act, politics now percolated down to the localities, which had largely remained peripheral to that point. The available evidence also suggests that the Act was the price the British paid for the continuity of the Empire. What thus appears to be a calculated generous gesture was very much a politically expedient step. In fact, the surrender of power, although at the regional level, caused consternation among the advocates of British power in India, who saw an eclipse of British authority in this endeavour.

An uncritical assessment of the major landmark constitutional initiatives during colonial rule may lead one to conclude that these were initiated by the British for the purpose of better administration for the Indians. But that would underestimate the spirit of nationalism. If one goes beyond the surface, what is evident is that public administration underwent changes largely because of the British effort to defuse popular discontent. Hence the argument that every constitutional drive was initiated by the Raj is totally unfounded. History reveals that there were situations that forced the British authority to adopt measures to control agitation. For instance, the Congress campaign in the 1880s contributed a lot to the introduction of the 1893 reforms. Behind the 1909 Morley–Minto Reforms lay the *Swadeshi* Movement and revolutionary terrorism. Similarly, the 1919 Montague–Chelmsford Reforms were attempts at resolving crises that began with the Home Rule League and climaxed in the 1919 Rowlatt Satyagraha and the Non Cooperation Movement of 1910–21. To a large extent, the Gandhian civil disobedience movement (1930–2) accounted for the introduction of constitutional measures seeking to involve Indian politicians in public administration.

Furthermore, the interpretation of these constitutional designs remains partial unless it is linked to the broader socio-economic and political processes in which they were conceptualized. An attempt to analyse the structure and dynamics of constitutional politics without reference to the broader social matrix and economic nexus is futile, because the politico–constitutional structure reflects economic and social networks, religio-cultural beliefs and even the nationalist ideology which impinged on the organized world of administrative and constitutional structure. So an urgent and unavoidable task for an analyst is not to completely ignore the broader socio-economic context but to ascertain its relative importance in shaping a particular constitutional initiative. For instance, the 1932 Communal Award was believed to have been initiated by the British to expand political activity among the Muslims in Bengal and Punjab. But, as studies have shown, it was also a concession the British were forced to grant in order to make the maintenance of the Empire easier. The sharing of power with the native elites was thus prompted by considerations other than merely British initiatives.

With independence, the nature and the spirit of administration were bound to be radically different since its moral foundation had undergone dramatic changes. The Indian historical experience, both during the British period and its immediate aftermath, has led to the emergence of a public administration that was ill-suited to the needs and aspiration of the people. The reasons are not difficult to find, as studies have shown that the bureaucrats who were brought up and trained in the colonial administrative culture were wedded to the Weberian characteristics of hierarchy, status and rigidity of rules and regulations and concerned mainly with the enforcement of order and the collection of revenues. For the colonial regime, this structure was appropriate; however, it was completely unfit to discharge functions in the changed environment of an administration geared to the task of development. As the Government became the main institution for development in the democratic set-up that India adopted following independence, the role of officials underwent changes. The sole objective of officials became to 'emphasize results, rather than procedures, teamwork rather than hierarchy and status, [and] flexibility and decentralization rather control and authority'.[7] Seen as 'the development administrator', a bureaucrat, endowed with 'tact, pragmatism, dynamism, flexibility, adaptability to any situation and willingness to take rapid, ad-hoc decisions without worrying too much about procedures and protocol'[8] was thus hailed as perhaps the most effective aid to accomplishing the ideological mission that an independent India had undertaken.

Following independence, government functions expanded in scope and content. With the introduction of the parliamentary form of government and the setting up of people's institutions right down to village level, there has been an inevitable rise in the level of expectation and government performance has been seen to vary. People's institutions were set up with the objective of creating self-governing institutions at village level. A true democracy, as advocated by Gandhi, ensures that local, state and national representatives are accountable to the people for local, state and national matters respectively, through effective transparency. Such one-to-one accountability may promote responsible politics and competent political professionals. That objective remains distant. Our present system based on diffused accountability, as mentioned in the consultation paper of the National Commission for Review of the Working of the Constitution, 'breeds corruption and attracts self-seekers to politics'. For this breed, the paper further underlines, 'interests of national development, welfare of the people and needs of good governance take lower priorities, if any'.[9] Similarly, independence and Five Year Plans were perceived by the people as synonymous with economic and social equity and well-being, and freedom from want and oppression. In the early days of the planning era, people did not quibble much about shortages, which they confronted with fortitude, because the future held hope and promise for them. With the passage of time, they felt their hopes had been dashed, and, as the paper indicated, they were 'nowhere near the promised land of honesty, plenty and happiness'. The era of self-governance, decentralization and community development was flagged in with considerable élan and fan-fare. For example, the three-tier *Panchayati Raj* system and the urban local bodies were conceived of as a properly meshed network of institutions to accelerate the development process. Revolutionary in scope, the Seventy-Third and Seventy-Fourth amendments (1992) to the Constitution sought to advance the concept of 'self-governance' by providing for (a) regular elections, (b) minimal suppression of *Panchayati Raj* bodies through an administrative fiat and (c) regular finances through statutory distribution by state finance commissions. But, for various reasons, the political process became what may be termed as 'reversed', and highly centralized and personalized systems of government developed both at the central and state levels. There has been a massive erosion of institutions, whether they are the Parliament and parliamentary institutions, or the party system and democratic procedures in the running of parties, or the judiciary, or indeed the press.

Given the new challenges of economic development and social change, the prevalent administrative set-up was both structurally inadequate and functionally unprepared in India's changed socio-political circumstances. So there was a need for administrative reforms whereby the structure would respond to the systemic changes in the Indian polity following the British withdrawal. While redefining the nature of civil service in independent India, Jawaharlal Nehru thus commented that since 'the state has become a dynamic state – not a static state – Services (administrators) have to adapt themselves to the changes ... have to adapt methods to the changed conditions of work and the changed objectives of work'.[10] Several steps were undertaken in the aftermath of the 1947 transfer of power.

The first step was undoubtedly the Secretariat Reorganization Committee, appointed by the imperial government even before the actual transfer of power. In its report, submitted in August 1947, the Committee commented extensively on 'the unresponsive' nature of the administration, that was simply 'incapable' of handling 'the new challenges' in the aftermath of the British withdrawal.[11] This line of thinking was pursued in 1951 in two subsequent reports – *Public Administration in India* and *Efficient Conduct of State Enterprises*, prepared by A D Gorwala for the Planning Commission. Recommending the introduction of the 'organization and method' procedure in government departments and public enterprises, Gorwala suggested steps to ensure 'efficiency' and 'discipline' in the civil service. What separates this report from the earlier ones is the considerable emphasis on 'the coordination between politicians and administrators' for 'smooth and efficient' functioning of public administration.[12] A D Gorwala's report was submitted on 30 April 1951. The report stated that, although the administrative machinery had remained sound, the increasing work load had been adversely affecting the performance of the personnel. The major recommendations included (a) maintenance of high standards of integrity and efficiency in administration, (b) that the machinery be reorganized to ensure speed, effectiveness and accountability (c) that some basic structural changes be introduced to improve the quality of services, and (d) that arrangements be made for training of officials and recruitment through the Public Service Commissions to avoid nepotism and patronage.

In his in-depth study of the Indian administration in 1953, Paul Appleby suggested radical reforms of an administrative structure that was 'archaic', 'feudalistic' and 'unimaginative' and hence was simply 'inadequate' to fulfill the primary goal of nation with 'a long history of colonialism'. In his report, Appleby criticized 'the structure which subordinated the national Government to State, district and municipal control making implementation of programmes of national importance difficult'. He therefore suggested some structural changes such as (a) creation of middle-level functionaries and recruitment of more executives at all levels, (b) a more flexible system of recruitment to meet particular needs and requirements, (c) the setting up of panels of qualified persons in place of the existing practice of selecting individuals, (d) arranging of refresher courses for serving personnel, (e) setting up of an Organization and Management Division in each Department to monitor the work, and (f) finding ways to improve the administration through specialized studies and reviews undertaken by the Institute of Public Administration. Moreover, he was critical of the tendency of the Ministry of Finance to centralize powers and not to delegate them to the operational ministries. Furthermore, while commenting on the nature of subordinates at the cutting edge level of bureaucracy, Appleby expressed concern at the growing level of corruption by saying that 'it is not surprising that it is at these cutting edges – post offices, district sub offices, in agricultural extension and in many places – where corruption is most common and where personal disgruntlement is the great handicap in the way of pushing on programmes ... actually undertaken and not merely verbalized'.[13] He referred to the diffusion of responsibility from the top to the lower levels and the lack of 'facilities for administrative delegation'. Because of this diffusion of responsibility, it was difficult to ascertain 'accountability'. There was, according to him, 'too much scrutiny and too many impediments before the fact and too little systematic review and scrutiny after the fact'.[14] What is thus required for administration to remain relevant, felt Appleby, is regular review of decisions by taking into account the contextual inputs.

What drove Appleby in this exercise was his concern for change, which was unlikely to happen in the administration given its colonial roots? In other words, an administration that had served the imperial rulers did not appear to be appropriate for a free nation with its own socio-political and economic agenda. In fact, it is clear in Appleby's report that the prevalent bureaucratic set-up that sustained foreign rule was a mismatch with India's national aspiration. What was most surprising to him was the acceptance of 'an administrative machine' simply because of its 'instrumental' significance. As a result, the later efforts at administrative reform appear to have focused more on structural changes that were believed to be crucial in radically altering the inherent ideology of Indian public administration. The report of the Second Pay Commission (1957–9) is illustrative here. Appointed in 1957, the Commission's primary task was to examine 'the principles' that should govern 'the structure of emoluments and conditions of service' of central government employees. In order to ascertain efficiency, the Commission suggested the classification of government offices into 'attached' and 'subordinate' offices on a functional basis and bringing the relevant Secretariat and the attached offices under 'a single headquarter organization'. The other notable recommendation, drawing on the British pattern of Whitley Councils, was the creation of machinery for negotiation and settlement of disputes between employers and employees. Although this recommendation was almost shelved, the growing corruption in administration led to the appointment of the 1964 Santhanam Committee that looked into the problem of administrative corruption. Its recommendations were largely procedural in the sense that the roots of corruption lay in the violation of the established systems and procedures. What was groundbreaking was the recommendation for the creation of a central vigilance commission, as a permanent administrative wing to keep a sustained watch on civil servants.

The most comprehensive enquiry ever undertaken in the aftermath of decolonization was the Administrative Reforms Commission that came into being in 1966 under the stewardship of Morarji Desai. Two important ideas seemed to have governed the constitution of this Commission: first, the changing nature of administration – from a mere law-and-order maintenance agency to an apparatus responsible for development – radically altered the traditional conception of administration; second, the ideological goal of a socialist pattern of society called for a drastic overhauling of the machinery of government that so far had discharged its responsibility in a very stereotypical manner. So the commission was given a very wide mandate and was entrusted with the task of

> giving consideration to the need for ensuring the highest standard of efficiency and integrity in the public services and for making public administration a fit instrument for carrying out the social and economic goals of development as also one which is responsive to the public.[15]

As is evident, the Commission sought to redefine public administration by recognizing the importance of the 'public' in administration. Furthermore, the adoption of a socialistic pattern of society brought about radical changes in conceptualizing the role of administration. Guided by the objective of establishing a socialistic pattern of society, the Commission was entrusted with a 41-point charter, grouped into ten specific areas of enquiry which are as follows: (1) the machinery of the government of India and its procedures of work; (2) the machinery for planning at all levels; (3) centre–state relationships; (4) financial administration; (5) personnel administration; (6) economic administration; (7) administration at the state level; (8) district administration; (9) agricultural administration; and (10) problem of redress of citizen's grievances. In 20 reports that the Commission submitted, there were altogether 581 recommendations that covered the entire gamut of Indian administration. The most important recommendations relate to the structural transformation of central government, including the composition of the cabinet and other governmental departments responsible for developmental plans and programmes. Suggesting a maximum strength of 45 for the central cabinet, the Commission defined the role of the prime minister as a guide, coordinator and supervisor of a collectivity, known as the cabinet. The commission also provided a checklist of what the prime minister should do, largely in conformity with the Westminster form of cabinet government, where the premier is the pivot of the government. The other substantive recommendation involved the minister–secretary relationships that lay at the root of an efficient administration. In other words, being critical of the 'neutrality' in the civil service, the Commission supported a bureaucracy that clearly upheld the political will of the country, as articulated by the prime minister and his cabinet. Since the government was committed to socialist principles, the civil service, which was responsible for the implementation of this goal, was expected to reorient its role in the changed circumstances. Although the Commission maintained the obvious distinction between policy making and its execution in public administration, there was no rigidity in its characterization of the role of the political and permanent executives. As both of them constituted integral parts of an organic whole, it would be simply unrealistic, the Commission held, to overlook the mutual interaction between the two.

While the Commission devoted a great deal of energy to the structural reform of central government, personnel administration also received attention for it was the human content that ultimately decided the character of public administration. Just as with the 1953–5 Hoover Commission, which believed that 'the government cannot be any better than the man and woman who make it function', the Commission also insisted that 'the road to the top must be open to every competent and qualified government servant [and] to higher management in the Secretariat, talent must be drawn from every cadre and class of government servants'. Drawing on this philosophy, the Commission articulated its suggestions in four different ways: first, a rational system needs to be devised for recruitment to policy-making positions, with the recruitment of personnel possessing the required qualifications and competence. This involves an optimum use of different services for secretariat assignments and also the adoption of special measures to build the necessary specialization in the secretariat; second, senior management personnel must be selected from all relevant sources – generalist and specialists – and, for this purpose, talent needs to be discovered and developed in all the services, especially among those who have not so far been inducted into the higher management positions in the secretariat to any significant degree; third, a rational pay structure requires to be installed so as to truly reflect the actual responsibilities associated with each job; and, finally, to boost morale in the civil service, talented lower rank personnel should be given greater scope than what exists now to move up in the hierarchy on the basis of competence and performance.

The Commission report is probably the most exhaustive checklist of steps to streamline the administration in the changed socio-political environment. Drawing on 'certain basic considerations', the most significant recommendation, apart from the introduction of the concept and technique of performance budgeting, is the appointment of *Lokpal* (at the centre) and *Lokayaukta* (in the states). Perhaps the two most important areas touched on by the Commission in its reports are (a) the minister–civil servant relationship, wherein it emphasized the need for the depoliticization of services; and (b) the creation of a climate and culture of administration, wherein the growth of personal relationship between individual civil servants and the minister should be stopped. However, a close look at the recommendations suggests that the Commission, instead of radically altering the structure, was favourably inclined towards mere 'cosmetic' changes within the administration. It is pertinent to mention here that administrative reform appears futile unless it is accompanied by political reform. In other words, since public administration is hardly neutral, its nature is contingent on that of the 'political' in which it is located. So the Commission report, despite being voluminous although not so illuminating, was scarcely effective in substantially transforming the Indian administration, which had, for obvious reasons, colonial roots. Notwithstanding the declared objective of making the administration responsive to the people, the report thus remained a well-researched document on Indian administration with no far-reaching impact.

During the period between the appointment of the Commission in 1966 and the inauguration of the Fifth Pay Commission in 1997, there were no major committees except three isolated attempts: (a) to improve the pattern of combined services, a competitive examination introducing a preliminary tier of examination to eliminate the large number of candidates having less potential for success, as a sequel to the 1976 Kothari Committee report; (b) to revitalize the *Panchayati Raj* system of governance at the grassroots by converting the three-tier structure into a two-tier structure (1979 Mehta Committee), which has contributed significantly to the adoption of the *Seventy-Third Amendment Act* in 1992, and (c) to change the system of economic administration (the 1986 Jha Committee). Following these efforts, the most dramatic administrative reform scheme was articulated by the 1997 Fifth Pay Commission that has, as shown below, radically altered the prevalent conceptualization of reform by tuning to the compulsion of liberalization and the emergence of a new economic order. Similarly, the reconstitution of the grassroots governance, in the light of the 1992 *Seventy-Third Amendment Act*, has introduced new dimensions in rural administration by seeking to bring in the hitherto peripheral sections of society in the decision making.

It is obvious that, even before the onset of liberalization, several measures were adopted to revitalize the administration that owe their origin to completely different socio-economic concerns. These reforms were largely internally generated, while post-liberalization efforts were mostly externally driven. In this series of reform schemes, the recommendations of the 1981 National Police Commission (NPC) are different not only in their thrust but also in raising probably very crucial questions in a context in which those possessing the legitimate instruments of coercive power tended to distort the public nature of their authority at the slightest pretext.

National Police Commission Report

A critical look at police behaviour reveals an important dimension of its history that continues to influence its nature even after 50 years of independence. It would not be an exaggeration to argue that the Indian police remains the same at least in substance as when it was formally inaugurated with the promulgation of the 1861 *Police Act* in the shadow of the 1857 armed struggle against the British and with the main objective of ensuring imperial rule. Replacing the old *daraga* system that had become redundant with the spread of the British ascendancy in India, the new system was introduced with a view to expanding its reach as widely as possible. The police were an instrument of control, an instrument that was, for obvious reasons, unsparingly used to advance the cause of British imperialism. It had therefore no societal trust. Despite the fact that the colonial state embodied the theory and practice of the rule of law in its constitutional deliberations, the police force was mired in partisanship, its role was vicious and its image was deliberately nurtured as adversarial to society. Notwithstanding severe indictment during its four decades of existence until the point of the 1902 Police Commission, no reform was allowed by the colonial government either of its organization or its work culture. The police therefore emerged as a time-tested instrument that was allowed to function almost without shackles.

It is not difficult to understand why the colonial state preferred the Irish constabulary model to the Metropolitan model, which had sought to provide a new image for the police, one in which they hardly ever used force. For obvious reasons, the British government had never allowed the colonial states to adopt the Metropolitan Bobby model, which drew upon a style of community policing that did not resort to coercion except under exceptional circumstances. Not only was the Irish Constabulary a time-tested force in Ireland, the model seemed to be the most appropriate in firmly establishing and maintaining British hegemony in circumstances in which the colonial state was most vulnerable. Primarily a coercive instrument, the police hardly had any interactions with the people, because it was believed that a well-defined distance from the people was necessary in order to ruthlessly implement the official decrees of the Raj.

For the colonial state, the choice of the Irish Constabulary model was an obvious one. What is surprising is the continuity of that same model, even after India became free. Despite being critical of the British police that had sustained the most oppressive administration, the nationalist leaders, including Vallabbhai Patel and Jawaharlal Nehru, allowed the system to remain, simply because of its efficiency in law enforcement under colonialism. Even Gandhi was not in its favour. Drawing on and inspired by *ahimsa*, he therefore perceived the police as conducive to a radically different socio-economic and political order in which 'the sprit of violence will have all but vanished and internal disorder will come under control'.[16] Those who opposed the continuity of the Irish Constabulary model because of its ideological underpinning seemed to have been persuaded in view of the sudden outbreak of communal violence immediately after the transfer of power. What was readily acceptable because of the exigencies of the situation became a permanent feature of independent India, since the political leadership – regardless of ideology – began to relish a partisan police force that allowed the government to use a legitimate coercive force as and when required to pursue a political goal. The 2002 Gujarat carnage is perhaps the best available illustration to show how the police went berserk at a critical juncture to please their political bosses. However, it would be wrong to suggest that the police always act in accordance with the ruling authority's dictation. Again, the Gujarat case demonstrates the extent to which the local police reflected the mood of the majority community. By getting involved in the mayhem, either through actions or non-actions, the Gujarat police had articulated its response to the riot merely as an integral part of the majority community. By sharing the emotions of the majority community, the police had hardly remained secular. Gujarat is probably the latest example of the police being an active partner in the Hindutva campaign. Perhaps the most glaring example of a police force that tends to become communal at the slightest provocation is the Provincial Armed Constabulary in Uttar Pradesh. Examples can easily be multiplied showing the complicity of that constabulary with those for Hindutva. What stands out was its role during the 1992 Ayodhya catastrophe, when it was reported to have directly participated in the demolition of the controversial Islamic historical relic.

In view of the growing communalization of the police force, perhaps this is an appropriate time to have a fresh look at the 1981 report of the NPC. Before the NPC was inaugurated, several police commissions were appointed by various states, with Kerala being the pioneer in instituting a Police Reorganization Commission in 1959. Appointed in the aftermath of the 1975–7 Emergency, the NPC made several recommendations on police reforms in its eight-volume report, submitted in 1981. What is ironical, however, is that those who argued strongly for police reform since they suffered most as a result of police brutality during the Emergency held power at the centre in 1996–7, and yet there was a complete silence on what was hailed as 'a groundbreaking document' that would radically alter our approach to the police and policing in India.

The NPC has touched on a wide range of issues concerning the police in India. The two areas that appeared to have bothered the Commission most were (a) the misuse of the police and (b) accountability and police performance. For the Commission, the Emergency was a reference point at which the bias of the ruling authority seemed to have determined police behaviour. The police were used not merely as an instrument of the state or the government in power, but also of the politicians who had lost their legitimacy to rule. Jayprakash Narayan's appeal to the police to disobey the illegal order of their bosses in the wake of the *Chhatra Sangarsh* movement in Bihar was perhaps the first articulated signal of the possible devastation resulting from police complicity with the government of the day.

According to the NPC, the police themselves at the behest of politicians distorted their role during the Emergency. The Commission thus exhorts that 'the police sub-culture should take into account the fundamental rights of the people, the supremacy of laws and not of executive fiat, and our constitutional goal towards a developed and egalitarian society'.[17] There are innumerable examples to show that 'putting down political dissent became a tacitly accepted objective of the police system in most of the states'. In order to express their loyalty to the ruling party, the police always dealt with the law and order situations 'with a political eye'. The NPC was candid in seeking to conceptualize 'the police brutality and its cancerous corruption' by underlining that

> no thinking and planning are in evidence because the senior administrative ranks are perpetually insecure and are exhausted by the continual effort to survive, in an atmosphere where their assessment by the executive – administrative and political – is not always based on merit. Clearly the police organization as it stands today is unfit to discharge its duties.[18]

To contain the misuse of the police, two major recommendations were made: (a) there should be a tenured office of the Chief of Police, selected by a panel drawn from a committee comprising the chairman of the UPSC, the Union Home Secretary, the senior most heads of central police organizations, the Chief Secretary of the state and the existing Police Chief of the state; and, (b) there should be a six member permanent State Security Commission with a fixed term of three years to review annually the performance of the police.

The other serious recommendation involved measures to ascertain police accountability for the discharge of their duties. There are three types of interlinked accountability – accountability to the people and to the law and organizational accountability – that the police should seek to ensure.

There is a well-defined mechanism within the organization to ascertain 'internal accountability' for the police. This, by itself, does not ensure accountability to the people, for which mere recommendations will not suffice. So, accountability in this context presupposes two-dimensional responsibilities: on the one hand, the police are to discharge their responsibilities in accordance with both organizational rationality and systemic rationality, based on the law of the land; on the other hand, accountability also requires the duties to be discharged to the satisfaction of the party for whose benefit they are being performed. What it suggests is the importance of certain well-defined norms whereby a constant watch is maintained by the people. Over the years, it has been observed that the police seem to be completely alienated from the people whose agents they are and to whom they are ultimately accountable. It is not surprising that the use of third degree methods and custodial deaths have been on the rise. The police seem to be the easily available coercive instrument of the elected representatives, whenever they are required to forcibly suppress mass agitation against those representatives' misuse of public office. The NPC noted that, on innumerable occasions, the police acted like a mercenary force and ignored completely its societal role in defending the people, regardless of religion, clan and creed.

There is no doubt that these recommendations, if implemented, would radically alter not only the image of the police but also their functioning in a multi-religious society such as India. What is most disturbing, however, is the reluctance of even those who suffered due to police atrocities to take care of the recommendations when they come to power. The reasons are not difficult to seek. The police appear to be a handy instrument at the disposal of the ruling authority to pursue sectarian interests with legitimacy. The roots of this blatant distortion therefore lie elsewhere. If society is affected by a communal virus so that an anti-Muslim bias gets translated into violent action with the slightest provocation, it would be wrong to blame only the police for those distortions in our secular fabric. The NPC recommendations seem to have provided a good reference point to deal with those fundamental socio-political issues which, though directly linked to the functioning of the police, are equally significant in grasping what provokes mass hysteria at regular intervals in India.

Recent conceptualization of ethics in governance

Concern for ethics in governance is being continuously pursued by those in authority in tandem with the demands that the wider socio-economic and political milieu make on the system. Reform efforts in government have thus been a natural response. As shown above, the Administrative Reform Commission (1966–70) in India produced a series of reports concerning almost all the departments of the government. Every Pay Commission report in India carried with it many recommendations for changes in public administration per se. What is important to note is that these reform proposals were discussed within the framework of traditional public administration. The accountability of the civil service to the elected element within the overall accountability structure laid down in the parliamentary system of government was not in question. There was general consensus that public administration could be reformed effectively by a combination of strategic management, structural organization and the development of better personnel management systems.

In the 1980s, the global socio-economic and political scene started changing rapidly. The failure to control the economy in the developed West led to the rejection of old solutions of control. There was an accompanying change in political ideology, particularly on the right, that broke with the old consensus. The state seemed to lose its preeminence in governance because the inputs from civil society and other national and global agencies were equally important in contemporary governance. Ethics in governance is no longer confined to the four walls of public governance; instead it is also being conceptualized in response to what emanates from the wider socio-economic and political contexts. Given the relative decline of the state in governance, public ethics cannot be appropriately comprehended in a state-centric discourse. Hence, one has to be sensitive to those factors that may not have been taken seriously in traditional approaches to public administration, but have now acquired tremendous significance in view of the growing importance of non-state actors. This is a significant change that needs to be conceptualized, keeping in mind the fact that public administration has ceased to be bureaucracy-centric.

As is evident, the concern for administrative reform in India is not of recent origin. What is new is the context in which this is being articulated. With the adoption of the New Economic policy in the early 1990s, there have been attempts at dismantling the centrally directed framework of economic development. This is also the beginning of the period when international donor agencies have exercised immense influence in the domestic economy by attaching conditions to the provision of aid. These conditions were, at the outset, merely prescriptions for the administration of that aid; later, however, they became mechanisms for reform of the overall framework of governance itself. Given the rising tide of 'neo-liberalism', no country is free from this. The changed empirical context has contributed to a new conceptualization in the form of 'reinventing government', which seeks to articulate the transformed role of public administration.

The reforms in administration in India in the 1990s have been basically driven by measures on economic liberalization. The Indian response was clearly articulated in the 1996 conference of Chief Secretaries, which suggested several corrective steps to arrest the drift in the civil service before it was too late. The basic concern of those participating in the conference was to transform an aloof, impersonal and paternalistic bureaucracy into one that was citizen friendly and sensitive to user needs. What was suggested in the conference had its roots in the arguments put forward by Rajiv Gandhi, the former prime minister, in favour of 'responsive administration'. In his series of speeches at the workshops for district magistrates and collectors that spanned almost two years between 1987 and 1988, Rajiv Gandhi argued that

> [the] paternalistic model of [our] administration is not suitable for a society where the main thrust of administration is on development. It was agreed that the regulatory functions of administration should not be seen as an end in themselves, as they tended to be in colonial times, but as a means of reinforcing and sustaining the processes of broad based development. [A] more representative and more responsive administration would be better placed to relate the purposes of administration to the larger goals of our national life – democracy, socialism, secularism and non-alignment.[19]

The other point that was made related to 'the dependency syndrome' of the people. Bureaucracy continues to remain 'a doer' and not 'an enabler'. The people in general wait for the government to do 'the simplest things which they can do themselves'. The system has become 'so top-heavy and top-oriented' that at every level, people look to the level above for a solution. What is therefore needed is 'to push the administration down, not just in the administration but also sometimes out of the administration to the community'. By involving people in both planning and executing developmental programmes at the grassroots, the administration will become both 'responsive' and 'representative' in character.

Given the new emphases in contemporary public administration, it is now clear that traditional public administration is hardly an appropriate tool to conceptualize contemporary governance. Critical of the pyramidal structure of administration, the new wave is articulated by a model in which 'centralization and top downs get edged out, compelling innovation and dictating empowerment of functionaries at the cutting edge'.[20] With the flow of power downwards, those who matter at the field level gain strategic importance, and administration is forced to shift its attention from a hierarchically informed and bureaucratically designed response to a citizen-friendly approach vis-à-vis public affairs. So, the mere instrumental importance of administration seems to be gradually phasing out, giving way to a proactive system of governance in which the citizens are not merely recipients but clients with significant influences on both the content and the style of governance.

So, in this changed perspective, the focus in these reforms is 'on reshaping the boundaries and responsibilities of the state, through privatization, the restructuring of public services, and the introduction of private market discipline into public administration'.[21] Contemporary public administration is not just about efficiency; it also upholds democratic participation, accountability and empowerment. There is therefore a constant tension between (a) how to make government efficient and (b) how to keep it accountable. There is also a corresponding tension between 'the conception of people as consumers in the context of relations between state and market' and the conception of 'people as citizens in the context of relations between state and society'.[22] What it suggests is the increasing importance of citizen participation in public affairs.

Several steps have been taken to restructure the administration in response to this impetus from both domestic and external sources. Of these steps, the adoption of the Seventy-Third and Seventy-Fourth Amendment Acts of 1992 and the implementation of the fifth Pay Commission report appear to be significant because of their impact on existing governance. Arising from the perspectives outlined above, these were momentous steps that were potentially groundbreaking and contained seeds for radical transformation of both the content and style of governance. Interestingly, these two measures – the Amendment Acts and the Pay Commission recommendations – coincided not only with the liberalization impetus of central government, but also with the World Bank's marked emphasis on 'good governance' and decentralization. As the fundamental impulse of policy making moves away from centralized state institutions towards the market, these amendments, in principle, should facilitate the creation of structures that devolve power to localized bodies. The underlying principle of *panchayati raj* is the use of local knowledge, popular experience and participation in the making of decisions that affect local people. There is no doubt that the reformed *panchayati raj* institutions are supposed to reconstitute the decision-making processes on the basis of local participation on a continuous basis and thus, in principle, represent an institutionalized shift in power towards lower, hitherto 'disempowered' sections of the rural population.

Notwithstanding the shortcomings of the prevalent system of local governance, which are linked to the existing social and economic bases of power, these amendments, especially the *Seventy-Third Amendment Act*, provide an alternative to the state-led and re-distributive developmental models. The renewed movement towards democratic decentralization and citizen-centric government has eroded the bureaucratic monopoly over the development processes and has shifted the locus of power to those who matter at the grassroots. This has been a reality due to variety of factors. With the constitutional recognition of rural and urban local bodies, state-level election commissions and finance commissions and the granting of mandatory status to the *gram sabahas*, the bureaucrats are seen as mere facilitators and promoters of development and not as regulators and directors. Within the theoretical format of democratic decentralization, bureaucracy is a catalyst for change rather than the agents of change. So, it is a significant step in eroding the overwhelming paternalistic authority hitherto enjoyed by the bureaucracy.

If the Seventy-Third and Seventy-Fourth Amendments denote 'the political route' to the people's empowerment, the Effective and Responsive Administration package that arose out of the 1997 Chief Minister Conference in New Delhi was an articulation of 'the managerial route' to redefine the power equation between government and citizens. The imperative need was for government at all levels to reinvent itself, redefine its roles and responsibilities and bring about reforms in all the areas in which it interfaced with the people. The public image of the bureaucracy, it was candidly confessed, was one of inaccessibility, indifference, procedure-orientation, poor quality and sluggishness, proneness to corruption and non-accountability for results. The pressing need was therefore 'to assure the people of India of an efficient, open, responsible, accountable, clean and dynamically adjusting administration at all levels'. Immediate steps should be taken to restore people's confidence in the capacity and fairness of the administration. Very significantly, the conference recognized that 'governance has to extend beyond conventional bureaucracies to involve actively citizens and consumer groups at all levels, to empower and inform the public and disadvantaged groups, and to ensure service and programme execution through autonomous elected local bodies'.[23] There were, thus, three important aspects of this new agenda for civil service reform: (a) there was a crisis in the administration, which was not people-sensitive or citizen-friendly; (b) there was an urgent need to bring about reform in administration to make it people-sensitive, efficient and cost-effective; and (c) there was also the need for a change in the mindset so that governing could be conceived afresh as 'governance' – a wider term than mere formal 'government' – opening, in the process, possibilities of the inclusion of other actors, such as citizens, consumer groups, elected local bodies or those who are linked with the administration in some way or the other. As is evident, a managerial reform package seeking to transform public administration needs the following three measures: (a) accountability-fostering measures; (b) measures for promoting transparency and openness and (c) measures directed at civil service performance and integrity. So, reform is nothing but an enlargement of opportunities for all, not just for the select few.

The recommendations of the fifth Pay Commission were another milestone in the direction of the above well-directed designs for civil service reform. True to the spirit expressed at the 1996 Chief Secretaries conference, the fifth Pay Commission recommended: (a) downsizing the government through corporatization of activities which involved the 'manufacturing of goods or the provision of commercial services'; (b) transparency, openness and economy in government operations through 'privatization of activities where government does not need to play a direct role' and also 'contracting out of services which can be conveniently outsourced to the private sector';[24] and (c) contractual appointments in selected areas of operation 'for the purpose of maintaining a certain flexibility in staffing both for lateral entry of experts, moderating the numbers deployed depending on the exigencies of work and ensuring availability of most competent and committed personnel for certain sensitive/specialized jobs.'[25]

The central government had been advised to go for a 30 per cent reduction in the strength of the civil service since, as the Pay Commission felt, it would be unwise to let the government sector continue as 'an island of inefficiency' and 'inertia'. The normal procedure of voluntary retirement after completing 20 years' service was to be continued. Alongside this, the Commission recommended a special scheme of voluntary retirement in those departments where surplus manpower had been identified. In such cases, there should be a provision for the selective retirement of persons, with the initiative always resting with the government over any 'golden handshakes'.

The other significant recommendation of the Commission concerned 'openness' in administration. This stated that, apart from what was detrimental to the interests of the nation, the security of the state or its commercial, economic and other strategic interests, 'nothing should be held back just to subserve the interests of individual bureaucrats and politicians'.[26] Everything else should be made public. Every important government decisions involving 'a shift in policy' should invariably be accompanied by a White Paper 'in the nature of an explanatory memorandum'. As an integral part of civil service reform, the Commission insisted on the formation of an efficient grievance redress machinery '[that] has to be effective, speedy, objective, readily accessible and easy to operate'.[27] Drawing upon the examples of Canada, the UK and Malaysia, where effective grievance redress systems had been functioning efficiently, the idea of a Citizen's Charter – defining the rights of the customers of government schemes and services – was mooted by the Commission. The recognition by the Commission of the citizen's right to information and the procedures suggested in this connection are of seminal importance from the point of view of debureaucratizing government and making it citizen-friendly. The issues raised by the Pay Commission figured prominently in the 1997 Conference of Chief Ministers at which an action plan was adopted to (a) make the administration accountable and citizen-friendly, (b) ensure transparency and the right to information and (c) cleanse and motivate the civil services.

The latest in government–citizen relationships is the concept of the Citizen's Charter. Democracy demands that the citizen's voice be heard and taken note of in the delivery of services to him/her, particularly if those services are rendered by government agencies. In fact, the parameters of the services need to be defined by the requirements of the citizens. It is at this interface between the citizen and the service provider that trust is demanded, and that is the point at which, very frequently, trust breaks down. Problems arise relating to transparency, accountability and the responsiveness of the public administration. The Citizen's Charter was perceived as an instrument that could be used to chisel out the possibilities of a healthier relationship between the service provider and its user. In India, it was also seen as a vehicle for building greater awareness of their mutual responsibilities among both the government and the citizen.

Under the Charter, citizens have been brought to the centre of all the government's activities, changing the prevalent concept of treating citizens as passive recipients of government service. The idea behind the Charter is to tap the citizens' responses to the actual working of government organizations. Normally, the Charter would cover all public services and aim at demanding from the government and service organizations (post office, railways etc., for instance) accountability, transparency, quality and choice for all the services provided by them to the people. The Charter is not, at all, a list of new principles of governance; instead, it has merely reiterated those norms that ideally should constitute the foundation of public administration. It is, therefore, an attempt to bring back the basic values of public administration that have been eroded for various socio-political reasons connected with the evolution of the political system.

Concluding observations

Administrative reforms and the concern for ethics in governance are dialectically connected: the latter sets in motion processes that the former articulates in the form of policy decisions. In order to conclusively address and resolve contemporary socio-economic and political issues, governance needs to be regularly reinvented; otherwise, it will lose its salience. So, administrative reforms are regular events that are usually undertaken with an ideological, but context-dependent, agenda since administration is also a problem-solving tool. Administrative reforms require negotiation and contestation, which further confirms that politics remains critical in their conceptualization. As shown above, administrative reforms in India contributed to the articulation of ethics in governance, defined differently in the different historical phases that India has encountered in her journey as a polity. During British rule, the issue of ethics did not seem to figure prominently, since colonialism had completely different ideological goals that ran contrary to the interests of the 'native' citizens. Nonetheless, the concern for ethics did initiate processes for reorienting administration in such a way as to give prominence to the prevalent rules of law, and not to customs, as had been the practice in the preceding years before British rule was firmly and legally established in India. For colonialism to flourish, the change from custom-based governance to one that derived its sustenance from well-defined constitutional principles appeared to be ethical to the Indians who had shown up till then their habitual obeisance to royal diktat, based generally on customs. As time passed, the colonial government agreed to accommodate Indians in the administration, as part of their ideological mission to rule India in accordance with the fundamental principles of the British Enlightenment. This certainly had a political angle which we cannot lose sight of. Nonetheless, the drive towards running the administration on the basis of codified rules and regulations seems to have been derived from the urge to establish ethics in governance. There is no doubt that colonial administration, however rule-bound it had been, was an exploitative system. Yet, by insisting on a rule-bound governance, colonial administrators did create an environment in which an alternative form of administration was not only conceptualized, but pursued, one that was contrary to the whimsical governance that they had inherited once they had established their hegemony in India. The fundamental point that governance no longer remained the prerogative of the ruler but was dependent on written laws seems to have instilled the idea that, to remain ethical, public administration had to be sensitive to the rules and regulations that were meant to serve 'the subjects of the Crown' in accordance with what the colonial rulers had construed as the best possible principles of governance.

Independent India has, as the above discussion has shown, different sets of challenges that are both inherited from the long colonial rule and also drawn from the obvious contextual constraints. The founding fathers, in order to fulfil their exclusive ideological priorities, had prescribed a system of administration that was tuned to the goal of development in accordance with the much-hyped socialist pattern of society. What did not seem to have received adequate attention from those who had presided over India's destiny at the dawn of India's rise as an independent polity was whether the existing administration bequeathed by the colonial power was sufficiently equipped to handle the administrative issues confronting India following the 1947 transfer of power. India's growth was not satisfactory and it was alleged that the economic model that the democratically elected rulers suggested was not suitable. The administration was charged with being prejudiced when several scams broke out in the first years of India's existence as an independent nation. Two issues seem to have become preeminent. On the one hand, questions were raised about the integrity of those holding power; the misappropriation of public funds could not have been possible without the complicity of top political bosses. On the other hand, this was identified as testimony to the breakdown of India's moral fabric, which encouraged individuals and groups to bend rules and regulations to achieve personal ends. Reiterating that ethics in governance was too critical to be neglected, several specific steps were undertaken: the most prominent among them was, as discussed at length in this chapter, the appointment of the first Administrative Reforms Commission in 1964. As will be shown in Chapter 5, it was felt that the decline of ethics and the increasing incidence of corruption in India were mutually supportive, an idea that the Santhanam Committee had, most critically, probed in its 1964 report on the prevention of corruption which provided a thorough analytical statement on the linkages between the decline of ethics and serious administrative lapses.

Despite the fact that committee after committee came out heavily against corruption and malpractices in governance, the situation has hardly improved; corruption continues to plague the system. It has thus been argued that the system could be improved once the roots of corruption receive no nourishment. This may not be an easy thing to achieve, because vested interests are too powerful to disappear so quietly. Administrative reforms in India thus get reduced to mere window dressing, since most of the radical recommendations are usually shelved given their possible adverse effect on the existent power-equations, which are nurtured by the politicians for their personal gain. This is, however, not to suggest that change is impossible; in fact, history is full of examples to prove otherwise. What innumerable instances from India show is how the release of mass energy for a cause radically alters the texture of a system even in adverse circumstances. While administrative reforms do not seem to be adequately equipped to bring about a complete overhaul of the system, since they usually have a limited mandate, they nonetheless articulate those significant inputs that are most critical in assessing the nature of contemporary governance. Indicative of the deterioration of the system, administrative reforms are thus possibly the most powerful steps to recharge its vitality, by following what is deemed to be appropriate in a specific context. Herein lies the importance of having administrative reforms at regular intervals to remind those in authority of their responsibility to exercise power in a way that upholds the fundamental ethical tenets of governance.

Administrative reform is a continuous challenge to those seeking to understand the processes of governmental renewal, which derive their impetus from the sense that the existing political and governmental systems do not meet contemporary demands. In other words, administrative reform does not take place in a vacuum and is always inspired by the failure of the existing system of governance to respond effectively to the social and political needs of the governed. In the context of 'breathtaking change', the bureaucratic institutions that developed during the industrial era seem to be inadequate and the importance of globalization as the conceptualization of new issues involving the government and the governed cannot be glossed over in such a scenario. So, a new perspective – underlining the role of market or market-type mechanisms in redefining the nature of governance – has emerged in which administrative reform is articulated. What is new here is a distinctive formulation, synthesizing traditions of public administration with contingent changes in public service provision and influences from the private and voluntary sectors. The process, known as the pluralization of the state has, as has already been shown, redefined the contours of reform so that the state is a mere agency along with others involved in public affairs. Administrative reform is thus a practical scheme of governance highlighting a clear theoretical advancement in the discipline of public administration.

Administrative change is inevitable because (a) public administration regularly negotiates with the changing priorities of the society of which it is a part, and (b) it seeks to incorporate not only the new administrative techniques but also the ideas that grow out of socio-economic and political churn. The constant governmental renewal thus appears to be the outcome of the search for an appropriate administration keeping pace with changing reality. So, it would not be wrong to argue that governmental renewal is primarily inspired by 'ideologies, philosophies and policy approaches on which interventions in society are based'.[28] Governance is a legitimizing device for government action that is justified by the rationale from which a government draws its sustenance. In a democracy, for instance, the administrative reform is usually articulated in measures reflective of the predominant politico-ideological values. Not only do they provide rationale for governmental action but they are also yardsticks for assessing policy alternatives. As has been shown, reform efforts in India reveal the extent to which the changing priorities of the political system act decisively in governmental renewal. Whether in the pre-liberalization phase or its aftermath, administration reinvents itself to accommodate the dominant values from which its legitimacy is drawn. Before the onset of globalization, the distinctive feature of public administration was that, despite having nurtured the colonial structure, it had successfully injected new dynamism into governmental activities reflective of a conscious search for an alternative both in spirit and content. Globalization, with its ideological package of 'structural adjustment', means an altogether different and intricate external environment that seeks to radically alter both the administrative set-up and the values on which it is based. Several steps have already been undertaken to undermine the bureaucratic grip over public administration in India. The recommendations of the fifth Pay Commission (1997) seem to have upheld this spirit while suggesting several steps for administrative reorganization in India. Changes in administration are, however, mostly cosmetic in nature. So, although the reform efforts have a direction, their lack of appropriate ideological backing appears to have weakened the entire project.

Notes

1 Niccolo Machiavelli, *The Prince*, Penguin, London, 1979, p. 59.
2 Gerald E Caiden, 'Administrative reform – proceed with caution', *International Journal of Public Administration*, 22 (6), 1999, p. 820.
3 Ibid., p. 827.
4 Gerald E Caiden, 'Development administration and administrative reform', *International Social Science Journal*, 2 (1), p. 8.
5 Gerald E Caiden's foreword in Mohammad Mohbbat Khan, *Bureaucratic Self-Preservation: failure of major administrative reform effects in the civil service of Pakistan*, University Press Limited, Dhaka, 1980.
6 The 1892 Indian Council Act – quoted in A Berriedale Keith (ed.) *Speeches and Documents on Indian Policy, 1750–1921*. Vol. II. Oxford University Press, London, 1922, p. 79.
7 Anil Bhatt, 'Colonial bureaucratic culture and development administration: portrait of an old-fashioned Indian bureaucrat', *Journal of Commonwealth and Comparative Politics*, 17(3), 1979, p. 259.
8 Ibid., p. 281.
9 *Review of Election Law, Processes and Reform Options*, (a consultation paper), National Commission to Review the Working of the Constitution, New Delhi, (no date), p. 19.
10 Jawaharlal Nehru's speech 'A word to the services', (delivered on 9 December 1955), *Jawaharlal Nehru and Public Administration*, Indian Institute of Public Administration, New Delhi, 1975, pp. 42–3.

11 *Report of the Secretariat Reorganization Committee*, Government of India, New Delhi, 1949, pp. 19–21.

12 A D Gorwala, *Report of Public Administration* and also *Efficient Conduct of State Enterprises*, Government of India, New Delhi, 1951.

13 Paul Appleby, 'History and precedent vs. reform' in U C Agarwal (ed.), *Public Administration: vision and reality*, Indian Institute of Public Administration, New Delhi, 2003, p. 33.

14 Paul Appleby, *Public Administration in India: report of a survey*, the Ford Foundation, Delhi, 1953, p. 38.

15 *Administrative Reforms Commission's Report*, Ministry of Home Affairs, New Delhi, 1966–70. A parallel is drawn with the 1953 Hoover Commission that made a series of recommendation to improve the US administration in the aftermath of the Second World War.

16 M K Gandhi's comment s on the nature of policing. *Harijan,* 1 September 1940.

17 *Eighth and Concluding Report of the National Police Commission*, Government of India, May 1981, ch. LXII, p. 14.

18 Ibid.

19 Rajiv Gandhi, 'Responsive administration', (speech on 18 June 1988 at Coimbatore), *The Times of India*, 19 June 1988.

20 Arvind Sharma, 'Administrative reforms in India: a synoptic view' in Pradeep Sahni and Uma Medury (eds), *Governance and Development: issues and strategies*, Prentice Hall, New Delhi, 2003, p. 111.

21 Martin Minogue, 'Changing the state: concepts and practice in the reform of the public sector' in Martin Minogue, Charles Polidano and David Hume (eds), *Beyond the NPM: changing ideas and practice in governance*, Edward Elgar, Cheltenham, 1998, p. 17.

22 Ibid.

23 *An Agenda for Effective and Responsive Administration*, (the agenda paper, circulated for the 1996 conference of Chief Secretaries of States and Union Territories), Department of Administrative Reforms and Public Grievances, Ministry of Personnel, Public Grievances and Pensions, Government of India, New Delhi, November 1996, pp. 1–2.

24 *The Report of the Fifth Pay Commission*, Vol. 1, Government of India Press, New Delhi, 1997, pp. 122–3.

25 Ibid., p. 175.

26 Ibid., p. 151.

27 Ibid., p. 157.

28 Nico Nelissen, Marie-Louise Bemelmand-Videc, Arnold Godfroij and Peter De Goede (eds), *Reinventing Government: innovative and inspiring visions*, International Books, Netherlands, 1999, p. 18.

4 Civil service reforms in India

An aid to ethics in governance

As shown in Chapter 3, administrative reforms play a critical role in transforming governance in accordance with the prevalent ideological dispensation. Governments need to be regularly reinvented; otherwise, they lose viability and relevance. In other words, in order to remain sensitive to contemporary demands, what is thus pertinent is to go for systemic changes. The idea of government renewal thus assumes tremendous significance in contemporary thinking about how to make public services relevant to the stakeholders. This is done in a context that appears to exercise a determining influence on the ideological texture of administrative reforms, one that does not suggest mere structural changes, but also sets in motion processes whereby new ideas for better public services are welcomed and appreciated. The basic point, as argued in the earlier chapter, is how to make the administration truly public by being attentive to what is deemed to be appropriate in a particular socio-economic and political milieu. It is true that the fundamental conceptual parameters informing administrative reforms in India may have been derived from wider concerns for citizen-centric public administration; nonetheless, the contextual influences always remain most critical in deciding the major thrust of administrative reforms. Two ideas are of significance here: on the one hand, administrative reform entails primarily specific measures for administrative renewal according to the prevalent ideological concerns of those in authority; on the other hand, they are futuristic too because reforms are said to set in motion processes for change which are reflective of what is required to be done to achieve administrative goals. Hence, administrative reforms cannot be a single shot phenomenon, but ones that need to be continuously pursued; otherwise, they will end up being mere context-bound technical devices.

One of the major components of administrative reforms is civil service reform. Besides specific committees, appointed to review the functioning of the Indian civil services, the Pay Commissions are also integrally connected to the processes of change that Indian bureaucracy has so far undergone since the constitution of the first Pay Commission in 1946. The Weberian form of hierarchical governance was critical in setting the ideological tone for the first four pay commissions; given the universality of the state-led development paradigm, bureaucracy had always had an edge in contemporary thinking, because of its assumed utility to accomplish the ideological goals that those in power sought to achieve. The situation underwent a sea change following the adoption of the 1991 New Economic Policy, which radically altered governmental priorities by giving precedence to the market in fulfilling the neo-liberal ideological directions of the state. Seeking to articulate the idea of governance in accordance with the World Bank-sponsored governance paradigm, the Pay Commissions since 1994 have suggested major measures for transforming Indian bureaucracy from being rent-seeking in the erstwhile Licence–Quota–Permit Raj to being a useful instrument for public services. Suggesting that the Weberian top-down model of administration is simply inadequate since citizens are also consumers, the governance model of governance is also an attempt to expand the base of public administration by taking into account the importance of external actors who had never had a role in the past. In order to remain truly public in its functioning, the government needs to be not only accountable to the stakeholders, but also attentive to their requirements. This is citizen-centric governance, as per the neo-liberal conceptualization of governance.

The chapter has two interrelated parts: given the overwhelming theoretical importance of the governance model, the first part of the chapter is devoted to the idea of governance, with a view to analytically assessing its viability in contemporary India. Despite being rooted in the World Bank endeavour, the idea of governance seems to have become critical in civil service reforms in India. With its analytical depth, the first part will be of tremendous use in comprehending the second part of this chapter, which focuses on the two pay commissions – the fifth and sixth Pay Commissions – appointed in 1994 and 2006 respectively. Although these are primarily review commissions, they are nonetheless major steps towards adapting the Indian civil services to the neo-liberal ideological dispensation in which the interests of the stakeholders always reign supreme. Besides suggesting significant structural changes, these two commissions are thus a watershed in so far as Indian public administration is concerned, because not only are they pay commissions in the conventional way, but they also seem to have translated the ideological intent of the ruling authority into concrete steps while reviewing the Indian civil services.

Despite having provoked debates and criticisms, the governance paradigm appears to have been accepted as perhaps an antidote to the decline of ethics in governance in India. Based on the drive towards making administration accountable to the citizens, there is a sense in saying that governance is likely to succeed as a paradigm, given the optimism that it has, so far, generated in developing countries, including India, where bureaucracy, by being rent-seeking, was always the captive of vested social, economic and political interests. Governance is thus a powerful challenge in a rather stultified environment in which the citizens' roles as active partners in governance have always been compromised. In view of this, it is highly appropriate to pursue a critical discussion of the concept of governance, which the chapter seeks to do in Part A. Drawing on the argument that governance is a determining influence in both the fifth and sixth Pay Commissions, Part B is devoted to a detailed discussion of the recommendations that these commissions made for streamlining Indian bureaucracy in order perhaps to articulate the idea of governance in spirit and depth. Both these parts, despite being analytically separate, hinge on the common argument that the clamour for ethics in governance seems to have become a natural call because of the well entrenched rent-seeking character of bureaucracy in the erstwhile era of state-driven and planned economic development. The fifth and sixth Pay Commissions may have had their limitations, but the drive towards setting new standards of governance, in which accountability, adherence to the rule of law and the commonly accepted ethical code of conduct remain supreme, is said to have drawn citizens, as Part B further argues, to public governance as active partners, because of their increasing faith that the instruments of governance will be tuned to what they require to gratify their individual and collective needs. Parts A and B are integrally connected, to show that governance, which is a conceptual category with practical implications, has gained salience in India where public administration gradually became an instrument which was neither public nor administratively effective. Hence there was a clamour for change, which the fifth and sixth Pay Commissions articulated in their recommendations. Whether these recommendations are adequate to halt the deterioration of ethics in governance is a question that cannot be easily answered. Nonetheless, there is no doubt that these pay commissions stand out in the annals of governance in India not only because of their attempt to alter the texture of Indian bureaucracy, but also because of the importance that they gave to the issue of ethics in governance as integral to the efforts towards building a corruption- and also prejudice-free governmental system.

PART A

Conceptualizing the idea of governance

Governance is not just a conceptual parameter, but a prescription to combat and also refashion a predatory state that has appropriated the government for partisan gain. This is also a shield for market-driven socio-economic regeneration, since an orderly governance creates political stability and also institutions which are critical to the smooth functioning of the market. So the notion of good governance in the neo-liberal realm supports and also expedites the processes for maintaining the status quo, for reasons connected with the market and its partisan functioning. By enhancing the state's capability within the neo-liberal predisposition, good governance accords a powerful conceptual justification to endeavours drawn from self-motivation, which is undoubtedly good provided there are well established mechanisms for such efforts. If such mechanisms are absent, they need to be created with state support, at least at the initial stages; hence, over emphasis on good governance may result in a situation in which the state withdraws hoping to be replaced by what is euphemistically characterized as 'popular initiatives'. Nonetheless, both as a conceptual category and a practical design, governance is a positive intervention in three fundamental ways: first, by shifting the focus from inputs to outcomes, it has radically altered our perception of public administration, so that it cannot be conceptualized as an event, but as an integral process in which government is just a, albeit significant, player. Challenging the hierarchical bureaucratic governance, it has further reemphasized the importance of the horizontal coordination of agencies involved in the delivery of public services. As against hierarchy, the principal concern here is to evolve teamwork involving the stakeholders. The second implication is far more serious, especially in a developing country such as India, where the colonial bureaucratic structure of the bygone era was more or less retained. Governance, despite it being a market-friendly design, has unleashed forces supportive of institutional pluralism which are most radical given the well-entrenched bureaucratic hegemony, notwithstanding the commitment of the founding fathers for creating a new India, free from bias and prejudices of any kind. This is an opportunity for the Indian public administration to be substantially refashioned in the neo-liberal context, in which governance is not merely an act, but a coordinated effort seeking to redesign public administration in a creative manner. In this sense, governance cannot be just a checklist of items, as per the World Bank, but a fresh wave of thinking based on a thorough critique of the age-old Weberian conceptualization of hierarchical and control-stricken public bureaucracy. Third, governance is also an institutional mechanism to address the well entrenched inadequacies in India's public administration. It is now common knowledge that endemic corruption not only undermines the moral fibre of the polity, but has serious and irreversible practical consequences for politics, economic development and governance. With the growing involvement of stakeholders in governance, any corrupt practices that are indulged in attract immediate attention. This means that an alert citizenry is perhaps the most effective shield against corruption. Governance, by catapulting people onto the centre of the stage, thus becomes an important vehicle for change in circumstances in which stakeholders are being linked together in the service of common goals.

Theory and practice of governance

In contemporary social science discourses, governance has acquired ubiquity. Governance does not simply mean 'rule' or 'administration'; it has a specific meaning in the context of globalization. Broadly speaking, governance is the manner in which power is exercised. It is different from public administration in that it underlines the importance of its 'purpose' as well as the structure and processes of administration. Governance is about 'the capacity' of the public authority and its accountability. Capacity includes the state's 'hardware', its financial resources and administrative infrastructure and its effectiveness in executing policy decisions. Accountability is 'the software' of the state whereby the political system is linked with its performance. Governance is thus another way of conceptualizing public administration in the changed global scenario. Before critically evaluating the phenomenon, the following three points seem most appropriate to put the discussion in perspective. First, governance as a concept and also as a paradigm is a practitioner's contribution to public administration, in the sense that it has been conceptualized by the World Bank in the context of sub-Saharan Africa at a particular historical juncture. Failure to repay the World Bank loans, among other things, led to its formulation. Second, the World Bank definition of governance is very limited and is associated with administrative and managerial arrangements seeking to instil 'efficiency' in public administration. Third, governance is also political, in the sense that it includes an insistence on 'competitive democracies' of the western variety. In a way, governance is therefore a well-defined administrative set-up that draws its sustenance from 'participatory democracy'. Its historical roots cannot be ignored, for governance was articulated when the state-led development that flourished in the former Soviet Union collapsed

Governance generally means 'the act or process of governing, specifically authoritative direction and control'.[1] To be more precise, governance can be further defined as 'the political direction and control exercised over the actions of the members, citizens or inhabitants of communities, societies and states'.[2] While conceptualizing good governance in the context of debt-ridden sub-Saharan Africa, the World Bank was guided by

> efforts to create an enabling environment and to build capacities that will be wasted if the political context is not favourable. Ultimately better governance requires political renewal. This means a concerted attack on corruption from the highest to lowest level. This can be done by setting good example, by strengthening accountability, by encouraging public debate, and by maturing a free press. It also means ... fostering grassroots and non-governmental organizations such as farmers' associations, cooperatives and women's groups.[3]

Underlining the above goal, the World Bank defined good governance in the following manner:

> Good governance is epitomized by predictable, open and enlightened policy making, a bureaucracy imbued with a professional ethos acting in furtherance of the public good, the rule of law, transparent processes and a strong civil society participating in public affairs.[4]

As is evident, there are four key elements: public sector management; accountability; legal framework for development; and information and transparency. Improving governance would begin with an assessment of the institutional environment (accountability, rule of law, openness and transparency) that determines the patrimonial profile of the country. Good governance is also contrasted with the 'poor governance' that is held responsible for lack of sound development in these sub-Saharan African nation-states. Poor governance is, according to the World Bank formulation, 'characterized by arbitrary policy making, unaccountable bureaucracies, un-enforced or unjust legal systems, the abuse of executive power, a civil society unengaged in public life and widespread corruption'.[5] According to the World Bank, some of the main symptoms of poor governance are as follows:[6]

- failure to make a clear separation between what is public and what is private, hence, a tendency to divert public resources for private gain;
- failure to establish a predictable framework of law and government; behaviour conducive to development, or arbitrariness in the application of rules and laws;
- excessive rules, regulations, licensing requirements, and so forth, which impede the functioning of markets and encourage rent-seeking;
- priorities inconsistent with development, resulting in a misallocation of resources;
- excessively narrowly based or nontransparent decision making.

Underlying the litany of Africa's development problems is thus 'a crisis of governance', the World Bank expressed concern for 'the lack of official accountability, the control of information and a failure to respect the rule of law'. Since governance is 'the conscious management of regime structures, with a view to enhancing the public realm' the Bank thus insists on 'independence for the judiciary, scrupulous respect for the law and human rights at every level of government, transparent accountability of public monies, and independent public auditors responsible to a representative legislature, not to an executive'.[7] Such a distortion in public institutions appears to be unavoidable because they, superimposed 'on political and economic systems in which they had no roots, continued to lack accountability, but were captured by clan pressures, politicized by booty [resembling largely] the kinds of patrimonial states common in early Europe'.[8] The tragedy of 'mismanagement' and 'corruption' seems to have its root in this colonial imposition of states and bureaucratic institutions, rather than 'their natural evolution through a process of citizen demands for accountability and ruler adjustments'.[9] Driven by concern for efficient governance, another World Bank document, *Governance and Development* (1992),[10] defines governance as 'the manner in which power is exercised in the management of a country's economic and social resources for development'. That denotes (a) the form of political regime (parliamentary or presidential, military or civilian and authoritarian or democratic); (b) the process in which the power is exercised; and (c) the capacity of the government to design, formulate and implement policies – to discharge the government functions. While the first aspect of governance falls outside the World Bank's ambit, the second and third aspects, as claimed by the World Bank, appear critical to the Bank.[11] However on a closer look at the subsequent elaboration of the concept by other international agencies endorsing the World Bank agenda, it is clear that these three aspects remain integral to governance. Absorbing the primary thrust of the World Bank prescriptions, the UN Development Programme (UNDP), for instance, elaborates the concept by underlining that governance is the essence of economic, political and administrative authority to manage a country's affairs at all levels. It comprises mechanisms, processes and institutions through which citizens and groups articulate their interests, exercise their legal rights, meet their local obligations and mediate their differences.[12]

Governance is also articulated by the UNDP in terms of the following major eight characteristics.[13] It is participatory, consensus oriented, accountable, transparent, responsive, effective and efficient, equitable and inclusive and follows the rule of law. It assures that corruption is minimized, that the views of minorities are taken into account and that the voices of the most vulnerable in society are heard in decision making. It is also responsive to the present and future needs of society.

Participation

Participation by both men and women is a key cornerstone of good governance. Participation could be either direct or through legitimate intermediate institutions or representatives. It is important to point out that representative democracy does not necessarily mean that the concerns of the most vulnerable in society would be taken into consideration in decision making. Participation needs to be informed and organized. This means freedom of association and expression on the one hand and an organized civil society on the other.

Consensus oriented

There are several actors and as many viewpoints in a given society. Good governance requires mediation of the different interests in society to reach a broad consensus on what is in the best interest of the whole community and how this can be achieved. It also requires a broad and long-term perspective on what is needed for sustainable human development and how to achieve the goals of such development. This can only result from an understanding of the historical, cultural and social contexts of a given society or community.

Accountability

Accountability is a key requirement of good governance. Not only governmental institutions but also the private sector and civil society organizations must be accountable to the public and to their institutional stakeholders. Who is accountable to whom varies depending on whether the decisions or actions taken are internal or external to an organization or institution. In general an organization or an institution is accountable to those who will be affected by its decisions or actions. Accountability cannot be enforced without transparency and the rule of law.[14]

Transparency

Transparency means that decisions taken and their enforcement are done in a manner that follows rules and regulations. It means that information is freely available and directly accessible to those who will be affected by such decisions and their enforcement. It also means that enough information is provided and that it is provided in easily understandable forms and media.

Responsiveness

Good governance requires that institutions and processes try to serve all stakeholders within a reasonable timeframe. By being responsive, governmental institutions gain 'legitimacy' in the public realm, which will automatically ensure their wider acceptance and thus effectiveness in governance. Apart from well-designed structural devices, responsiveness of public institutions can only be meaningfully ascertained if there is a serious civil society engagement in public affairs.

Effectiveness and efficiency

Good governance means that processes and institutions produce results that meet the needs of society while making the best use of the resources at their disposal. The concept of efficiency in the context of good governance also covers the sustainable use of natural resources and the protection of the environment.

Equity and inclusiveness

A society's well-being depends on ensuring that all its members feel that they have a stake in it and do not feel excluded from the mainstream of society. This requires all groups, but particularly the most vulnerable, to have opportunities to improve or maintain their well-being.

Rule of law

Good governance requires fair legal frameworks that are enforced impartially. It also requires full protection of human rights, particularly those of minorities. Impartial enforcement of laws requires an independent judiciary and an impartial and incorruptible police force.

Strategic vision

Leaders and the public have a broad and long-term perspective on good governance and human development, along with a sense of what is needed for such development. There is also an understanding of the historical, cultural and social complexities in which that perspective is grounded.[15]

Governance is thus a checklist of criteria for managing public affairs, following certain well-defined codes of conduct based on the concern for ethics in public life. As Lewis T Preston, the World Bank President, categorically stated in his foreword to *Governance and Development*,

> good governance is an essential complement to sound economic policies. Efficient and accountable management by the public sector and a predictable and transparent policy framework are critical to the efficiency of markets and governments, and hence to economic development.[16]

Broadly speaking, good governance is conceptually three dimensional. First, it refers to certain espoused principles of public administration, namely, accountability, transparency and participation. Second, it also dwells on the processes through which political power is articulated and exercised. The process involves a complex interplay among the prevalent values, policies and institutions that are critical to making and implementing decisions for the society in question. Governance also recognizes the importance of interactions between state, market and civil society. Third, the successful application of governance, both its principles and processes, is contingent on the regulatory capacity of the state. While control without good governance is oppressive, good governance without the capacity to apply it is an empty slogan. A perusal of these features suggests that governance is not a magical formula. Instead, it seeks to articulate a device to improve governmental functioning in areas where government is apparently minimal and is largely appropriated by 'partisan' interests where it does exist. Hence it is stated that

> Governance is a continuum, and not necessarily unidirectional, it does not automatically improve over time. It is a plant that needs constant tending. Citizens need to demand good governance. Their ability to do so is enhanced by literacy, education and employment opportunities. Government needs to prove responsive to those demands.... Change occurs sometimes in response to external or internal threats. It also occurs through pressures from different interest groups, some of which may be in the form of populist demands. Although lenders and aid agencies and other outsiders can contribute resources and ideas to improve governance, for change to be effective it must be rooted firmly in the societies concerned and cannot be imposed from outside.[17]

To sum up the discussion on the definition of good governance, one can safely make the following points. Governance is a conceptual approach (a) concerning 'big questions' of a 'constitutional' nature that establish the rules of political conduct; (b) involving creative intervention by political actors to change structures that inhibit the expression of human potential; (c) emphasizing the nature of interactions between state and social actors and among social actors themselves; and (d) referring to particular types of relationships among political actors which are socially sanctioned rather than arbitrary.[18] Taking all these features together, governance refers to 'the traditions, institutions and processes that determine how power is exercised, how citizens are given a voice and how decisions are made on issues of public concern'.[19] Governance is thus inherently 'political', since it involves 'bargaining and compromise, winners and losers, among actors with different interests and resources'.[20] Thus governance is also a platform for interaction between stakeholders and government that is always frictional due largely to the obvious incompatibility of interests among them. Informed by this concern, governance is also defined as 'engaged governance', whereby engagement between government and civil society is formally recognized. The primary focus is on the policy cycle of the government within a value-driven governance system.

If assessed superficially, governance is just another mode of public administration. But if one locates governance in the global neo-liberal thrust for social, economic and political homogeneity, the concept acquires completely different connotations. This becomes a way of articulating the neo-liberal agenda and seeking to fulfil the neo-liberal goal. Anchored in specific theoretical reasoning, governance is not at all an innocent construction of administrative practices. Instead, it is loaded with specific ideological preferences, supported by the so-called unipolar world drawing from 'neo-liberalism'. The neo-liberal thought found favour with the Western donor agencies such as the World Bank and IMF that were engaged in the funding of the development projects of the 'debt-ridden' Third World. The convergence of thought with regard to change reached its apogee in the newly emergent phenomenon of globalization, facilitated by the free flow of funds, goods and services as dictated by the new conditionalities laid down by the WTO, and by the new IT revolution (internet, fax, and web-based communication).

Governance as an aid to ethics in public life

Governance is a policy-making device that underlines transparency, accountability, integrity and legitimacy of the institutions, rules, practices and values on which a society is based. These characteristics are relative to the society in question, because they cannot be articulated in absolute terms. But what is critical is the process whereby citizens favourably link with governance because it generates trust and confidence in them. Governance is thus a mechanism involved in (a) 'the formation and propagation of values'; (b) 'the creation and distribution of wealth'; and (c) 'the emergence and consolidation of institutions'.[21] In the governance paradigm, the traditional governance process, with the state as supreme actor, is now heavily influenced by international organizations with a growing number of regulations formulated at the supra-national level. These supra-national policies travel across 'languages and cultures, framing and positioning local discourses and being translated by the local configurations of resources and ideas'.[22] As shown, the growing but critical importance of governance both as a technique and an agenda can easily be attributed to two important developments in the global order in recent times: first, the disintegration of the former Soviet Union, suggesting not only the weaknesses of Marxism–Leninism as a cementing ideology in diverse societies, but also the failure of the state-directed development model in mitigating the basic human social, economic and political needs. This apparent vacuum is being filled in by the consolidation of the neo-liberal discourse in which 'states should become commodified and marketized in their outlook and give way to the "market discipline" [paving the way for] governance without government'. The governance without government that is market discipline can be seen as the 'governmentality of neo-liberal globalization'. Drawing on Foucault, governmentality includes 'mental and practical levels of governance'. Governmentality is 'a result of mentality and the organization of conduct that composes the art of governance'.[23] Drawing on 'the internalization of practices of governing', governmentality is a mechanism for policing the self 'according to existing conceptions of truth grounded in knowledge about the self'.[24]

The second, and perhaps more significant, factor is the remarkable technological advances that shrink distance and the interdependencies that arise from much wider and deeper global economic integration. In these changed circumstances, if they do not reorient themselves substantially, the decision-makers can hardly remain appropriate in governance. As a result, public administration is bound to undergo radical changes because of the historical circumstances in which the idea of 'contextual' public administration seems to have lost its viability. The ecological view is replaced by the 'neo-Taylorist' philosophy of 'one best way' to organize public affairs. Neo-liberal values surged ahead, predicting 'the end of history' and the natural emergence of capitalism as 'the sole' arbiter of the fate of the world. In the contemporary socio-economic milieu, 'management' and 'market' seem to be inbuilt in public administration, redefining 'public' in a radical way.

There is no denying that governance has refashioned the contemporary debate on public administration by raising certain major critical questions. However, the primary goal that remains at the core of this new dispensation in the World Bank-sponsored model is to seek to champion universal goals within particular constraints in which the role of politics is minimal, if not entirely outlawed. Despite the formally apolitical stance of the World Bank on this question, 'there is little doubt that underlying even this limited vision of governance is a Western model, ringing with Weberian ethos, with its emphasis on free markets, individualism and a neutral but efficient public administration, subject to a legitimate government'.[25] Without politics, democracy has a restrictive meaning. Politics is the only social process of negotiation and contestation – politics as consisting of all the processes of conflict, cooperation and negotiation involved in the use, production and location of resources. Hence John J Kirlin argues that 'as long as democracy is valued the big questions of Public Administration must go beyond the big questions of Public Management'.[26] Public Administration's role in society is diminished if it is understood primarily in terms of managing public agencies. The Minnowbrook I Conference (1968) and the Blacksburg Manifesto have both raised this issue of democratic governance in the public interest. What is relevant in the context of the 'Third World' is that public administration is being crippled in the name of structural adjustment, invoking more and more 'the market model' of governance in utter disregard of the crucial social developmental role of the state in developing countries. The interests of public administration are no longer people-related but capital-related. And herein lies the perils of externally induced administrative reform, through which most of the Third World countries are passing today. Hence Leftwich rightly argues that

> the primacy of politics in development should not ... be disguised any longer behind a technicist language about governance and management. For while no one would deny the importance of institutions and rules, it is political processes which bring them into being and crucially, which sustain them.[27]

Governance, by absorbing the urge to govern following the well-established dictums, thus misses altogether the overarching perspective of a democratic polity. The sustained capacity of the political system for collective action, effective citizenship and developing and nurturing the civic infrastructure for protecting citizens' rights and promoting collective life is of vital significance for any public administration in a democracy. The new governance cult is particularly ominous for Third World public administration, as it tends to strengthen bureaucracy further, impeding the development of the alternative people's institutions so necessary for both generating social capacity to govern and creating more democratic spaces independent of bureaucratic administration. Characterized as 'neo-Taylorism', good governance seems thus a rehash of 'the one-best-way principle' of the classical administrative theory, which is a complete mismatch, for obvious reasons, with the contemporary global context that demands more 'open-endedness' in governance than rigidity of any kind.

PART B

Civil service reforms in India in a neo-liberal context

Discussion on civil service reform is generally confined to changes in bureaucracy. Administrative reforms are, as shown in Chapter 3, efforts towards transforming bureaucracy within certain well-defined theoretical parameters, reflective of the ideological underpinning of the polity in question. A perusal of major administrative reforms in India reveals how the wider ideological concern of the polity shapes their nature: so long as the idea of a socialist pattern of society remains dominant, administrative reforms generally prefer those structural changes which uphold the determining role of bureaucracy in governance. Given the wider acceptance of state-led developmental planning, the role of bureaucracy, as perhaps the most effective instrument in the entire process, was far more appreciated. The scene had, however, undergone dramatic changes following the adoption of the 1991 New Economic Policy in which the neo-liberal approach to the economy gained precedence. The growing ascendancy of the market as a determinant of public policy resulted in conceptualizing bureaucracy as one of the many critical instruments that contributed to successful governance. Being recognized as a collective venture, governance creates an environment in which the so-called external actors also remain significant. The idea that governance is not at all bureaucracy-centric leads to a new conceptualization of bureaucracy that cannot be understood in the traditional theoretical format of public administration. So, there are two different phases in India's civil service reforms: until the appointment of the fifth Pay Commission in 1994, all pay commissions had recommended steps to further strengthen the hold of bureaucracy on governance, by suggesting multiple packages of salary improvements and other facilities. The issue of accountability was always raised, but was sought to be streamlined by improving the mechanisms for internal accountability; the idea of external accountability was considered to be an anathema. That was what provoked the Second Administrative Reforms Commission to argue that 'the functioning of the civil service [in India] is characterized by a great deal of negativity, lack of responsiveness to what the people want and the dictates of democracy'.[28]

Conceptualized within the governance paradigm, the fifth Pay Commission is perhaps one of the most thoughtful statements on the importance of neo-liberal ethics in governance. As such, the fifth Pay Commission is not a pay commission in the conventional sense, given its efforts to reinvent the Indian civil service in the light of global inputs. The recommendations can be said to have drawn on the governance agenda, seeking to redefine bureaucracy merely as 'an enabler', and not 'a doer', as was the case in the past. By discarding the paternalistic idea of bureaucracy being a benevolent guardian, since it had become a rent-seeking instrument, the fifth Pay Commission also recognized the importance of external actors which had until then remained peripheral to governance. Ethics is now conceptualized with wide connotations, because governance is no longer an exclusive bureaucratic domain, but entails processes in which the bureaucracy collaborates with other actors. As shown above, governance is about those qualities that need to be uncritically appreciated to reorient public administration as an instrument for public well-being. Whether these measures are appropriate for inclusive development in India is a question that has no easy answer, since there is a strong argument that rights-based social provisions cannot be so easily dispensed with in India where the proportion of families living below the poverty line continues to cause alarm to the policy makers. Nonetheless, by recognizing governance as multidimensional and not monochromatic, the fifth and sixth Pay Commissions seemed to have set the ball rolling in a direction in which concern for ethics continues to remain critical in governance.

As argued so far, even before the onset of liberalization, several measures were adopted to revitalize the administration, which had owed its origin to completely different socio-economic concerns. The early reforms were largely generated by internal concerns, while the post-liberalization efforts were mostly driven by external considerations. There has been a clear shift towards a reduced role for the government in all countries. In the words of the fifth Pay Commission, 'Thatcherism in UK and Reagonomics in USA tried to pull out the State from the morass of over-involvement. The decline of Communism in Eastern Europe has furthered the trend towards economic liberalization and disinvestment in public sector enterprises'.[29] So, the impetus for reducing the role of government came from outside, as the Commission admits by mentioning that 'India could not have remained unaffected by these global trends'.[30] What was, however, most critical in the entire process was

> the deep economic crisis of 1991 which pushed [India] on to a new path of development, [which meant that] Government should confine itself primarily to the core functions that cannot be performed by the market. Everything else must be left to private initiative.[31]

Underlining the reduced role of the government, the fifth Pay Commission clearly articulates 'a new path of development'. Critical of 'the over-involvement' of government, the Commission demarcates certain 'core functions' for the government, keeping aside a wide range of functions for private enterprises. Conceptualizing government within the governance paradigm, the Commission also seeks to negotiate with the neo-liberal thrust in public administration and accordingly suggests 'reform packages' to adapt the civil services in India to the changed milieu. The government retreats, giving space for private operators to discharge functions which it had performed traditionally for 'public well-being'. By redefining the role of government, the Commission seems to have equipped the state to keep pace with the changes in an interdependent world.

The appointment of the fifth Pay Commission in 1994 by the Government of India is significant for two important reasons: (a) this is a Pay Commission which undertakes its exercise at a time when globalization seems to have influenced, if not shaped, human life to a significant extent; and (b) there is no doubt that the governance paradigm (which is clearly an antithesis to the state-directed development model) provides a critical reference point to civil service reform in most of the developing countries seeking loans from international agencies. The primary goal of the civil service is, as the Commission identifies, to 'understand customer needs'. Based on this fundamental concern, the mission statement[32] of the Commission thus runs as follows. To:

- clarify the goals of the organization in the mind of the management;
- clarify for staff the purpose of their jobs in meeting the organizational goals;
- make clear the policy of the government to ensure that it is interpreted accurately by staff;
- engender pride in belonging to the organization;
- provide targets to aim for, against which results can be assessed.

These are not new ideas: in the 1996 Chief Secretaries Conference, they had been emphasized to reinvent civil services in the context of the changed neo-liberal socio-economic and political environment in which citizens became the prime movers in governance.

The fifth Pay Commission is a watershed in the evolution of India's civil service for a variety of reasons. This is not a pay commission in the ordinary sense of the term, since it has also sought to reshape the bureaucracy in the light of emerging global trends especially after the collapse of the Soviet system. By suggesting significant changes in the administrative hierarchy, the Commission translates into reality the drive towards 'de-bureaucratization'. There are two immediate consequences. (a) It draws our attention away from the 'steel-frame' to other agencies that are equally crucial in the 'public service', but have not been formally recognized so far. In this sense, the Commission provides a powerful critique of a Weberian bureaucracy that is strictly hierarchical and largely status quo-ist. (b) By recognizing the importance of civil society organizations in public administration, the Commission gives formal recognition to cooperation between the governmental bureaucracy and these organizations. Such cooperation was discouraged because of 'the sanctity' of the governmental domain, in which the state bureaucracy appears to be 'the only legitimate agency' in discharging responsibilities on behalf of the state. Underlining the importance of agencies that are not exactly linked with the government and its peripheral organizations, the fifth Pay Commission has not only redefined Indian bureaucracy but has also expanded its sphere of influence by seeking to involve various non-governmental agencies, whose role was never recognized under traditional theories of public administration.

The fifth Pay Commission is also a significant comment on the nature of Indian administration, which has a clear colonial hangover. Critical of hierarchical Weberian administration, the Commission is clearly favourably disposed towards a 'decentralized' administration that provides room for organizations that are not exactly within the government. In structural terms, decentralized administration underlines the importance of various layers of decision-making process. What cripples public administration in the post-colonial India, as World Bank document underlines, is 'overregulation', which is both 'a cause and an effect of bloated public employment and the surest route to corruption'.[33] Apart from 'contracting out of the state', the World Bank suggests several specific measures to 'motivate' the civil servants 'through a combination of mechanisms to encourage internal competition'.[34] That the Pay Commission recommendations have not been accepted *in toto* by the government of India clearly suggests that the Indian response to the governance-initiated civil service reforms is a guarded one. In India's planned economy, the role that the civil service has discharged is that of 'a regulator' and not 'a facilitator'. And yet, the civil service was not severely challenged, because of its structural requirement in governance. The mood does not appear to have changed radically in the context of an interconnected global order. This can perhaps be linked with India's response to globalization, which is equally tempered by her peculiar socio-economic and political circumstances. Hence two contrasting scenes are visible: on the one hand, there is evidence of a growing free market in India; on the other hand, the Indian state is still very interventionist and the Indian economy is still relatively closed to external goods, finance and investors. The policy trend is thus 'better interpreted as a rightward drift in which the embrace of the state and business continues to grow warmer, leaving many others out in the cold'.[35]

Irrespective of whether the recommendations of the fifth Pay Commission are rightward drifts or not, the fact remains that it has drawn on the neo-liberal theoretical thrust towards globalization. Accepting that bureaucracies in the developing countries are also 'rent-seekers', the Commission has raised issues that are pertinent in redefining its role in the changed environment of governance. What is sadly missing is the context in which the recommendations are to be implemented. India is perhaps a unique example, showing a peculiar combination of roles in public bureaucracy that has a distinct colonial flavour, due to its obvious historical roots. Structured in the Weberian mould, Indian bureaucracy, however, reinvented its role and character following the adoption of the state-directed planned economy. Now, governance offers new challenges. The fifth Pay Commission, by seeking to reorient the Indian civil service, is responding to these challenges. Given the historical nature of Indian bureaucracy, most of the recommendations of the Commission may not be appropriate and thus not worthwhile. Nonetheless, there is no doubt that the Commission has played a historical role in the sense that it has drawn our attention to the weaknesses of a well entrenched bureaucracy and also the advantages of critically assessing its utility in the globalization-inspired social, economic and political circumstances.

In some sense, the fifth Pay Commission brings back the Wilsonian dichotomy between politics and administration, in which administration is defined as an unalloyed technical exercise. Whether there is a conclusive resolution of this debate, which had its roots in the 1887 article by Woodrow Wilson, is debatable. However, one can confidently argue that administration without politics (denoting values or ideologies) is like a fish without water. Administration is a guided action. Hence values seem to be critical in its articulation and manifestation. The fifth Pay Commission does not seem to have paid adequate attention to this dimension of civil service reform. Instead, it has generally endorsed the ideal of governance in its recommendations. There is no doubt that the recommendations of the Pay Commission are historical in the sense that they approximate to neo-liberal values; they are a-historical as well, because they are non-contextual responses to an environment where globalization continues to remain, for valid socio-economic and political reasons, an anathema.

The Sixth Pay Commission, 2006

What the fifth Pay Commission suggested was further reiterated by the sixth Pay Commission, which was constituted in 2006 with its final report submitted in 2008. It is the first Central Pay Commission that came into being in this century of rapid technological advances and after the coming into force of the RTI and

Fiscal Responsibility and Budget Management Acts. The government machinery, therefore, had to gear up for better performance under stricter fiscal discipline and delivery mechanisms. These imperatives are reflected in the terms of reference of the sixth Central Pay Commission which made it incumbent on the Commission to recommend systematic changes for (a) transforming the central government organizations into modern, professional and citizen-friendly entities that are dedicated to the service of the people; and (b) harmonizing the functioning of the central government organizations with the demands of the emerging global economy.

The sixth Central Pay Commission, therefore, had not only to evolve a proper pay package for government employees but also to make recommendations rationalizing the governmental structure with a view to improving the delivery mechanisms for providing better services to the common man. The main recommendations of the commission that have a bearing on good governance are as follows.

Reduction of layers

The commission recommended a reduction in the layers within the government structure so that decision making and delivery is expedited. From 35 standard pay scales, the grades have been reduced to 20 spread across four distinct running pay bands, one Apex Scale and another grade for the post of Cabinet Secretary/equivalent.

Restoring pride in public services

Government employees have to be motivated to take pride in public services. Thus the Commission recommended various measures for job enhancement and job enrichment. The functions presently being discharged by Assistants and Private Secretaries will now be carried out by Executive Assistants. The upgrading of all posts in Group D in the government to Group C, along with retraining and multitasking, will provide enlargement and enrichment of functions and responsibilities for a large section of government employees.

Delegation with accountability

Restoring delegation, with accountability at each level in the decision-making process, is one of the main proposals from the commission. Upgrading critical cutting-edge jobs such as teachers, staff nurses, and police constables has been recommended. Strengthening the decentralized levels with parity between field offices and the secretariat has also been recommended as the motivation and performance of the field and programme officers is critical to improving service delivery.

Ensuring the availability of the best possible talent for government

The Commission has recommended performance contracts, and lateral entry at higher levels in the government to ensure the availability of the best possible talent from within and outside government. It suggests a shift from career-based to post-based selection in the higher echelons of government in order to get the best domain-based expertise. A higher starting salary and better incentives have been given at initial entry level so as to attract younger talented staff. No increase in the retirement age is recommended, as an active younger employee profile is best suited for the tasks ahead. Additionally, the Commission argues for a market driven compensation package for young scientists and posts requiring special expertise and professional skills

Performance related incentive scheme

The introduction of a performance-related incentive scheme is designed to reward performance, innovation, creativity and the responsive administration of relations with stakeholders to create inclusive outcomes and effective service delivery. This will be a budget-neutral tool for results-based management with performance targets, standards and indicators and greater accountability.

It may not be an easy task to define de-bureaucratization in precise terms because it is semantically multi-dimensional with a variety of nuances attached to it. In general, it is characterized by a situation that is devoid of bureau-pathologies (red tape and delay); it also means downsizing, delayering (as opposed to a hierarchy), decentralization designed to enhance the importance of the lower strata of administration, and strengthening the cutting-edge functionaries (street-level bureaucracy) that are involved in executing the policies in the field. The term also refers to the efforts to bring about attitudinal change (from the typical indifferent bureaucratic response to one of extending as much help as possible) and articulate strategies to demystify governance through the simplification of procedures, rules and regulations. The idea is to democratize governance by involving the stakeholders who, with their inputs, make governance contextually relevant and meaningful. By insisting on citizen-centric public authority, governance is, as the Pay Commission suggests, no longer a distant entity, but one that is integrally connected with one's life.

Concluding observations

Contemporary governance is not just about efficiency; it also upholds democratic participation, accountability and empowerment. There is therefore a constant tension between (a) how to make government efficient and (b) how to keep it accountable. There is also a corresponding tension between 'the conception of people as consumers in the context of relations between state and market' and the conception of 'people as citizens in the context of relations between state and society'.[36] What it suggests is the increasing importance of citizen participation in public affairs. So, institutional reforms are but a significant step of 'strengthening [people's] voice in general – and the voice of the poor in particular'. This strategy, as the 2000 World Bank report endorses, emphasizes that

> the institutional reform is not simply a matter of changing the ways in which public hierarchies are arranged. Its focus is on the broad array of 'rules of the game' that shape the incentives and actions of public actors – including the 'voice' mechanisms that promote the rule of law and the accountability of government to its citizens.[37]

What this perspective underlines is the need for a citizen-centric government. The only flaw in this argument is that the village-based institutions continue

> to reflect unequal social and economic structures ... and higher castes and economically powerful groups within the village continue to be the de facto leaders in *panchayats*; while the women, despite the reservation, remain 'proxies' to male counterparts who participate in *panchayat* affairs and decisions.[38]

Notwithstanding the obvious structural constraints, the *Panchayati Raj* institutions provide a form of governance that is based on community resources. At the grassroots, community is the organic unit of cultural, social, economic and political organization. In view of the growing popularity of the *Panchayat* institutions, there is no doubt that a better administration can easily be achieved by building on community resources rather than trying to import 'managerialization' of public services.[39]

So, civil service reforms entail designs for extending opportunities for all and not just for a select few. This will mean in a country like India, as a former chief minister elaborates, 'creating opportunities for people for education, health, employment and general well-being. If these are not the focus of concern, the reforms will face a very rocky path because their very logic will be questioned. If reform cannot provide people [with] better education, health care and job opportunities, it will belie its very name'.[40] Governance is thus an endeavour to ensure public well-being, and reform measures should be directed towards that, although it is easier said than done, given the well entrenched vested interests challenging rather instinctively efforts towards building ethically sensitive governance. Civil service reforms are important but not sufficient because administrative debasement is deep-rooted. It can be conclusively tackled only by creating parallel social movements in favour of ethics in governance as perhaps the only means to arrest the decadence in public administration.

There is one final point. Civil service reforms are a testimony to the desire for change in bureaucracy because bureaucracy-led governance seems to have lost its vitality from the time that it was well equipped to bring about development in the real sense of the term. Poverty shows no signs of abatement and the benefits of development are being appropriated by the elite at the cost of far more deserving segments of Indian citizenry. As the trajectory of India's development in the twentieth century shows, state-led development planning failed to bring about the changes as the founding father felt. The inadequacies of the erstwhile reform packages can be said to have contributed to the growing acceptance of an alternative model of development, insisting on localizing governance in a decentralized and people-centric self-development mode. Development is not the brainchild of the experts; it is an outcome, drawn on inputs from the grassroots. What is critical in this conceptualization is the role of civil society that has emerged as a third sector along with the state and the market. This is a new venture in societal problem solving in which governance is less bureaucratic. A significant departure from the conventional approaches to public authority, civil society-centred governance creates a space for voluntary action in areas where the state has already retreated.

Governance and civil service reforms seem to have gone hand in hand in India. Despite being rooted in the neo-liberal justification for the withdrawal of the state from social sectors, the contribution of the model of governance is enormous in reiterating the importance of ethics in public authority. It is being increasingly felt in every walk of life in India that one of the major reasons for the lack of expected growth is an inefficient and insensitive civil service that needs complete overhauling. The recommendations of the fifth and sixth Pay Commissions are instructive here: in order to make the Indian civil service an ethics-driven instrument of governance, these pay commissions, besides fulfilling their traditional role of adjusting pay packages in the light of the changing price index, seem to have upheld the fundamental tenets of the governance paradigm while seeking to reinvent civil services in India as both civil and responsible for providing quality services to the citizens. From the point of view of the recommendations which these pay commissions have made to revamp the civil services, they have certainly fulfilled their mandates, although the fact remains that, without a complementary mindset, the transformative design that they have articulated is unlikely to be put into effect. Nonetheless, by showing concern for ethics in governance, these pay commissions seem to have unleashed processes whereby principles of accountability and responsiveness have been persuasively espoused as critical for public authority.

Notes

1　Webster's *New Universal Unabridged Dictionary*, Dorset & Baber, London, 1979.
2　*Random House College Dictionary*, (revised Edition), Random House, New York, 1984, p. 571.
3　*Sub-Saharan Africa: From Crisis to Sustainable Growth: a long-term perspective study*, The World Bank, 1989, p. 18.
4　*World Development Report*, The World Bank, Oxford University Press, New York, 1992, p. 29.
5　*The World Bank in Governance: the World Bank Experience*, The World Bank, Washington DC, 1992, p. 27.
6　*Government and Development*, The World Bank, Washington DC, 1992, p. 9.
7　*Sub-Saharan Africa*, p. 192.

8 Deborah Brautigam, 'Governance and economy: a review', Working Papers, Policy and Review Departments, The World Bank, December 1991, p. 8.

9 Ibid., p. 9.

10 *Governance and Development*, p. 3.

11 Ibid., p. 58 (footnote 1).

12 UNDP, *Reconceptualizing Governance*, discussion paper 2, New York, January 1997, p. 9.

13 Ibid., p. 19.

14 This section is drawn from *Human Settlements*, a report prepared by the United Nations Economic and Social Commission for Asia and Pacific, unless otherwise stated. Source:www.unescap.org/huset/gg/governance.html.

15 The summary is drawn from the UNDP Report, *Governance for Sustainable Human Development*, 1997.

16 Lewis T Preston's foreword in *Governance and Development*, The World Bank, Washington DC, 1992, p. v.

17 *Governance and Development*, pp. 11–12.

18 Drawn from 'Governance barometer: policy guidelines for good governance', prepared by the National Party of South Africa, *www.gdrc.org/u-gov/governance-understand.html*.

19 This is how governance is defined by The Institute on Governance, Canada. Source:www.iog.ca/about.html.

20 Lawrence E Lyer, Jr, Carolyn J Heinrich, Carolyn J Hill, *Improving Governance: a new logic for empirical research*, Georgetown University Press, Washington DC, 2001, p. 10.

21 Daniel Tarschys, 'Wealth, values, institutions: trends in government and governance' in *Governance in the 21st Century: future studies*, OECD, Paris, 2001, p. 28.

22 Dorte Salskov-Iversen, Hans Krause Hansen and Sven Bislev, 'Governmentality, globalization and local practice: transformation of a hegemonic discourse', *Alternatives: social transformation and human governance*, April–June 2000, p. 188.

23 Elina Penttinen, 'Capitalism as a system of global order' in Henri Goverde, Philip G Cerny, Mark Haugaard and Howard Lentner (eds) *Power in Contemporary Politics: theories, practices, globalizations*, Sage, London, p. 211.

24 Paul R Brass, 'Foucault steals political science', *American Reviews of Political Science*, 3, 2000, p. 318.

25 Adrian Leftwich, 'On the primacy of politics in development' in Adrian Leftwich, (ed.), *Democracy and Development: theory and practice*, Polity Press, Cambridge, 1996, p. 16.

26 Jonh J Kirlin, 'the big question in a democracy', *Public Administration Review*, September–October 1996, p. 217.

27 Adrian Leftwich, 'on the primacy of politics in development' in Adrian Leftwich, (ed.), *Democracy and Development: theory and practice*, Polity Press, Cambridge, 1996, p. 20.

28 *Refurbishing of Personnel Administration: scaling new heights*, Tenth Report, The Second Administrative Reforms Commission, November 2008, p. V.

29 *Report of the Fifth Central Pay Commission*, Vol. 1, Government of India, New Delhi, January 1997, p. 95.

30 Ibid.

31 Ibid., pp. 95–6.

32 Ibid., p. 117.

33 'The State in a changing world', *The World Development Report* (Summary), 1997, The World Bank, Washington DC, 1997, p. 14.

34 According to the 1997 World Development Report (summary), there are three ways in which the civil service can be radically reformed: (a) a recruitment system based on

merit, not favouritism; (b) a merit-based internal promotion system, and (c) adequate compensation. 'The State in a changing world', p. 9.

35 Atul Kohli, *State-Directed Development: political power and industrialization in the global periphery*, Cambridge University Press, Cambridge, 2004, p. 285.

36 Martin Minogue, 'Changing the state: concepts and practice in the reform of the public sector' in Martin Minogue, Charles Polidano and David Hume (eds), *Beyond the NPM: changing ideas and practice in governance*, Edward Elgar, Cheltenham, 1998, p. 17.

37 *Reforming Public Institutions and Strengthening Governance, a World Bank strategy*, November 2000, Public Sector Group, Poverty Reduction and Economic Management (PREM) Network, p. 2.

38 Supriya Roychowdhury, 'Globalization and decentralization', *The Hindu*, 5 January 2002.

39 Elaine Kamarck pursues this argument in her 'Government innovations around the world', Faculty Research Working Paper Series, John F Kennedy School of Government, Harvard University, 2004, p. 32.

40 Digvijay Singh, (former Madhya Pradesh Chief Minister), 'Public ownership of reforms: the experience of Madhya Pradesh', in Stephens Howes, Ashok Lahiri and Nicholas Stern (eds), *State-level Reforms in India: towards more effective government*, Macmillan, New Delhi, 2003, p. 31.

5 Institutional responses to the decline of ethics in governance in a historical perspective

History has shown that efforts have constantly been made to arrest systemic degradation. As the argument runs, systems are bound to falter for contextual reasons, while they are articulating their ideological priorities. What is thus needed is to evolve effective mechanisms to halt the debasement that a system suffers from time to time. This is a powerful lesson of history: it cannot be disputed, because the roots of the derailment of the system are too well entrenched to be eradicated easily. This is a view that also draws our attention to the wider socio-economic and political milieu in which the reasons for the systemic failure are located. Despite the fact that the dislocation of the system has its roots in the immediate context, the importance of the wider environment to which the system is organically linked cannot be ruled out. The processes leading to the deviation of the system from the fundamental canons of ethics in governance are complex. It is now accepted that a decline in any system is inevitable, since the environment in which the system is located is not perfect. So, the problem and its source have been identified. This is one part of the story. The other part – underlining the efforts against tendencies to undermine, if not derail, the system – is about those major serious attempts which seek to re-establish the values of ethics in governance as perhaps most useful in realizing the core beliefs of liberal democracy.

What is fundamental here is that the challenges from the reduction of ethics in public life usually refuel the debate, which is always helpful in re-conceptualizing the approaches and tools of analysis. As will be shown below, institutional decay and social degradation are dialectically connected: the former is as much a push-factor as an outcome of the processes, which are rooted in the wider social environment. This makes the situation far more complicated, because institutions contribute to significant changes by playing defining roles; similarly, society is a source of dramatic flux in institutions when it accommodates new demands, which are usually articulated by various types of social movement. As an ongoing process, governance is being constantly reinvented, sometime for internal reasons, sometime as a result of external pressure. The purpose is to uphold the publicness of public authority, which, if compromised, strikes at its foundation. Solutions must be found; otherwise, the edifice of governance crumbles. Given the contextual complexities in which governance unfolds, there cannot be tailor-made solutions to the problems responsible for government derailment; this idea is supported by the failure of the so-called universal models of governance, sponsored by the World Bank, to arrest the decadence in governance in a large number of developing countries. What it reemphasizes is the fact that, since problems have clear contextual roots, solutions are to be identified by keeping in view the contextual peculiarities of the system, which can never be comprehended through derived wisdom.

Historically speaking, there are two major ways in which governance loses its public character. On the one hand, corruption and malpractices, which are always hailed by vested interests as complementary to the gratification of partisan interests, continue to plague governance to a significant extent in most developing countries, including India. On the other hand, the slackening of governance is also due to the misuse of public authority through circumstances in which the political leadership conveniently bypasses even its constitutional obligations to pursue and fulfil private goals and objectives, at the cost of those of the governed. This is indicative of the decline in ethics in governance. Disheartened by the distortions in governance, S Radhakrishnan, who became India's President in 1962, thus suggested in as early as 1947 that

> unless we destroy corruption in high places, root out every trace of nepotism, love of power, profiteering and black marketing which have spoiled the good name of this great country in recent times, we will not be able to raise the standards of efficiency of administration as well as in the production and distribution of the necessary goods in life.[1]

Governance is thus not so much an instrument for public well-being, as an apparatus for self-gratification for those in power and authority.

Implicit in the above argument is an insistence on institutional devices to contain the derailment in governance; this further requires resistance when governance is appropriated by vested interests. It is difficult to capture those challenges in a chapter, given the paucity of space. Hence this chapter selectively focuses on three major endeavours that the government of independent India undertook to address the sources of the decline of ethics in governance. The aim was identical, because all these efforts were directed at reforming governance, which had significantly lost its public character. Reasons for the governmental degradation, however, varied: while the 1977 Shah Commission attributed the decline in ethics in governance to the deliberate misuse of power due to the arrogance of the prevalent political leadership in view of the numerical majority that it had in parliament, the 1962 Santhanam Committee and the 2005 Second Administrative Reforms Commission, also known as the Moily Commission, focussed on increasing corruption in public life as being responsible for its decadence.

Constituted in 1962, the Santhanam Committee was the first of its kind, because corruption in public offices did not seem to have received so much attention in the past. Unlike the Shah Commission or the Second Administrative

Commission, the aim of the Santhanam Committee was also to create an environment in which bribery and corruption would not flourish. The report was an eye-opener, although, by providing purely institutional solutions to the debasement of public authority, the Committee did not seem to have paid adequate attention to the social roots of the phenomenon.

For the Shah Commission, the debasement of public authority was conditioned by circumstances, being supported by the rise of a dictatorial leadership. As the Commission saw, there was neither a military coup nor the consolidation of an extra-constitutional authoritarianism that usually contribute to the rise of an absolutist political authority; the design that justified the misuse of public authority was absolutely constitutional. Guaranteed by the Constitution of India, the then Congress leadership at the behest of its leader, Indira Gandhi, resorted to specific constitutional provision to create and consolidate what could be readily characterized as constitutional authoritarianism. The Shah Commission report is a thorough statement of how public authority was misused at the drop of a hat during the two-year period, between 1975 and 1977, when a constitutional Emergency was declared to quell opposition to the ruling authority. Besides narrating how authority was personalized and political leadership became hegemonic in public life, the Commission also reiterates that the decline of ethics in public authority can be conclusively arrested once the Constitution of India reigns supreme in so far as governance is concerned.

In contrast to the Shah Commission, which was constituted to look into the excesses committed by the existing ruling authority, the 2005 Moily Commission, as the Second Administrative Reforms Commission was known, obviously had had a wider mandate. Like the Santhanam Committee, it was also aware that, unless there was a robust culture of integrity, it would be difficult for the institutional mechanisms to take root. The crux of ethics in public life does not entail the mere declaration of a commitment to ethical behaviour, but its adoption in one's behaviour while discharging public roles. Corruption is a deviant behaviour that can successfully be tackled by (a) strengthening institutional checks and balances; and (b) creating a culture of integrity. So, while devising mechanisms to arrest administrative decline in India, the Second Administrative Commission, unlike the other two interventions, seems to have taken a wider view of the phenomenon by being sensitive to India's peculiar socio-political compulsions. Conceptually, this was most innovative attempt, since it paid adequate attention to the social factors behind the decline of ethics in governance in India. The decline had a very distinct contextual flavour, and cannot be persuasively explained in terms of the derivative models highlighting institutional decay.

By thoroughly analysing the reports of these three important government initiatives in independent India, the chapter argues that institutional reforms may not be a sufficiently appropriate shield against the debasement of governance in India. What is required is to create an environment in which public authorities with a tendency towards appropriating benefits for themselves are despised and hated. So, there has to be a cultural solution along with the creation of appropriate institutional mechanisms that are strong enough to contain corruption and mal-practices in governance. The aim of this chapter is to lay out the arguments that these Commissions made while dealing with the decline of ethics in governance and also to assess them with reference to a context which was not inclined in favour of creating a robust culture of integrity. By dwelling on each of the reports separately, the chapter further makes the point that what links all these efforts, despite their being prepared in different eras, was their concern for ethics in governance which, it was strongly felt, had been considerably eroded in inde-pendent India.

Divided into two parts – Part A and Part B – this chapter is a thorough study of the reports that specific Commissions/Committees prepared to weed out cor-ruption from public life and create an institutional fabric supportive of a robust culture of integrity. The chapter makes two arguments, one historical and the other conceptual. The argument hinges on the ideas that the approach to the issues of ethics and integrity is history specific and that the conceptual under-standing of the phenomenon evolved accordingly. The discussion in Part A revolves around the Licence–Quota–Permit Raj as the possible root cause of cor-ruption in public authority, since it encouraged the unrestricted discretionary power of public personnel, usually exercised in exchange for a premium. Part B, which seeks to conceptualize the derailment of public authority in the context of a globalizing India, dwells on the phenomenon against the background of a com-pletely different socio-ideological milieu, which was appreciative of the gradual opening up of the Indian economy. Besides accepting the importance of the institutional mechanisms in containing corruption and malpractices in govern-ance, the new era also emphasised the role of other social actors in transforming the environment, a role in which the concern for ethics and integrity in govern-ance reigned supreme. Although the discussion is formatted chronologically, there is a common conceptual theme that links Parts A and B that, regardless of the radical changes in India's ideological texture following the acceptance of the 1991 New Economic Policy, the governments that followed have paid consider-able attention to the containment of corruption and those indulging in malprac-tices for self-aggrandizement.

PART A

The Santhanam Committee and the Shah Commission: institutional counters to corruption and malpractices in governance

Corruption is unavoidable in governance, as history has shown. Is it due to lack of public morality or institutional decadence or both? Explanations vary, although there is hardly any disagreement about the fact that corruption is omni-present in public life. While seeking to understand the nature of corruption in India, her erstwhile Prime Minister argued that there is no protection if the fence starts eating the crops. We have government servants who do not serve but oppress the poor and helpless ... who do not uphold the law ... but connive with those who cheat the State and whole legions whose only concern is their private welfare at the cost of society. They have no work ethics, no feeling for the public cause, no involvement in the future of the nation, no comprehension of the national goals, [and] no commitment to the values of modern India. They have only a grasping mercenary outlook, devoid of competence, integrity and commitment.[2]

This is a most revealing statement underlining the decadence of the system of governance that India has endured since independence. The problem is clearly internal, since it is the public officials who are condemned as corrupt because of their scant respect for the fundamental principles of ethics in governance. Public authorities have ceased to be public, given their pronounced lack of commitment to public well-being or enthusiasm for fulfilling their partisan interests and the sacrifice of their public missions. What was stated at the highest level of governance in 1985 was echoed in the Tenth Plan (2002–2007) that, by pinpointing the overall decadence in public life, argued that

while the functions of the State in India have steadily widened, capacity to deliver has steadily declined over the years due to administrative cynicism, rising indiscipline and a growing perception that the political and bureaucratic elite views the state as an area where public service is to be used for private ends. In almost all [Indian provinces], people perceive bureaucracy as wooden, disinterested in public welfare and corrupt.... Weak governance, manifesting itself in poor service delivery, excessive regulation and uncoordinated and wasteful public expenditure, is seen as one of the key factors impinging on growth and development.[3]

The idea that corruption is a threat to public authority was pursued with increasing zeal in the Eleventh Plan as well. While probing into what ails governance in India, it was thus mentioned that 'corruption ... that has assumed serious dimensions in public services ... is a major factor in the wastefulness, inefficiency and inequities we find in public administration [in India] today'.[4] As will be discussed later in this chapter, the derailment of public services in India was a source of concern for the Second Administrative Reforms Commission, which also made a thorough analysis of the phenomenon in one of its reports. The fact that corruption figured prominently in the government discourses also suggests that it had not escaped public notice; the voluminous reports that were produced since independence to address the issue are a testimony to the seriousness with which the government sought to understand the issues. By providing a critical analysis of two important reports – the 1964 Santhanam Committee Report and the 1977 Shah Commission Report – this chapter is about the institutional mechanisms that the Indian policy makers used to arrest the growing incidence of corruption, in a context in which the state's hegemony was hardly questioned.

One of the earlier attempts to meaningfully address the issue of administrative corruption was made in 1964, when the Government of India constituted a fully fledged committee to look into the phenomenon of the corruption that was assumed to have significantly crippled governance as an instrument for public well-being. Headed by K Santhanam, a member of the lower house of the Indian parliament, the committee is perhaps one of the first serious endeavours to understand and combat the menace of corruption. Appointed by the parliament, the committee was given very specific tasks in the terms and conditions of its appointment:[5]

- to examine the organization, set-up, functions and responsibilities of the vigilance units in the ministries and departments of the Government of India and to suggest measures to make them more effective;
- to examine the organization, strength, procedures and methods of work of the special police establishment and the difficulties experienced by it, and to suggest measures to further improve its functioning;
- to consider and suggest steps to be taken to emphasize the responsibilities of each department for checking corruption;
- to suggest changes in law that would ensure speedy trial of cases of bribery, corruption and criminal misconduct, and make the laws otherwise more effective;
- to examine the rules relating to disciplinary proceedings and to consider what changes are necessary in order to expedite these proceedings and to make them more effective;
- to suggest measures calculated to produce a social climate both amongst public servants and in the general public in which bribery and corruption may not flourish;
- to examine the government servants' conduct rules and to recommend changes necessary for ensuring maintenance of absolute integrity in the public services;
- to suggest steps for securing public support for anti-corruption measures; and
- to consider special measures that may be necessary in corporate public undertakings to secure honesty and integrity amongst their employees.

As the terms of appointment suggest, there were three complementary tasks that the Committee was asked to undertake: to conceptualize the nature of corruption in public life; to suggest specific laws to combat that corruption, identified as a key to the deterioration of values in public life; and, given the clear social roots of corruption, to create an environment in which corruption and malpractices would be considered serious aberrations in a value-driven public life and thus to be abhorred. Since it was a parliamentary committee and was formed following a declaration by the then Minister for Home Affairs Lal Bahadur Shastri, it had the backing of parliamentarians, who appeared to have been equally alarmed at the pace at which corruption was becoming part of public life. So, the appointment of the Santhanam Committee was a wake-up call in response to a public outcry against corruption and the undermining of ethics in governance.

For the Committee, corruption connoted the 'improper or selfish exercise of power and influence attached to a public office or to the special position one occupies in public life'.[6] It was aware that corruption, as was explained above, needed to be conceptualized as a social phenomenon rooted in the wider social, economic and political milieu. This was not, however, the task that the Committee was given; what it was expected to do was to understand the phenomenon with reference to the Union Government, which had apparently lost its vitality due to corruption. Guided by this vision, the approach that the Committee had adopted was clearly institution-based and also clearly Weberian because it drew upon the belief that the systemic decay could be arrested by ascertaining internal accountability. The argument was simple: the rising importance of corruption in public life was proportionately linked to the weaknesses of the mechanisms for internal accountability. So, the solution was to strengthen the mechanisms where they existed and put them in place where they did not.

Corruption had historical roots. As Committee felt, 'the high water-mark of corruption was reached in India ... during the Second World War [since] ... propriety of means was no consideration if it impeded the war effort'.[7] This was perhaps the beginning of what gradually became a source of concern, as it challenged the foundational ethical principles of public administration in India. What accounts for the growing incidence of corruption? In the Committee's view, 'where there is power and discretion, there is always the possibility of abuse, more so when the power and discretion have to be exercised in the context of scarcity and controls and pressure to spend public money'.[8] While it would not be possible, as the Committee understood, 'to completely eliminate discretion, it should be possible to devise a system of administration which would reduce to the minimum ... the need for exercise of personal discretion consistent with efficiency and speedy disposal of public business'.[9] What was most alarming was the attempt to short-circuit governmental procedure by offering bribes, which the Committee characterized as 'speed money' – an amount given to government officers by those seeking to bypass the procedures of administration. It was a means to avoid the cumbersome procedures to arrive at a decision. Speed money was, as the Committee reported, 'a fairly common type of corrupt practice particularly in matters of granting of licenses and permits'.[10] As the Committee further noted, '[t]he anxiety to avoid delay has encouraged the growth of dishonest practices like the system of speed money.... Generally the bribe giver does not wish, in these case, to get anything done unlawfully, but wants to speed up the process of the movement of the files and communications relating to decision ... even by bypassing the normal procedures, if necessary'.[11] A product of the famously construed 'License–Quota–Permit Raj',[12] speed money created a quid pro quo arrangement whereby both the benefit seeker and giver gained advantage. Hence the arrangement continued at a cost to the system, because of the loss of vitality, which was not a deterrent to those willing to make the system captive for their personal gain.

According to the Committee, the willingness to corrupt and the capacity to corrupt go hand in hand. This was a menace that was found in large measure in the industrial and commercial classes. In the Permit Raj, they flourished by indulging

> in evasion and avoidance of taxes ... by various methods such as obtaining licenses in the names of bogus firms and individuals, trafficking in licenses, suppressing profits by manipulation of accounts to avoid taxes and other legitimate claims on profits, accepting money for transactions put through without accounting for it in bills and accounts, and under-valuation of transactions in immovable property.[13]

Corruption thus became integral to commercial transactions; in fact, it was perhaps the most effective means, the Committee was surprised to notice, 'to get things done'.[14] Hence it was suggested that the only way to eliminate corruption was to 'fight these unscrupulous agencies of corruption'.[15] The most devastating impact of widespread corruption was manifested in the public 'losing faith in the integrity of public administration',[16] and the idea that public administration functioned only through corrupt practices gained ground. Here two points seem critical: on the one hand, it was firmly established that excessive state control enabled 'the middle men' to be effective, because of their access to those responsible for the issue of licenses and the granting of other facilities; on the other hand, their rise seemed to have been helped by the apparent slackening of the efforts of the government machinery to contain such tendencies.

How to combat corruption?

With an extensive study of the roots of corruption, the Santhanam Committee drew the conclusion that corruption in governance is rooted in 'wide discretionary powers which are exercised by the executive in carrying on the complicated work of modern administration'.[17] Once the root of corruption was located, it was easier for the Committee to devise mechanisms for its eradication. The Committee thus suggested two types of mechanism: on the one hand, in order to arrest the institutional decay resulting from the lack of integrity of the personnel, the Committee recommended an institutional agency to take punitive measures against errant government and public sector employees if their complicity with corruption was proved. The Committee was of the view that since 'the detection, investigation and punishment of corruption and misuse of authority by individual government servants is of utmost importance'[18] for a vibrant public administration, there was a need for a powerful institution to be responsible for punishing the deviants. Following this sentiment, the Committee recommended the setting up of a Central Vigilance Commission with a branch that would deal with general complaints and redress and another to deal with vigilance activities. This was an improvement on what had existed in the past: as part of the Ministry of Home Affairs, the previous Administrative Vigilance Division had been authorized to look into the cases of alleged corruption in public personnel associated with the Home Ministry, whereas the Central Vigilance Commission was legally authorized to deal with cases in each and every department and also in the public sector units within the government. Besides its expanded scope of function, the Vigilance Commission was also an independent organization with an exclusive task. The Committee also felt the need to strengthen the existing Special Police Establishment to intensify the action against bribery and corruption. For the Committee, despite being endowed with adequate legal power, the Special Police Establishment lacked the power because it did not receive as much attention from the political authority as had been expected. It was thus recommended that it get support from the government to make it self-sustaining; otherwise, the basic purpose of its creation was likely to be defeated.

Besides suggesting the creation of an institution meant exclusively for handling the cases of corruption and strengthening the Special Police Establishment, the Santhanam Committee also recommended revamping the wider sociopolitical environment which is a key to ensuring the probity in public services. The Committee was alarmed to notice that

> there is a widespread impression that failure of integrity is not uncommon even among the Ministers and some Ministers who have held office during the last 16 years have enriched themselves illegitimately, obtained good jobs for their sons and relations through nepotism, and have reaped other advantages inconsistent with any notion of purity in public life.[19]

According to the Committee, absolute integrity on the part of the ministers who were supposed to set the trend in public life was an indispensable condition for the establishment of a tradition of probity in public life. The institutional mechanisms that the Committee had proposed would be futile unless there existed a social climate in which corruption was despised and those indulging in corruption were hated and socially ostracized. The Committee felt that, by setting healthy precedents, public office holders could create an environment supportive of integrity in public governance. The ministers were required to be impeccably honest and thus incorruptible; otherwise, public administration could never become an instrument to ensure public well-being. Tuned to the Weberian preference for mechanisms of internal accountability to ascertain ethics in governance, the Santhanam Committee suggested the following steps,[20] which were critical in fulfilling the core principles of public administration:

- A code of conduct for ministers ... relating to acquisition of property, acceptance of gifts and disclosure of assets and liabilities should be drawn up. This code of conduct should be placed before Parliament and State Legislatures. The Prime Minister and Chief Ministers should be responsible for enforcing the code of conduct.
- A specific allegation of corruption on the part of a Minister at the Centre or in a State should be promptly investigated by an agency whose findings would command respect. We recognize that irresponsible allegations cannot be taken serious note of. We therefore suggest that if a formal allegation is

made by any ten members of Parliament or a Legislature in writing addressed to the Prime Minister or Chief Minister, through the Speakers, ... the Prime Minister or Chief Minister should consider himself obliged, by convention, to refer the allegations for immediate investigation by a Committee, constituted for this purpose.

This would be in addition to the responsibilities of the Prime Minister and Chief Minister of States to take note of allegations made in the Press or which otherwise come to their notice. In respect of such allegations also the Prime Minister and Chief Ministers should be free to refer the matter to the proposed Committee. In all other cases, the Minister against whom the allegations are made should, as a rule, institute legal proceedings by filing a complaint for criminal defamation and the Minister concerned should be given legitimate assistance by the Government of which they are Ministers.

- In cases, where the Ministers are unwilling to take legal action, the Prime Minister or the Chief Ministers of States, as the case may be, should consider themselves obliged by convention, unless there is irrefutable proof of the integrity of the Minister concerned, to advise the President or the Governor, as the case may be, to withdraw his pleasure which would mean that the Minister will have to go out of office unless he himself resigns.

Apart from the ministers, the integrity of the members of parliament and state legislatures was, the Committee felt, integral to the creation of a social climate against corruption and malpractices in governance. Besides suggesting a code of conduct for the legislators, the Committee empowered the parliamentary Committee of Privileges to enquire into cases of corruption involving the lawmakers. Once guilt was proved, the members had no option but to quit and to face the consequences for their breach of conduct. The idea was to control deviant behaviour through punitive actions. Again, what guided the Committee was the fact that, once a precedent had been established, the legislators were likely to behave in such a fashion as to generate respect from the stakeholders for their conduct. Implicit here was also the hope that punitive actions against the errant legislators were sure to cause damage to their social standing, which they would want to avoid at any cost. That would be far more effective, the Committee underlined, with an alert media spreading the message to the public. So, in the scheme of things that the Committee sought to create, the media was also a critical player in ensuring ethics in governance.

The Santhanam recommendations are in a class by themselves simply because, besides suggesting a formula for strengthening the institutional fabric of governance, they also talked about a conducive social environment in which corruption cannot flourish. They are also a class part because they referred to an important source of corruption, which is being talked about with even greater emphasis in the twenty-first century: it is strongly believed that corruption in governance will disappear to a significant extent once public funding of elections is accepted as a principle. The Committee thus noted that 'the public belief in the prevalence of corruption at high political levels has been strengthened by the manner in which funds are collected by political parties, especially at the time of elections'.[21] As is evident, fighting an election is an expensive proposition and the parties in the fray raise funds, through legal and illegal means, to take care of the expensive campaign that they undertake. Corporations and businessmen always come up with the offer of funds to support the candidates in the hope that, once they are elected, they would act as their representatives when a favour is sought. It was therefore essential, as the Committee stated, that 'the conduct of political parties should be regulated in this matter by strict principles in relation to collection of funds and electioneering'.[22] Debarring corporations from supporting the candidates financially, the Committee insisted that 'funds for fighting elections should come openly from supporters and sympathizers'.[23] This was a powerful recommendation with future implications, because one of the major sources of corruption in India was election funding by private enterprises. With their liberal funding of the election campaigns of political parties, corporations create a symbiotic network with the candidates, which they squeeze once their chosen ones are in power. Usually, when it comes to funding, businesses do not appear to discriminate between the parties because the outcome of an election generally remains uncertain. This is an unwritten rule that seems to govern the system of election funding in India. This is also an effective strategy that always places private interests at an advantage when it comes to the extraction of benefits from those holding political power.

An analytical scan of the recommendations reveal that institutional protections do not seem to be adequate in containing corruption to a significant extent unless they are equally strongly backed by a social climate in which corruption is hated and hence has no chance to flourish. In the ultimate analysis, the role of the public is critical in sustaining a propitious environment, supportive of high moral values, for creating and consolidating an edifice of governance drawing on them. This is what came out when the Committee suggested that 'it is desirable to create a situation in which those officials who have been found guilty of corruption feel not only that they have lost their jobs but also feel socially degraded'.[24] Emphasizing the importance of public opinion against persons who indulged in corruption, the Committee thus reiterated a fundamental principle of public administration, which always gave supremacy to the public to ensure its core.

Corruption in India acquired the status of folklore, as Gunnar Myrdal argued while seeking to understand the peculiar nature of India's development trajectory. As folklore, it has, as Myrdal further argued, 'a crucial bearing on how people conduct their private lives and how they view their government's efforts to consolidate the nation and to direct and spur development'.[25] As corruption was integrally connected with Indian public life, so were efforts towards understanding and also effectively combatting the phenomenon. So if corruption was an action, to use a metaphor from Newtonian laws of gravity, anti-corruption campaigns were a reaction. The 1964 Santhanam Committee needs to be conceptualized in this context. Corruption raised its ugly head to the certain detriment of the system that the founding fathers sought to build; it also led to various efforts aimed at eradicating its sources. It was more or less accepted by the people at large that corruption was a way of life – or, to use Myrdal's expression, folklore – which was so deeply entrenched in Indian administration and its socio-political milieu that it cannot be rooted out. In such an atmosphere, the recommendations that the Santhanam Committee made were most refreshing for two reasons: on the one hand, by seeking to refashion the prevalent system of administration, the Committee suggested several institutional mechanisms which, despite having figured in public discourse, had never received governmental support. In that sense, the Committee was a very crucial intervention in administrative reforms, in accordance with the public desire to govern ethically and constitutionally. Mere institutional reforms are not effective. Hence the Santhanam Committee emphasized, on the other hand, the importance of the social climate in creating and consolidating the forces that were challenging those who flourished by being corrupt.

What is most striking is the fact that the 1964 Santhanam Committee had, besides devising preventive institutional instruments, also set in motion processes whereby corruption was to be analysed in perhaps its most complex manifestation. Its contextual roots were located in the License–Quota–Permit Raj, in which functionaries of government bureaucracy held disproportionate power over granting licences and permits. So, a controlled polity led to the creation of a corrupt regime. This was possible because, as the Committee further argued, the prevalent social climate supported corruption in growing organic roots in Indian society. By striving to locate the social roots of corruption, the Committee made recommendations which were thus transcendental; corruption continues to remain a serious menace to governance, though its nature has undergone a sea change, as will be shown below in the consideration of the report of the 2005 Second Administrative Reforms Commission. In conceptualizing ethics in governance, what always remains critical is the role of the social climate in creating an ambience in which values for ethics in governance are not only well entrenched, but are also strong enough to evolve complementary practices in its support. By being sensitive to this aspect, the Santhanam Committee has made a very useful contribution to comprehend and also to conceptualize how corruption and the decline of ethics were dialectically inter-connected in the specific historical context of India. The recommendations are not entirely contextual, but transcend the historical era by drawing our attention to the social roots of corruption. Thus a fundamental theoretical formulation for the eradication of corruption is conceptually possible once this is accepted as a social goal. In other words, once corruption loses its social backing, it can never be a threat to governance because, for those involved in its execution, it becomes, instead of being a source of self-gratification, a source of hatred and social degradation.

The Shah Commission: an antidote to privatization of governance

Appointed in 1977 in the aftermath of the end of the Emergency in which democracy had been shelved, the Shah Commission was constituted to look into the excesses that the ruling authority had indulged in. There were cases of gross violation of constitutional propriety while fulfilling personal whims, especially by those who held the highest constitutional positions in India. The Commission was thus

> to inquire into several aspects of allegations of abuse of authority, excesses and malpractices committed and action taken or purported to be taken in the wake of the Emergency proclaimed on the 26th of June, 1975 under Article 352 of the Constitution of [India].[26]

The Commission was, it was further stated, 'also not concerned to determine the infraction of any laws involving imposition of any penalty upon a person charged with the commission of infraction of law'.[27] The function of the Commission was to determine facts relating to 'matters of public importance and by adopting a procedure, which is not adversarial in character, but inquisitorial in character'.[28] It was primarily a fact-finding commission which was authorized to assess the impact of the privatization of governance on public life. The report is revealing, and it would not be an exaggeration to suggest that a study of the history and politics of the Emergency will remain elusive if the report is ignored. The purpose here is to build the story on the basis of the findings of the report, which unfortunately have not received, so far, adequate scholarly attention.

What led to the Emergency needs to be understood first. Since the aim here is not to provide a detailed account of the Emergency, I shall refer to two major events which reportedly created the conditions in which the Emergency was declared on 25 June 1975.[29] One can pin down two tumultuous events that largely accounted for the imposition of the constitutional decree for the suspension of the democratic constitutional machinery that had taken root in India since her political freedom in 1947. Scholars point out that the events on 12 and 13 June seemed to have decisively tilted the political balance in favour of a declaration of Emergency. On 12 June, Indira Gandhi's election to parliament from Rae Bareilly was declared null and void because of proven indulgence in 'corrupt electoral practices on two counts, namely using her private secretary in her election campaign and employing state and local government officials to manage her campaign for winning the parliamentary seat from Rae Bareilly'. Her election was invalid, although she later got a little respite from the Supreme Court of India, which, instead of granting complete and absolute stay of the earlier judgment, granted conditional stay by enabling her to remain as Prime Minister without the privileges that a member of Lok Sabha, the lower chamber of the Indian parliament, enjoys.

The second event was the result of the Gujarat assembly election which her party, the Congress, lost miserably to a motley conglomeration of parties, known as the Janata Front. It was simply unthinkable to the Prime Minister, given her declared confidence of winning the state election, since it was she who had campaigned vigorously to garner votes. These two events were powerful testimonies to her dwindling popularity. The situation became worse for her when the united opposition mounted a scathing attack on her, which became virulent as soon as the media got involved in this campaign. She was determined to improve her political image by measures to gag the opposition, regardless of the obvious ideological consequences. On 25 June, a massive meeting of the opposition parties was organized in Delhi, which was addressed by Jayaprakash Narayan, also known as J P to the people. As he had done in the past, possibly in a less direct way, J P appealed to the military, the police, and the civil service to put loyalty to the Constitution above loyalty to the government. This gave a handle to the Prime Minister, who construed it as an attempt 'to incite our armed forces to mutiny and police to rebel'. It was clearly stated in her radio broadcast on 26 June, when she justified the imposition of the Emergency to scuttle an armed rebellion that the opposition parties were planning to organize in India. She thus presented her case by saying that

> The President has proclaimed an Emergency. This is nothing to panic about. I am sure [that] you are conscious of the deep and widespread conspiracy which has been brewing ever since I began to introduce certain progressive measure of benefit to the common man and woman of India. In the name of democracy, it has been sought to negate the very functioning of demo-cracy.... How can any government worth the name stand by and allow the country's stability to be imperiled?[30]

To avoid further deterioration, as Indira Gandhi had put it, the constitutional Emergency was imposed which led to the suspension of the democratic function-ing of the state. Ordinary citizens realized with shock, as a commentator has most perceptibly commented recently, that 'they had no rights whatsoever under the new system'.[31] A democratic governance was soon replaced by an authorit-arian system of administration because 'politicians surrounding [Indira Gandhi, the Prime Minister] became small dictators [and] ... the new style of exercising control was copied all the way to the municipal level'.[32] The system was sub-verted to champion one's whims and it was done so easily, which confirms how vulnerable the democratic system was in India; the well-nurtured institutions that held democracy so high lost their vitality and became stooges of the ruling authority in their grand plan to make India part of its fiefdom.

The arguments defending constitutional propriety were forcibly muted in cir-cumstances when even the figment of opposition was considered a serious threat to Indian polity. Governance became leader-centric, even though that was con-trary to the fundamental precepts of Indian democracy. In order to sustain and consolidate its hegemonic political control, those in power undertook three measures that aimed at the personalizing of public authority: (a) widespread arrest and illegal detention of many political activists for their alleged involve-ment in anti-state activities, (b) the stringent control of the press by pursuing press censorship; and (c) adoption of retroactive amendments and the use of law and the Constitution to endorse the draconian measures that the ruling clique had indulged in. Justifying these steps as necessary to retain India's democratic fabric, the state never wavered while arresting or detaining even those individuals who never took part in anti-government agitation but were implicated with the charge that they harboured ill feelings towards the state. The press was not allowed to function, because it was a threat to those involved in privatizing governance for partisan ends. Journalists were indiscriminately incarcerated. The government kept amending a draconian law, the *Maintenance of Internal Security Act*, to allow the custodians of law and order enormous power to execute what the top administrative authority willed. Parliament became a stooge at the hands of the Prime Minister and others, including her son Sanjay Gandhi, who did not even hold a constitutional position. In an environment of personalized governance, India clearly lost her democracy and also the principles of constitutional propriety, which were never challenged so strongly in the past. As shown in the literature, it was not merely a dark period in India's recent political history; it also showed how values of ethics in governance became a casualty, since those in power had hardly had any respect for them.

Analysis of the consequences of the Emergency

The Emergency was proclaimed in response to pressing circumstances, as Indira Gandhi stated to defend her action. Critical of such an interpretation, the Shah Commission charged her with violating constitutional propriety, even while she was preparing the ground for the declaration on 26 June 1975. In this act, her confidante was her cabinet colleague S S Ray, who admitted before the Commission that, when he met her, she seemed to have already chosen the course of action to contain the opposition campaign against her administration. As Ray pointed out,

> she told me on two or three occasions [in the immediate past] that in view of the all-round indiscipline and lawlessness ... India required a shock treatment and something had to be done ... and some sort of emergency power or drastic power was necessary.[33]

On the basis of the reports that Indira Gandhi had received, she firmly believed that India was drifting 'towards chaos and anarchy'.[34] Ray was reportedly reluctant to go for an emergency declaration because he, as the Commission's Report underlines, told her that 'they could manage [the opposition challenges] with the laws which are already on the statute books' which he defended by mentioning 'the success with which they tackled the law and order problem of West Bengal within the framework of the laws then in force'.[35] Indira Gandhi did not seem persuaded; she wanted strong measures. When pressed further by the Prime Minister, Ray suggested that she could consider, if she so desired, Article 352 of the Constitution for the purpose of imposing an internal Emergency. This was accepted by her and adequate steps were soon undertaken to execute the constitutional provision for the Emergency.

There were two types of impropriety that Indira Gandhi had committed to justify her whimsical decisions. She seemed to have made up her mind when she had had a discussion with her cabinet colleague, S S Ray. Notwithstanding Ray's faith in the prevalent law and order machinery, he could not oppose what the Prime Minister had suggested. As he himself admitted before the Commission, 'there were certain things, which, when they came from the Prime Minister, he could not say that they were totally wrong'.[36] This is reflective of how vulnerable her cabinet colleague was, who was perhaps too scared to say what he felt otherwise; by personal authority, she managed to run the state with the aid of a cabinet which hardly had an independent voice, and virtually became a collection of people parroting the leader's views. The second serious impropriety consists of her efforts to simply bypass the cabinet by seeking presidential approval for the proclamation. In her note of 25 June to the President of India, she herself mentioned that, although she would have liked to have consulted her cabinet colleagues on this matter, it was not possible due to pressing circumstances. Taking serious note of this omission, the Commission strongly felt that it was another illustration of whimsical decisions that were the natural outcome when authority was personalized. People tended to violate the basic values of ethics in governance because of their arrogance in circumstances in which their authority was hardly questioned. The Commission thus unambiguously stated that

> it is clear that some of the important functionaries in the Home Ministry, Cabinet Secretariat and the Prime Minister's Secretariat, who should have been consulted before such an important decision was taken, did not know anything about the proclamation of Emergency till very late and some of them learnt about it only on the morning of June 26, 1975.[37]

The Emergency was thus declared in contravention of the fundamental ethos of collective responsibility that was the core of the Westminster form of parliamentary democracy. Instead of regret, Indira Gandhi strongly defended her decision by saying that, if the Emergency had not been put in place, a duly-elected government would have been 'pulled down by threats of violence and demonstrations in the streets and by inciting the army and police to revolt'.[38] For her, it was perhaps the only plausible solution to avoid the colossal devastation likely to happen if preventive measures had not been undertaken in advance. This was the shock treatment that she conceived of to perpetuate the personalized rule, the Commission lamented. Besides violating the fundamental tenets of constitutional propriety that the cabinet form of government entails, there is another serious constitutional lapse that confirms how parliamentary procedures were bypassed. The Commission had in fact found out that the 1975 declaration of Emergency was redundant because the Emergency that was proclaimed in 1971 during the war with Pakistan which finally culminated in the rise of Bangladesh as an independent nation was never withdrawn; the Defence of India rules were in operation; the provisions of Article 358, which included the suspension of the right to freedom (Article 19 of the Constitution), were also operational. The Constitution, according to the Commission, 'does not contemplate the issue of an Emergency upon an Emergency already existing, nor prevents the courts from entertaining any challenge to the declaration of this additional Emergency'.[39] The decision cannot be declared illegal as the Constitution is silent, although it reveals that Indira Gandhi's declared objective of inflicting 'a shock treatment' to those indulged in 'anti-government activities' must have persuaded her to undertake such a feat which, as one's common sense suggests, was not required when an Emergency was already there. So the proclamation of Emergency was not a knee-jerk reaction, but one that was based on serious thinking, which was supportive of her design for personal authority at the cost of the fundamental values of parliamentary democracy and collective responsibility of the Westminster form of authority. It was possible for her to bypass the constitutional checks and balances, because the institutions holding India's democratic structure of governance were too weak to contain authoritarian tendencies and also because of the fact that those associated with Indira Gandhi did not find it prudent to challenge her decisions. Nothing was thus reason driven; everything was governed by power, which created a different kind of politics, in which values became less significant and hardcore pragmatism seemed to have ruled the roost. A new era had thus been ushered in in which an individual, if endowed with extraordinary personality, could easily be authoritarian within the constitutional boundary of the 1950 Constitution of India, as Indira Gandhi had shown during the two-year period of Emergency.

Along with the tuning of the constitutional provisions to support the Emergency, the political authority guided by Indira Gandhi devised elaborate plans to control the media which had been held responsible for the chaos preceding the 25 June proclamation by alerting citizens to the government's plans, which the Congress leadership had undertaken to further personalize power at the cost of basic democratic rights. Indira Gandhi contrived the plans to create a reign of terror against the journalists and media houses that did not appear to be pro-government. She believed, as the Commission noted, that 'the agitation was only in the newspapers and once the newspapers were placed under censorship there was no agitation'.[40] The concerned minister was thus instructed to make laws 'to prevent scurrilous, malicious and mischievous writings in the newspapers'.[41] This was all-out war against the deviant newspapers that were involved in exposing the authoritarian government's designs that fulfilled the leader's whims. The reasons for the administrative measures taken against the media in general and the Press in particular was, as the Commission noted, 'to keep the public in ignorance and instil fear in them thereby suppressing dissent in every form, individual, political, parliamentary and judicial, and that it was used as an instrument of news management aimed at thought control'.[42] The journalists who were harassed during this period testified to the atmosphere of fear that surrounded everyone in the profession.

It was believed that the media needed to be controlled to avoid further trouble. The government left no stone unturned to make it happen. As the Commission highlighted, there were three ways in which the political authority executed its plan, which were: (a) censorship, (b) pressure tactics, and (c) creation of an agency – *Samachar* – to exert better administrative control over the dissemination of news. It was obvious that stringent guidelines were formulated to impose rigid censorship: the media, both print and visual, was not allowed to circulate items which were not supportive of government activities; later, it was decided, as the Commission confirmed, that the media was forbidden to carry any news items other than those which had, according to the Ministry of Information, publicity value for the government. The media was also pressurized to toe the government line of thinking through discriminatory policies in the booking of advertisements, which was likely to affect the financial health of the media houses. For this, the government prepared strict guidelines for the Directorate of Advertisement and Visual Publicity, the sole public agency responsible for fixing the amount of money to be given for advertisements. It was decided, as a pre-emptive measure, that 'newspapers which indulged in virulent propaganda, inciting communal passion or offending socially accepted conventions of decency or morality were not to be used for advertisement'.[43] Accordingly a list was prepared which showed that the Information Ministry had segregated those newspapers which had shown an inclination towards the political parties opposed to the Congress. The grading of newspapers in terms of being 'friendly, neutral and hostile' was based on ideological inclination and also proprietorial affiliations to political parties.[44] A scan of the amount of advertisement support that was given to take care of the publication costs of political parties other than the Congress party reveals that the policy was clearly discriminatory. The Commission thus noted that

> the Government during this period utilized its advertising policy as a source of financial assistance or denial of financial assistance to newspapers and journals, among others, in complete variance with the policy, approved by the parliament; ... there were glaring examples to show that newspapers that supported the government policy ... were given advertisement beyond their legitimate due.[45]

Similar was the formation of *Samachar* out of the merger of four news agencies, United News of India, Press Trust of India, Hindustan *Samachar* and *Samachar* Bharati. The purpose was to exert centralized control over these news agencies. Bringing them together would give the government a free hand in controlling news dissemination. As is evident, the motive behind this merger was not to attain administrative efficiency, but to streamline control over the news agency, which could then easily be prevented from being errant. It is also clear that the Emergency had created an environment in which the political authority hardly showed any concern for the values of democratic governance. What primarily motivated those in authority was individual desire for personal power, perhaps for self-gratification. How did individuals become so powerful? The reasons can be located in the weakness of the institutions of democracy, which hardly acted as a deterrent when efforts were made to manipulate their functioning in accordance with a personal agenda. It was easier for Indira Gandhi, in other words, to undertake such a feat, because whatever she did apparently had the support of the parliament; she put all the decisions before parliament for ratification and, given her hegemonic role in the Congress Party and also in parliament, none of her colleagues in the party or government ever dissented to what she had decided. This was democracy in its perverted form because a democratically elected leader virtually became authoritarian in a context in which democratic checks and balances were severely compromised. A regime of constitutional authoritarianism had emerged which gradually lost its appeal, because of its failure to appreciate the values of ethics in governance, which then became significantly compromised.

The Emergency was, as the Commission concluded, an aberration. Administration became a captive of those holding power and those at the periphery remained deprived of even what was legitimately due to them. The system, the Commission further laments, was subverted to enable the powerful to exercise authority in accordance primarily with personal whim. It was a tragic scenario, in which government machinery was appropriated to advance causes that were usually justified as necessary to sustain the system and to prevent it from being totally derailed by opposition-sponsored anti-state activities. While commenting on the excesses during the Emergency, the Commission forcefully argued that 'with the press gagged and a resultant blackout of authentic information, arbitrary arrests and detention went on apace. Effective dissent was smothered, followed by a general erosion of democratic values. Highhanded and arbitrary actions were carried out with impunity'.[46] This is perhaps the most clearly spelt-out account of how the Emergency functioned to subvert the democratic processes of governance, which caught the nation by surprise. Public authority ceased to be public since the civil service remained neither civil nor service driven, but became a stooge of those holding political authority. The system seemed to have been completely derailed because, as the Commission underlined,

> tyrants sprouted at all levels overnight – tyrants whose claim to authority was largely based on their proximity to the seats of power. The attitude of the general run of public functionaries was largely characterized by a paralysis of the will to do the right and proper thing.... The fear generated by the mere threat and without even the actual use of the weapon of detention under MISA [Maintenance of Internal Security Act] became so pervasive that the general run of public servants acted as willing tools of tyranny.[47]

The execution of the Emergency-related measures was so sudden that the Commission felt that they were seen to be insurmountable long before public functionaries realized their implications. To this was added the fear that seemed to have gripped those involved in running the administration at the lower levels. The inevitable consequence was a massive decline of ethics inherent in their behaviour which was in many cases, the Commission noted, 'beyond the mental grasp of many of the public functionaries'.[48] In the Commission's perception, the impact of the Emergency was devastating because, besides the unconditional surrender of public servants to the political leadership of the Congress, the government machinery was allowed to be appropriated by Indira Gandhi's son Sanjay Gandhi, who held no constitutional position. While commenting on the massive demolition that the Delhi administration had carried out to fulfil its 'beautification of Delhi plan', the Commission attributed the decision 'to pander[ing] to the whims of Sanjay Gandhi who was not answerable to anybody and who held no position whatever in the administrative scheme'.[49] This was illustrative of how institutions of governance got derailed once authority was encouraged to be personalized. Various examples can be cited to show how the Emergency created an environment in which the values of democratic governance were severely jolted and the voice for their retention was too feeble to receive serious attention. Given its varied implications and manifestations, the Emergency can be said to be multidimensional in character, which confirms the argument that the two years of derailment of the value-based administration was both an offshoot and a product of the decline of ethics in governance, which had clear social roots. Despite obvious disheartening implications for citizens' individual and collective lives, the Emergency is thus a creative experience in the sense that it enables us to understand the decline of ethics as integral to the cultural deficit confronting India in the context of the state-centric governance of the previous era.

The report of the Shah Commission stands out not only because it is an analytical statement of what had happened during the Emergency, but also because it looked into the possible factors which justified the arbitrariness and recklessness in governance. In the words of the Commission,

> arbitrariness and reckless disregard of the rights of others and the consequent misery which characterized a number of actions of the different public servants over a period of nearly 19 months, terrorized the citizens resulting in a complete loss of the faith of the people in the fairness and objectivity of the Administration generally.[50]

The Administration, by becoming a stooge of the politicians and those officers who aligned with them, lost its character of being an instrument for public well-being. Whether it was inevitable or made to happen is a debatable issue, as the Commission underlined the difficulty of what the officers had undergone once they were instructed to do certain things by saying that

> some of the officers did apparently a series of wrong things, being powerless to resist the pressures in the prevailing conditions and being afraid of the consequences, if they were not to do what the politicians or higher authorities expected or ordered them to do.[51]

Given the fact that the public servants were complicit in the desire of the personalizing authority, there had emerged a situation in which the basic administrative values of integrity and care for public well-being seemed to have lost their viability. Politicians and their collaborators hijacked the administration to pursue and consolidate tendencies towards undermining what constituted the fundamental ethos of democratic governance. This was an unwarranted intervention, which should not have been allowed to prosper to guarantee the legitimate functioning of public administration in its true spirit. How to create such an atmosphere, in which the public authority remains tuned to the public interests, is another important issue that the Commission looked into. It is true that 'there was an all-pervading fear of consequences among the officials which ... inhibited many of [them] from acting in the only way which would have been conducive to the health of the administration primarily and of the nation generally'.[52] On the basis of an analysis of considerable evidence, the Commission had suggested that the most effective antidote to a degenerating civil service was to create an environment in which tendencies to overshadow integrity and ethics in governance were not allowed to take root. Political leadership had a significant contribution to make, given their critical role as opinion makers at the grassroots. So had the officials, who were trained to translate the political values that politicians upheld in their interactions with the people at large. So, a good administration was elusive unless these components of governance were dialectically interconnected. The Commission thus strongly felt that

> it is [therefore] imperative to ensure that the officials at the decision-making levels are protected and immunized from threats and pressures so that they can function in the manner in which they govern with one single consideration – the promotion of public well-being and the upholding of the fundamentals of the Constitution and the rule of law.[53]

What is emphasized here is the importance of institutional watchfulness in sustaining the core of governance. This is a fair argument that needs to be understood in the wider socio-political context, because values are created and sustained provided there exists a supportive environment. So the fact that tendencies towards personalizing authority at the cost of the governed have social roots is critically important in conceptualizing administrative decadence. India is no exception. The Emergency was the epitome of the administrative distortions that India had encountered during those tumultuous 19 months. By probing thoroughly into what led to these distortions, not only has the Shah Commission provided sufficient inputs to comprehend the phenomenon, it has also given insights on how to tackle it before it becomes unmanageable.

The Emergency was a wake-up call for the citizens because it alerted them to the adverse consequences of the personalization of administration at the cost of the core principles of democratic governance being nurtured in an independent India. Democracy is 'an ethic' and not 'just a machine', and the core of democratic politics is to create the conditions for individuals in a society to develop to their fullest potentials.[54] Although the core loses salience on occasions, history has shown that it is revived by the people, once they understand the importance of democratic principles as perhaps the best shield for protecting individual rights against the ruling authority's hegemonic design. The emergency was an occasion in which individual rights were taken away, which perhaps contributed significantly to the attempts to get them back through sustained politico-ideological movements. Thus a commentator metaphorically suggested that although 'the fragile balance between reason and power was jolted during the Emergency, [the fact is that] ultimately reason returned'[55] due to the campaign drawing on the public's concern for democracy and prejudice-free governance. The Emergency is also about a human existence appreciative of contrasting tendencies. It had shown 'how easily [Indians] could accept the loss of their freedoms and how obediently [they] agreed to being herded into submission'.[56] The very fact that the desire for freedom ultimately prevailed also demonstrates that 'the comfort with submission and the desire to live with freedom seem to exist side by side;… democracy [thus] lives in the space between capitulation and resistance, and the Emergency offered [Indians] an opportunity to experience both'.[57] The Emergency was a peculiar experience that Indians had undergone following the 25 June proclamation. It prepared India for democracy, which, unless properly nurtured, loses its vitality, as the Emergency had shown. The real legacy of the Emergency has thus been wholly unintended because, as argued by an analyst,

> it has made India conscious, as never before, of civil liberties, of the right to freedom of expression; the Emergency, by robbing India for a while of the soul of republicanism, has made it a truer Republic than it was before 1975 when the Emergency was put into effect.[58]

It was thus a defining moment not only for citizens who, by confronting a systemic attack on their rights, learnt that rights needed to be protected but also for the nation which was likely to be subservient to the political authority if it lost its vitality.

What accounts for the complete collapse of democratic governance in India during the Emergency was not a systemic failure, but the capacity of the ruling authority to utilize the prevalent constitutional arrangement to its advantage. This is an important lesson of the Emergency, for what had happened in the wake of the June proclamation was endorsed by the 1950 Constitution of India. Emergency was not, at all, an extra-constitutional design, but one that was justified by the provisions of the Constitution. It has thus been aptly characterized as a regime of constitutional authoritarianism. Being armed with a constitutional guarantee, those who had ideologically sponsored the Emergency utilized the legally backed available rules to fulfil their partisan goals. It is argued that the horrors of mass detention during the Emergency were indeed 'built into the preventive detention legislation initiated by [India's first Prime Minister], Jawaharlal Nehru'.[59] Underplaying this aspect of governance, the Shah Commission attributed the Emergency to the abuse of the system by an individual and the coterie around her. This is surely making 'a monster of Indira Gandhi',[60] an easy escape from objectively assessing the Emergency as a systemic failure to build the institutional pillars capable of defending democratic governance in adverse circumstances. So it is possible to argue that what happened was not the subversion of a system of administration, 'but its apotheosis'[61] and that what the Commission characterized as misuse and abuse which sprang directly 'from the very provisions and rules and traditions built into that system'.[62] This is a conundrum that cannot be resolved easily, because it is surprising that democratic governance was made to disappear during the Emergency by the same Constitution that protected and nurtured its well-being. What it suggests is perhaps the fact that the constitutional guarantee, by itself, can never be an adequate safeguard unless the institutions are strong enough to stand by the constitution, which is not merely a codified version of the rule of law, but also upholds its spirit. The Emergency was undoubtedly a constitutional design, but it was clearly an aberration in the processes of governance, challenging the very foundational values informing the Constitution of India. An analytical scan of the period thus reveals how constitutional values lost their viability for constitutional reasons, and how the consolidation of an authoritarian regime was justified as the best shield against the opposition-engineered efforts to undermine those very constitutional values.

Concluding observations

In independent India, the 1964 Santhanam Committee Report and 1977 Shah Commission findings reveal that the root of administrative decay was unrestricted discretion, exercised by individuals usually in connivance with the political authority. For the Santhanam Committee, the vicious atmosphere that had emerged in the wake of the Licence–Quota–Permit Raj was perpetuated because of the benefits that both politicians and civil servants accrued from the system. There were hardly any organized movements against the abuse of authority, since the issue of administrative corruption did not seem to have caused alarm to the public. So, the situation was propitious for corruption to grow, but was not conducive to provoke anti-corruption campaigns. Driven by internal concern for a corruption-free governance in India as a necessity for the young nation to develop as per the exalted nationalist aspirations, the Santhanam Committee was thus a milestone in India's efforts towards creating adequately strong internal mechanisms to effectively combat corruption or malpractices in governance. By referring to the importance of a social climate supportive of corruption-free governance, the Committee was also aware that the institutional mechanisms, however effective they were, remained simply ornamental unless there was adequate social backing.

Unlike the Santhanam Committee, the 1977 Shah Commission had a very limited mandate to look into the excesses that made public authority a personal fiefdom of the Congress leaders who conveniently bypassed the well-established rule, regulations and conventions to fulfil their personal mission. By proclaiming an Emergency as per the Constitution of India, the elected political authority had constitutional backing to sustain an authoritarian rule. Within a span of two years, the administration was substantially re-oriented to strike down the edifice of democratic governance that India had developed over the years. The report was a timely warning that gave us enough inputs to understand that lack of public watchfulness was responsible for the creation and perhaps the consolidation of a Frankenstein's monster regime, because individuals holding public authority tended to become authoritarian if they were not sufficiently democratic in spirit and commitment.

An analytical scan of these two reports confirms that social context cannot be neglected while seeking to comprehend administrative decay and derailment in India. The internal Emergency of two years (1975–7) was a specific instance in which public governance was made a captive of the ruling party, especially its top leaders, though that was possible because the idea of discretionary power that those in authority held, especially in the context of the Licence-Quota-Permit Raj, continued to remain effective. The concern that the Santhanam Committee had expressed in the early 1960s was reiterated in the mid 1970s by the Shah Commission, which confirms that they had the same conceptual inclination while identifying the discretionary exercise of authority as a significant determinant of administrative decadence in India.

PART B

The Second Administrative Reforms Commission (or the Moily Commission) and Ethics Committees: delineating a design for ethics in governance

This part consists of two complementary sections which will be discussed in the following pages: on the one hand, it offers a critical analysis of the design that the Second Administrative Reforms Commission (also known as the Moily Commission) provides to ascertain the importance of ethics in governance; on the other hand, it also considers how the *Rajya Sabha* and *Lok Sabha* Ethics Committees handled the decline of ethics in public life. In an India that is tilted in favour of neo-liberal ideology, these endeavours represent serious efforts on the part of those involved in governance to create and consolidate institutions capable of arresting the decline of ethics. It is true that institutional designs, however strong they are on paper, will be futile unless they have organic roots in society. Nonetheless, these are useful inputs to comprehend how issues of ethics and corruption are being dealt with by those holding substantial authority in governance.

Based on the need to reform the administration, the second Administrative Reform Commission was set up by the Government of India in 2005, under the chairmanship of Veerappa Moily, to look into the issues crippling public administration in India. The Commission attributes the visible decline of ethics to a whole range of factors, including the socio-psychological decline of the individuals responsible for the redrawing of India's path for development. In the light of a general decline in public administration, the Commission thus observed that 'in our case, at times public office is perceived to be an extension of one's property. That is why sometimes, public offices are a source of huge corruption and a means of extending patronage'.[63] The Commission was thus asked to suggest measures to achieve a 'proactive, responsive, accountable, sustainable and efficient administration for the country at all levels of the government'. The Commission presented 15 reports to the government for consideration. Among them, the report on *Ethics in Governance* should be of particular interest to all those who clamour for an ethical framework for politics in the country. The Commission, while taking cognizance of the salutary measures introduced in recent years at the prompting of the Supreme Court and a pro-active Election Commission, has made a host of recommendations to usher in stability and accountability in the field of politics.

For the Commission, 'ethics is a set of standards that society places on itself and which helps guide behaviour, choices and actions'.[64] In order to arrest the decline of ethics in governance, the Commission adopts two principles. On the one hand, it has been emphasized that values and good moral character are important keys to meaningfully combat tendencies to support malpractices in administration. On the other hand, there should also be exemplary punishment for those involved in corruption; only then can the menace of corruption, the Commission feels, be effectively tackled. With these preliminary remarks, the Commission lays out the historical context of what led to the massive decline of ethics in public life. According to the Commission, there are three factors which seem to have aggravated the situation: first, the obvious pernicious legacy of colonialism supportive of 'unchallenged authority and the propensity to exercise power arbitrarily'[65] created a context in which those holding public authority became shackle-less and deviated from ethical conduct. Second, the enormous asymmetry of power also accounted for the excessive importance of public servants especially in India's state-led and bureaucracy-centric governance. As poverty was so rampant, government support was always most sought after; by being an authority disbursing favours in the form of assistance, public servants created an aura at least to those seeking for government help that allowed them to bypass the basic code of conduct. Third, by creating a state-centric governance, Indian policy makers upheld the view that the state cannot do anything wrong, which was responsible for making Indian bureaucracy all the more powerful as perhaps the only effective instrument to articulate the best of the state's intentions. These three factors, stated the Commission, created an environment in which the idea of ethics never took root. As the environment was propitious, corruption grew disproportionately in India. Critical of discretion and monopoly in exercising public authority, the Moily Commission also made a scathing attack on over-centralization because 'the more remotely power is exercised from the people, the greater is the distance between authority and accountability'.[66] In the erstwhile system of state-centric governance, local governments were never allowed to take root and power was concentrated both horizontally and vertically in a few hands. The net result of this was, the Commission laments, 'weakened citizenry and mounting corruption'.[67] As the description suggests, the decline of ethics in governance in the previous era was attributed to the exclusive control that Indian bureaucracy had exercised at the cost of stake-holders in a polity which considered the state-led development paradigm as perhaps the only meaningful design for inclusive development. So, corruption in public life was a history-driven phenomenon, which raised its ugly head since the environment was conducive to that.

How to arrest derailment in governance?

Values are the soul of public governance. The study and practice of governance can never be just technical or managerial. Governance has to be ethics-conscious since it entails effort towards ensuring public well-being. According to the Commission, so long as public servants are not accountable, the steps towards creating an ethics-driven administration will never be effective. What is thus required most is the empowerment of citizens in order to hold those in authority accountable and make them sensitive to their duties and responsibilities. Empowerment of citizens is easier said than done. Hence the Commission referred to certain powerful instruments which are useful in making citizens integral to governance: the right to information, effective citizens' charters, opportunity and incentives to promote the proactive approach of citizens, stakeholders' involvement in the delivery of public services, public consultation in decision making and social auditing are some of these devices of accountability that not only catapult the citizen to the centre stage of governance, but also promote integrity and prejudice-free decision making. What is striking here is the fact that, unlike the Weberian notion of accountability, which seeks to bring about a compatibility of interests between top-down policy and bottom-line implementation, the Commission insists on instruments that are driven by external agencies. Hierarchical governance is detrimental to public participation in decision making since hierarchy 'creates more ethical problems than it solves, by fostering inequality, an inappropriate level of instrumentalism on the basis of technical rationality, and agency inattention to the needs of the community'.[68] Hence the argument for participatory governance gains far more credibility by insisting on creating a situation 'for encouraging participation of the citizenry in the process of planning and providing public goods and services'.[69] Known as designs for external accountability, these instruments involve citizens as governance is articulated and executed. With their integral role in rule setting and execution, citizens have become, in the new dispensation, critical towards public authority. It has thus been argued that 'by involving citizens in monitoring government performance, demanding and enhancing transparency and exposing government failures and misdeeds,... [these] accountability mechanisms are potentially powerful tools against ... corruption tendencies derailing governance'.[70] This is the core of social accountability that relies on 'civic engagement, i.e. in which it is ordinary citizens and/or civil society organizations who participate directly or indirectly in exacting accountability'.[71] Complementary to the internal mechanisms of accountability, social accountability mechanisms allow ordinary citizens to access information, voice their needs and demand accountability between elections ... [and also] enhance the ability of citizens to move beyond mere protest toward engaging with bureaucrats and politicians in a more informed, organized, constructive and systematic manner, thus increasing the chances of effecting positive change.[72]

These ideas were reflected in what the Commission felt while devising mechanisms for arresting the debasement of governance in India. As the administrative and ideological steps that the Commission had proposed to revamp Indian administration show, serious attempts were made to re-conceptualize governance in the globalizing world in which governance is no longer a captive of bureaucracy but is also drawn from what citizens feel is most appropriate for their well-being.

The report begins with the ethical values in politics. It says that politics, and those engaged in it, play a vital role in the legislative and executive wings of the State whose acts of commission and omission in working on the basis of the Constitution and the rule of law become the point of intervention for the judiciary. Being aware that 'it is unrealistic and simplistic to expect perfection in politics in an ethically imperfect environment; there is [however] no denying the fact that the standards set in politics profoundly influence those in other aspects of governance'.[73] Impressed by the so-called Nolan principles,[74] which the 1994 Nolan Committee on Standards in Public Life in the United Kingdom identified as necessary for governance, the Commission refers to these principles as perhaps foundational ideas in any thinking on ethics in governance. The principles are as follows:

- *Selflessness*: holders of public office take decisions solely in terms of public interest. They should not do so in order to gain financial or other material benefits for themselves, their family or their friends.
- *Integrity*: holders of public office should not place themselves under any financial or other obligation to outside individuals or organizations that might influence them in the performance of their official duties.
- *Objectivity*: in carrying out public business, including making public appointments, awarding contracts or recommending individuals for rewards or benefits, holders of public office should make choices on merit.
- *Accountability*: holders of public office are accountable for their decisions and actions to the public and must submit themselves to whatever scrutiny is appropriate to their office.
- *Openness*: holders of public office should be as open as possible about all the decisions and actions they take. They should give reasons for their decisions and restrict information only when the wider public interest clearly demands.
- *Honesty*: holder of public office have a duty to declare any private interests relating to their public duties and to take steps to resolve any conflicts arising in a way that protects the public interest.

- *Leadership*: holders of public office should promote and support these principles by leadership and example.

Following the Nolan principles, the Commission thus stipulates the following steps[75] to ensure ethical behaviour in public life:

1   Codifying ethical norms and practices;
2   Disclosing personal interest to avoid conflict between public interests and personal gain;
3   Creating a mechanism for enforcing the relevant rules; and
4   Providing norms for qualifying and disqualifying a public functionary from office.

On the basis of the above directions, the Commission felt that there should be a Code of Ethics for the public office holder or ministers who are meant to serve the public, since they owe their position to them, in addition to the Code of Conduct, which also ascertains their accountability. The Code of Ethics should be based on the Nolan principles suggesting, 'the overarching duty of Ministers to comply with the law, to uphold the administration of justice and to protect the integrity of public life'.[76] Appreciative of the ideas implicit in the Nolan principles, the Commission provides a long checklist of the activities while articulating the Code of Conduct[77] that the ministers are expected to uphold or avoid, which is as follows:

- Ministers must uphold the highest ethical standards;
- Ministers must uphold the principle of collective responsibility;
- Ministers should have a duty to account to Parliament, and be held to account, for the policies, decisions and actions of their department and agencies;
- Ministers must ensure that no conflict arises, or appears to arise, between their public duties and their private interests;
- Ministers in the Lok Sabha must keep separate their roles as Ministers and as constituency member;
- Ministers must not use government resources for party or political purposes; they must accept responsibility for decision taken by them and not merely blame it on wrong advice;
- Ministers must uphold the political impartiality of the civil service and not ask civil servants to act in any way, which would conflict with their duties and responsibilities;
- Ministers must comply with the requirements that the two Houses of Parliament lay down from time to time;
- Ministers must recognize that misuse of official position or information is violation of the trust reposed in them as public functionaries;
- Ministers must ensure that public money is used with utmost economy and care;

- Minsters must function in such a manner as to serve as instruments of good governance and to provide services for the betterment of the public at large and foster socio-economic development; and
- Ministers must act objectively, impartially, honestly, equitably, diligently and in a fair and just manner.

A checklist notwithstanding, the Code of Ethics also represents efforts to create an environment in which public functionaries are made to abide by certain basic rules while discharging their roles. These are not new ideas, but what is distinctive about them is the force with which they were articulated; they can be said to be state-sponsored ideas, which were upheld to redesign governance by establishing a specific Code of Ethics for those involved in governance. Nonetheless, not only are these steps well directed, they are also context driven since the decadence in governance in India was the result of the abdication of ethics by those holding public office. In that respect, the Commission has set in motion processes whereby the Code of Ethics became integral to the Code of Conduct, especially for the ministers who are primarily public servants in a democratic form of governance. It is true that 'the enunciation of ethical values and code of conduct puts moral pressure on public functionaries'.[78] They require effective monitoring and need to be backed by an enforcement agency within the legislature; otherwise, they lose their meaning, especially between elections when the voters have an opportunity to punish the deviant legislators.

The other serious recommendation relates to Article 311 of the Constitution of India that accords a special constitutional guarantee to those in the civil service; even if they are implicated by charges of corruption, they cannot be dismissed by an authority subordinate to that by which they were appointed. This is a continuation of the past position, as the guarantee was introduced by the *Government of India Act* of 1919. The immunity granted to civil servants in case they are charged with serious offences seems to have been utilized to placate them. The 1964 Santhanam Committee expressed concern over this undue protection for civil servants, which, the Committee felt, was a source of corruption.[79] Persuaded by the fact that corrupt officials need to be weeded out to generate public faith in public authority, the Commission was reluctant to extend the favour to the civil servants. In a democratic system where power emanates from the ballot box, an extraordinary protection for the civil service amounts to contributing to a prejudiced system of governance. The Commission thus believes that

> the rights of a civil servant under the Constitution should be subordinate to the overall requirement of public interests and contractual rights of the State. It cannot be an argument that a corrupt civil servant's rights are more important than the need to ensure an honest, efficient and corruption-free administration. Ultimately, the public servant, an agent of the State, cannot be superior to the State and it is his fundamental duty to serve the State with integrity, devotion, honesty, impartiality, objectivity, transparency and accountability.[80]

Article 311 thus leaves enough scope for it to be misused. The founding fathers did not confront the situation that has emerged now when the constitutional guarantee is being misconstrued as an instrument to consolidate one's fiefdom in governance. In the words of the Commission, there exists

> a fairly common perception that explicit articulation of protection in the Constitution itself gives an impression of inordinate protection [which led the Commission to suggest that] 'on balance, Article 311 need not continue to be a part of the Constitution.[81]

In order to withdraw this undue protection to the civil service, the Commission made the unequivocal recommendation of 'the repeal of Article 311' and enactment of appropriate legislation to provide protection to public servants against arbitrary action, which is guaranteed by Article 309. This is a very useful recommendation with a far-reaching impact on public governance. Bureaucracy has, by instinct, an urge for unwarranted power and it happens so often, especially when the politicians lack the required technical ability to translate into action their ideological commitments to the stakeholders. By way of helping them, the bureaucrats become policy makers and tend to bend or distort rules to please their political bosses; this becomes a habit that is inculcated due to circumstantial needs. In view of their constitutional protection (à la Article 311) and India's cumbersome judicial processes, civil servants in India seem to have been encouraged to resort to malpractices to manipulate the well-established rules and regulations. The honest members of the civil services remain marginalized, while their colleagues, because of their complicity with the political masters, hog the limelight. In such a gloomy scenario, the de-constitutionalizing of Article 311 will have serious implications in the drive towards creating and consolidating an ethics-driven public governance.

Election-related expenses: a source of corruption

According to the Commission,

> excesses in elections (in campaign-funding, use of illegitimate money, quantum of expenditure, imperfect electoral rolls, impersonation, booth-capturing, violence, inducements and intimidation), floor-crossing after elections to get into power and abuse of power in public office became major afflictions of the political process over the years.[82]

What seems to have aggravated the situation is large, illegal and illegitimate expenditure in elections which is, the Commission underlines, 'another root cause of corruption'.[83] Hence the Commission recommends that 'cleansing elections is the most important route to improve ethical standards in politics, to curb corruption and rectify maladministration'.[84] What is so striking is that what caused alarm to the 1964 Santhanam Committee continued to remain a source of irritation for the Second Administrative Reforms Commission: indiscriminate and illegal funding of the elections by business and corporations creates an environment in which there emerges a quid pro quo arrangement between the winning candidates and the funding agencies that never allows the system to function appropriately. Hence the Commission has made the following suggestions[85] to introduce reforms in the political system:

- A system for partial state funding should be introduced in order to reduce the scope for illegitimate and unnecessary funding of expenditure for elections.
- The issue of disqualification of members on grounds of defection should be decided by the President/Governor on the advice of the Election Commission.
- Section 8 of the *Representation of the People Act, 1951* needs to be amended to disqualify all persons facing charges related to grave and heinous offences and corruption, with the modification suggested by the Election Commission.
- The Constitution should be amended to ensure that, if one or more parties in a coalition with a common programme mandated by the electorate either explicitly before the elections or implicitly while forming the government, realign midstream with one or more parties outside the coalition, then Members of that party or parties shall have to seek a fresh mandate from the electorate.

Decadent moral fabric

Similar to the 1964 Santhanam Committee report that attributed the decline of ethics in governance to 'the lack of moral alertness ... [hampering] the growth of strong traditions of integrity and efficiency',[86] the Second Administrative Reforms Commission insisted on 'the inculcation of values facilitating the subordination of the self to a larger societal good'.[87] This cannot be achieved overnight. But a conducive environment can be created by adopting complementary rules and regulations in which these values are well appreciated. The Commission is thus of the view that there should be a set of public service values that should be stipulated by law. As in the case of Australia, there should be a mechanism to ensure that civil servants constantly aspire towards these values. The commission appreciated the values prescribed in the draft Public Services Bill 2006, which was later made into an Act. The salient 'values'[88] informing the Act are:

- allegiance to the various ideals enshrined in the preamble to the Constitution
- apolitical functioning;
- good governance for betterment of the people to be the primary goal of civil service;
- duty to act objectively and impartially;
- accountability and transparency in decision making;

- maintenance of highest ethical standards;
- merit to be the criteria in selection of civil servants, consistent, however, with the cultural, ethnic and other diversities of the nation;
- ensuring economy and avoidance of wastage in expenditure;
- provision of healthy and congenial work environment;
- communication, consultation and cooperation in performance of functions i.e. participation of all levels of personnel in management.

Envisaging a public code of conduct and a public service management code insisting on specific duties and responsibilities, the Act is a watershed in so far as public service is concerned. Keeping in view the importance of the public in public services, the Act thus lays out its basic goal by suggesting that (a) good governance is an inalienable right of the citizens in a democracy, (b) good governance should be participatory, accountable, governed by the rule of law and informed by equity and inclusiveness in governance, and effectiveness and efficiency in service, and (c) a politically neutral, professional, accountable and efficient public service is an essential instrument for promotion of good governance.[89] In order to fulfil its aim, the Commission thus recommends a Public Service Authority to ensure that the code of conduct is sincerely followed. If stringent punitive measures are applied to punish those deviating from the code of conduct, corruption in public services, the Commission emphatically believes, will be significantly reduced.

As the above description adumbrates, the arrangement that the Commission proposed is perhaps the best one in putting the civil services in India back on the rails. This also confirms that institutional back up appears to be an adequate shield against the debasement of public services. Implicit here also is the argument that institutional support can never be effective unless there is adequate social back up, which means that social values supportive of corruption-free civil services need to be streamlined and also strengthened wherever necessary. It has thus been argued that

> a strong and vigilant civil society can be a check on corruption and form the basis for countervailing action.... Even the most comprehensive set of formal democratic institutions may not be in a position to produce the needed accountability in the absence of a strong and vigilant civil society to energize them.[90]

Civil society in India does not seem to be well enough organized to create a powerful voice. Nonetheless, there have been recent instances, as will be shown in Chapter 6, of civil society activism being very effective in forcing the state to agree to consider and also deliberate on demands that had roots in civil society. These are however stray instances, because civil society-driven participatory governance is still in its infancy in India. Hence social disapproval is hardly a deterrent here, unlike in Japan where the social shaming of civil servants of questionable integrity is an effective form of controlling the deviant public officials. Besides social shaming, political embarrassment acts as an effective deterrent to the errant public authority. The Indian situation is, however, different, and the deviation from the established code of conduct causes embarrassment and may also evoke punishment, if caught, though it cannot be a permanently effective deterrent to those who tend to resort to corruption for personal gain.

Effective civic engagement in governance is definitely a useful step towards creating an ethics-driven administration, which is designed to decisively challenge sources of corruption. According to the Commission, the role of whistleblowers is critical in exposing corrupt public servants. This is possible if there exists an alert citizenry, which is also sensitive to its moral commitments and responsibility. There is every possibility that the whistleblowers restrain themselves, fearing adverse consequences. This can be addressed meaningfully provided there is a complementary social environment in which these efforts are always appreciated and widely respected. As this is clearly a social cause, the citizens should feel empowered when they are involved in such acts. This is one way of encouraging those who appear to be less fearful about the consequences. There is another way, as the Commission strongly argues, suggesting that the whistleblowers need to have adequate legal protection in case they suffer due to their role in unearthing the roots of corruption. In its recommendations, the Commission, by reiterating the views of the Law Commission of India, forcefully argues for the following steps[91] to protect the whistleblowers:

- Whistleblowers exposing false claims, fraud or corruption should be protected by ensuring confidentiality and anonymity, protection from victimization in career, and other administrative measures to prevent bodily harm and harassment.
- The legislation should cover corporate whistleblowers unearthing fraud or serious damage to public interest by willful acts of omission or commission.
- Acts of harassment or victimization of, or retaliation against, a whistleblower should be criminal offences with substantial penalty and sentence.

These are very useful suggestions that the Commission makes, while seeking to provide legal protection. Such legal protection may not, however, be meaningful if there is not adequate social back up. Being aware of this dialectical interconnection between what society transmits and the role of the whistleblowers, the Commission thus points out that what is critical in arresting the governance debasement is

> the citizens' voice which can be effectively used to expose, denounce and restrain corruption. This calls for the engagement of civil society … in educating citizens about the evils of corruption, raising their awareness levels and securing their participation by giving them a voice. This also introduces a new dimension of accountability [which is contrary to] the traditional horizontal mechanisms of legislative and legal accountability of the executive and internal vertical accountability.[92]

There are two fundamental points that the Commission has raised here. Besides underlining the importance of external accountability, the Commission insists, on the one hand, on constant civic engagement as definitely a deterrent to practices thriving on corruption. On the other hand, as a result of civic engagement, the Commission also feels that a powerful citizens' voice emerges, which also acts as an effective hurdle for those preferring corrupt means for self-aggrandizement. These are generally spontaneous endeavours that have 'emerged out of an urge to serve the needs of the common man ... [although] the state can create an environment whereby citizens' groups can effectively participate in its efforts to root out corruption'.[93] The idea is manifested in the citizens' charter, which, being based on citizens' inputs, is an administrative design to make administration accountable and citizen friendly. Insisting that citizens should be made integral to governance to combat tendencies towards appropriating administration for private interests, the Commission thus recommends[94] that

- The Citizens' charter should be made effective by stipulating the service levels and also the remedy if these services are not met.
- Citizens may be involved in the assessment and maintenance of ethics in important government institutions and offices.
- Reward schemes should be introduced to incentivize citizens' initiatives.
- School awareness programmes should be introduced, highlighting the importance of ethics and how corruption can be combated.

These are likely to be instrumentally appropriate. The Commission is also aware that adequate social backing for these means is an insurance for their effective articulation. Governance is a collaborative act, which succeeds not because of the institutions, but because of the support that it receives from the citizenry. The more ethically sensitive the government is, the more support it generates among those endorsing its spirit. One of the powerful instruments to ascertain ethics in governance is a social audit, as per the Commission. Appreciative of the means, the Commission thus expresses that

> social audit through client or beneficiary groups or civil society is a check on the wrong doing in procurement of products and services for government, in the distribution of welfare payments, in the checking of attendance of teachers, students in schools and hostels, staff in hospitals and a host of other similar citizen service-oriented activities of government.[95]

As elaborated, social audit is an interface between the state and citizens, in which the latter play a critical role in fulfilling what the former is expected to do to articulate its role as a service provider. The idea that citizens are integral to governance is further reconfirmed. This is most fundamental in conceptualizing governance as a philosophy of collective action, and the Commission, by reiterating the idea, has reconfirmed once again how important it is in fulfilling the primary ideological goal that a government represents.

The discussion on ethics in governance, though selective, would remain incomplete without a brief note on the Commission's recommendation on the importance of Lokpal as an Ombudsman to effectively address the issue of corruption in India. In consonance with the suggestion of the 1964 Santhanam Committee, the Central Vigilance Commission came into being in 1964. Effective in raising a voice against corruption, the Vigilance Commission did not appear to be adequate to root out corruption in India's public life. The other agency that is critical in corruption-related cases is the Central Bureau of Investigation. Established in 1941 as the Special Police Establishment, responsible for domestic security, it was re-christened the Central Bureau of Investigation in 1963. Deriving its authority from the 1946 *Delhi Special Police Establishment Act*, the Bureau is responsible for investigating certain specified offences or classes of offences pertaining to corruption and other kinds of malpractices involving public servants. Although there are institutions for addressing cases of corruption in public life, 'the working of many of these anti-corruption bodies', the Commission laments, 'leaves much to be desired'.[96] In the light of the rather disappointing performances of the available instruments, the Commission feels the need to create a national Ombudsman, Lokpal in Indian parlance, which was also recommended by the First Administrative Reforms Commission in 1964. The Lokpal Bill was not made into law for various politico-ideological reasons, although it was believed that Lokpal could have become an effective instrument to weed out corruption from public life. As will be shown in Chapter 6, the demand for a Lokpal was widespread and provoked a Delhi-based campaign in 2011 that had national implications. Similar to the institution of Ombudsman in the Scandinavian countries, which acts as a bulwark of democratic government against the tyranny of officialdom, the Lokpal was also conceptualized as a watchdog responsible for ascertaining the values of integrity among the ministers and also the members of parliament. In order to discharge its role most effectively, it was also authorized to punish errant members for violating the code of ethics. Although a serious endeavour, the Bill has so far been shelved, since policy makers have failed to arrive at a consensus because of the obvious attack on their impunity. The expression, 'Lokpal' has been replaced by 'Rashtriya Lokayukta', which is the Commission's preferred vocabulary. By insisting on guaranteeing constitutional status and according appropriate constitutional safeguards, the Commission thus recommends[97] that

a   The Constitution should be amended to provide for a national Ombudsman, to be called the Rashtriya Lokayukta. The role and jurisdiction of the Rashtriya Lokayukta should be defined in the Constitution while the composition, mode of appointment and other details can be decided by Parliament through legislation.

b   The jurisdiction of Rashtriya Lokayukta should extend to all Ministers of the Union (except the Prime Minister), all state Chief Ministers, all persons holding public office equivalent in rank to a Union Minister, and Members of Parliament. In case the enquiry against a public functionary establishes

the involvement of any other public official along with the public functionary, the Rashtriya Lokayukta would have the power to enquire against such
public servant(s) also.

c   The Prime Minister should be kept out of the jurisdiction of the Rashtriya
Lokayukta.

d   The Rashtriya Lokayukta should consist of a serving or retired Judge of the
Supreme Court as the Chairperson, an eminent jurist as Member and the
Central Vigilance Commissioner as ex-officio Member.

e   The chairperson of the Rashtriya Lokayukta should be selected from a panel
of sitting Judges of the Supreme Court who have more than three years of
service, by a Committee consisting of the Vice President of India, the Prime
Minister, the Leader of the Opposition, the Speaker of the Lok Sabha and
the Chief Justice of India. In case it is not possible to appoint a sitting Judge,
the Committee may appoint a retired Supreme Court Judge.

f   The same Committee may select the Member (i.e. an eminent jurist) of the
Rashtriya Lokayukta. The chairperson and member of the Rashtriya Lokayukta should be appointed for only one term of three years and they should
not hold any public office under the government thereafter, the only exception being that they can become the Chief Justice of India, if their services
are so required.

g   The Rashtriya Lokayukta should also be entrusted with the task of undertaking a national campaign for raising the standards of ethics in public life.

As suggestions, these recommendations are fine and probably reflective of the
public concern for effective anti-corruption measures. In terms of substance,
these suggestions are not new, but are repeated in a different language. Corruption continues to remain a menace in public life, because of the clear absence of
a complementary social climate in which corruption will not flourish as a debilitating social phenomenon. This has two serious policy implications: on the one
hand, the creation of multiple institutions for the containment of corruption
seems to be vacuous unless they have organic roots in the polity, being engaged
in rooting out corruption. The *Lokpal* or *Rashtriya Lokayukta* seems to have
institutional polish, but is likely to receive the policy makers' nod simply
because of the threat that they would lose their political immunity once these
institutions are put in place. So the politico-ideological constraints are impediments to even constitutionally recognizing these agencies. This also directs our
attention to how their partisan aims prevail over the public's concern for
corruption-free governance in India. This is a reality, though there have been
constant endeavours to make these instruments part of the constitutional set-up
to root out corruption by giving exemplary punishment to those indulging in corruption and malpractices.

Evaluation

Like earlier efforts, the 2005 Second Administrative Reforms Commission is a serious attempt to weed out corruption from public life. As shown above, the Commission strongly feels that institutional devices are inadequate unless backed by social accountability, which means administrative accountability will merely be cosmetic in nature in the absence of social accountability. A socio-psychological phenomenon, social accountability cannot be created overnight; it requires sustained efforts directed towards creating an environment in which corruption is culturally hated. Institutions responsible for arresting the decline of ethics in governance become far stronger once they are supported by popular will which is manifested in a series of endeavours, articulated by both government and other public agencies. There is no doubt that social accountability is a powerful anti-corruption device; but it needs to be nurtured by creating a culture of political transparency and probity. This is to be supplemented by access to information, because secrecy kills the very drive towards evolving a transparent administration; by ensuring the availability and reliability of information, governance no longer remains a captive of the bureaucrats, but becomes an instrument for public well-being. As is evident, the acceptance of the 2005 RTI radically altered the texture of public governance in India, simply because it allowed the stakeholders to have access to information which Indian bureaucracy never allowed to become public.

Along with access to information, there are agencies that are critical in creating and strengthening social accountability. One of them is the media, which

> has a crucial role in the preservation, monitoring and control of corruption ... [by informing and educating] the public on corruption, [exposing] corruption in government, private sector, civil society organizations and [helping] monitor codes of conduct while policing itself against corruption.[98]

So, media is a powerful medium through which social accountability is articulated. By raising awareness around public issues, disseminating findings and creating a platform for public debate, a sensitive media gets connected with governance, which newly spreads its tentacles beyond the formal bureaucracy.

That social accountability is a force to reckon with is possible only when an equally strong and alert civil society backs it up. The success of civil society initiatives is contingent on their legitimacy and representability and also their level of responsiveness and accountability to their own members. In other words, not only do they promote an enabling environment in which citizens get drawn to governance, they also provide useful inputs to the policy makers, which they derive out of their engagement with grassroots activities. The role of the state is equally critical because 'the success of social accountability initiatives also depends upon the capacity and effectiveness of the state ... [which, by being appreciative to] a political or administrative culture that values notions of public ... probity, accountability and equity' lays out a complementary system in its support.[99] One has to remember, however, that on its own neither the state nor civil society is adequately equipped to articulate social accountability in its substantial sense. Hence what is required is 'state–civil society synergy' because 'unilateral state action normally ends up in manipulation, while unilateral social action often ends in repression and violence by the state, and that the most productive results arise when both sides actively participate'.[100] As argued, independent of the state, civil society is futile and vice versa. To make social accountability an effective instrument to ascertain ethics in governance, what is thus required is an interface involving both the state and societal actors. There is one final point here. Social accountability initiatives are required to be institutionalized; otherwise, they become part of the vocabulary with little or no substance. It has thus been argued that 'the impact is greatest and most sustainable when social accountability mechanisms are institutionalized – in other words, embedded with and systematically implemented by a civil society, state or hybrid institution'.[101] As shown, conceptually, social accountability is an effective means to consolidate an environment supportive of drives towards instilling the values of ethics in governance. By creating new effective vertical mechanisms of accountability and strengthening the prevalent devices for horizontal accountability, social accountability can be said to be useful for better governance in which the role of the stakeholders is as critical as those who are officially responsible for translating into legislative decision of the political bosses' ideological priorities. With a focus on accountability and the machinery for its inculcation in public life, the 2005 Second Administrative Reforms Commission thus stands out not merely for its penetrating recommendations, but also for creating a momentum for change by raising a debate in the public domain on the dialectical linkages between the decline of ethics in governance and the moral decadence of India's social fabric.

The role of the ethics committees

Apart from the above major institutional steps, Lok Sabha and Rajya Sabha, the two chambers of the Indian parliament also expressed concern over the decline of ethics in governance. Inspired by the functioning of the ethics committees in both houses of the US Congress, the upper chamber of the Indian parliament took the lead and formed an Ethics Committee in 1997 to address the concern. The *Lok Sabha* soon followed and, in 2000, the *Lok Sabha* Ethics Committee came into being. Based on their desire to revive public faith in the institutions of governance, these committees made useful recommendations, which are partly drawn from some of the available codes of conduct and partly derived from practices being followed elsewhere. Since the *Rajya Sabha* Ethics Committee was formed earlier than its *Lok Sabha* counterpart, we will deal with the former first, to be followed by a discussion of the latter.

The Rajya Sabha Ethics Committee

In response to the findings of the 1994 Vohra Committee highlighting the nexus between criminal gangs, police, bureaucracy and politicians, the 1995 All Party meeting felt the need for the setting up of a parliamentary committee on ethics, as distinct from the Committee of Privileges which would act as a guardian on the activities of members of parliament. It was also decided by the participants that Rajya Sabha needed to have 'an internal mechanism' which would act as 'a self-regulatory body' for the members of India's second chamber. The idea was justified by stating that 'a well-functioning Ethics Committee and well laid out procedures were the best guarantee for a correct perception in the public about an in-house mechanism for ensuring the ethical conduct of members'.[102] In his welcome address, S B Chavan, the Chairman of the *Rajya Sabha* Ethics Committee, justified the formation of the committee by saying that

> by and large, the ideological base and the spirit of service which activates most of the politicians is getting eroded and the kind of elements who are trying to influence the political parties and political system at large, make everybody think as to how we can possibly bring about probity in the entire system. The formation of the Ethics Committee as one of the instruments to ensure value-based politics has become imperative in the present situation.... The Committee will persuade the members not to do such things which, perhaps, were beyond the accepted norms of behaviour.[103]

In tune with the same spirit, the leader of the opposition, Rajya Sabha, Sikander Bakht, became far more categorical in his condemnation of the politicians who were held responsible for the decline of ethics in public life. He thus stated that

> our character is viewed with suspicion. Our tribe lost the faith of the people. Corruption has permeated not only the tribe of politicians but also society at large ... [and] I believe the constitution of the Ethics Committee is the need of the hour. The politicians are on the receiving end of people's criticism and complaints. There is a great need to improve this image of politicians. The Ethics Committee may perhaps be of some help'.[104]

The Ethics Committee, constituted in 1997, remains a milestone in India's parliamentary politics for two reasons: on the one hand, it articulated the concern of the parliamentarians who felt terribly alarmed at the rapid decline of ethics in governance; on the other hand, it also reinforced, the public outcry against the abuse of governmental machinery for personal gains. In its first report of 1999, the Committee attributed the decline of moral values among those in public life to the rather lackadaisical attitude of the political parties in selecting candidates to fight elections on their behalf. The Committee observed that it was mainly the responsibility of political parties to prevent persons with criminal antecedents from entering the political process. Hence the Committee urged that political parties needed to be selective when recruiting candidates for membership in the

Rajya Sabha or other political outfits, being engaged in public work. Like the 1964 Santhanam Committee, the All Party meeting also endorsed the need for electoral reforms, including 'the revision of the ceiling on election expenses, corporate or State funding of political parties, foreign donations to them, among others'.[105] The decline was evident; but the Committee did not seem alarmed because, by following the 1994 Nolan Committee on Standards in Public Life of the United Kingdom, it felt that once the loopholes in the procedures were sealed, most of the public grievances could satisfactorily be addressed.

Like the Vohra Committee, the *Rajya Sabha* Ethics Committee took serious note of (a) criminalization of politics and (b) the felt need for massive electoral reforms. While criminalization of politics cannot be weeded out so easily, given its deep roots in socio-political processes, it will be easier to undertake meaningful electoral reforms. The Committee thus felt that 'the laws and rules ... have not had the desired effect ... and the problem of criminalization of politics and its causes and effects cannot be tackled by legislation alone'.[106] Instead of taking a legalistic view, the Committee decided to interact with the political parties to evolve a code of conduct for the members. Insisting that the political parties should avoid nominating those with criminal records, the Committee echoed the suggestion made by the 1964 Santhanam Committee. The most serious problem that attracted serious attention of the Committee was the role of the power of money in elections. It was admitted that 'large sums of money and other monetary benefits encourage the electorate for [parliamentary elections] leading sometimes to the defeat of the official candidate belonging to their own political party'.[107] The solution was simple: there was a need 'to incorporate suitable provisions in the existing electoral laws with a view to breaking the nexus between the power of money and elections'.[108] This is easier said than done, since the vested interests are too powerful to give away the advantages of being financially supported during the election, though the campaign seeking to break the nexus between the power of money and elections appears to have gained a momentum which cannot be wished away so easily.

The concern about ethics for its members figured prominently in the recommendations of the *Rajya Sabha* Ethics Committee, which strongly felt that

> the Members of Rajya Sabha should acknowledge their responsibility to maintain the public trust reposed in them and should work diligently to discharge their mandate for the common good of the people. They must hold in high esteem the Constitution, the Law, Parliamentary Institutions and, above all, the general public. They should commonly strive to translate the ideals laid down in the Preamble to the Constitution into a reality.[109]

For the *Rajya Sabha* members, the Committee had set out a specific code of conduct, which drew on the desire to establish high moral standards. This is an elaborate checklist of dos and don'ts, applicable to the members who are elected to serve the public. Unless they share the motivation of public service, they are unable to appreciate the code of ethics that the Committee had proposed.

Comprising 15 items, the code of conduct is primarily a set of authoritative directions to the members, who need to follow them to morally justify their role as part of public policy making. There are three major instructive items, which are reproduced below[110] to highlight the thrust of the recommendations:

- In their dealings if Members find that there is conflict between their personal interests and the public trust, which they hold, they should resolve such a conflict in a manner that their private interests are subordinated to the duty of their public office.
- Members should always see that their private financial interests and those of the members of their immediate family do not come in conflict with the public interest and if any such conflict ever arises, they should try to resolve such a conflict in a manner that the public interest is not jeopardized.
- Members should never expect or accept any fee, remuneration or benefit for a vote given or not given by them on the floor of the House, for introducing a Bill, for moving a resolution, putting a question or abstaining from asking a question or participating in the deliberations of the House or a Parliamentary Committee.

As is evident, there have been continuous efforts to create an environment that is appreciative of the importance of ethics in public life. The growing criminalization of politics is certainly a source of serious concern. How to halt the processes of criminalization? It was suggested by the *Rajya Sabha* in a resolution that 'meaningful electoral reforms be carried out ... [so that] political life and processes be free of the adverse impact on governance of undesirable extraneous factors including criminalization'.[111] What is being emphasized here is institutional reforms that are capable of reforming the habits of members of India's second chamber. Undoubtedly, institutional reforms are an effective means, provided they are backed by equally effective mechanisms that are not guided by partisan political priorities. Unless this is appreciated by those involved in policy making, institutional reforms will hardly be meaningful.

The decline of ethics in governance cannot be completely done away with by mere institutional reforms; what it requires is also to undertake appropriate steps to create processes for change in the wider social environment. The inculcation of ethics by the Ethics Committee will be futile unless the values of ethics are sincerely upheld by the people at large. Hence it is suggested that the exercise will completely be wasted unless it is complemented by parallel endeavours in evolving practices appreciative of ethics in public life. While identifying the Ethics Committee as certainly a definite step towards strengthening the campaign for ethics in public life, it was thus argued that

> the Ethics Committee is not intended as an essay in idealism, but as an exercise in pragmatic politics. It does not seek to usher in a moralistic regime in Parliament, but common ethical standards and decency in the conduct of its members, including, of course, ministers.... It will help in dissipating the

widely held belief that 'politics are a dirty game' repeated often by politicians and the public with some sort of acceptance of the inevitability of unethical behaviour in the practice of the political game.[112]

As has been argued, the appointment of the Ethics Committee is a significant step towards seeking to ensure ethics in public life. This is not enough if public life is vitiated to a significant extent. Only through 'continuous and proactive efforts,... greater transparency, probity and accountability in public life [are] ensured'.[113] These are values which are critical in evolving conditions appreciative of ethics-driven governance. Key to such a system of governance is the citizen, who holds the substance of participatory democracy. Conceptualizing citizens as proactive members in administration, the arguments in support of ethics in public life endorse the view that 'citizens are equal partners in all spheres of national endeavours, and not simply the beneficiaries of governmental initiatives'.[114] What it reinforces is the fundamental argument that institutional initiatives do not seem to be effective unless they receive adequate backing from the wider social environment. This is, however, not to argue that the former is absolutely futile; on the contrary, they remain critical in raising issues of ethics in the public domain, which may further expedite effective campaigns in their favour. So it will not be an exaggeration to suggest that the dialectical interconnection between internal initiatives and the wider social milieu help build a momentum for ethics in public life.

The Lok Sabha Ethics Committee

While the Rajya Sabha Ethics Committee was formed in 1997, the Lok Sabha counterpart came into being in 2000. Unlike the Rajya Sabha Ethics Committee, it took a rather narrow view in suggesting the remedies for decadence in governance. In its first report of 2001, the Ethics Committee of Lok Sabha thus reiterated that

> norms of ethical behaviour for members of the legislature had been 'adequately provided for' in the rules and procedures, directions by the Speaker and in the conventions which have evolved over the years on the basis of the recommendations made by various Parliamentary Committees.[115]

For the Committee, the steps towards containing the decadence were very simple: the remedy with regard to unethical behaviour on the part of the legislators lay 'in the strict enforcement of the existing norms'.[116] Apart from the prevalent norms, the members should, according to the Committee, abide by the following general ethical principles:[117]

- members must utilize their position to advance well-being of the people;
- in case of conflict between their personal interest and public interest, they must resolve the conflict so that personal interests are subordinate to the duty of public office;

- conflict between private financial/family interest should be resolved in a manner that public interest is not jeopardized;
- members holding public offices should use public resources in such a manner as may led to public good;
- members must keep uppermost in their mind the fundamental duties listed in the Part IV [Directive Principles of State Policy] of the Constitution; and
- members should maintain high standards of morality, dignity, decency and values in public life.

The approach that the *Rajya Sabha* Ethics Committee adopted was all-inclusive because, simultaneously with creating and also consolidating institutional backups, it also suggested changes in the wider social environment, because of its complementary role in creating a propitious environment for reform. The *Lok Sabha* counterpart held a contrary view, by emphasizing that internal institutional mechanisms were adequate to guide the members in accordance with the best of ethical values. The rules are in place; since they are not properly implemented, the system suffers. This is a difficult proposition with a very limited appeal, though it is true that tendencies towards encouraging deviation in governance are likely to be reduced to a significant extent if the rules are stringently applied regardless of class, caste and ideological inclinations. These tendencies, instead of being discouraged, seem to have been continuously boosted due to very specific socio-economic and ideological circumstances being nurtured in India, which also had a long colonial past. Despite being politically free, India is one of those countries in the developing world that keeps on suffering due to the elite capture of political authority, which impedes, to a great extent, the processes towards democratizing governance resulting in the marginalization of a large segment of the populace. This is probably the key to understanding the decline of ethics in public life, because, if governance is democratized, it will create space for the peripheral sections that, despite being franchised, continue to remain mere pawns in the chess of politics. Since ethics is a socio-psychological phenomenon, endeavours towards its creation by institutional means can never be successful; what is thus needed is a substantial overhauling of the social environment, in which individuals are psychologically inclined to uphold those ethical values ensuring public well-being. Although there is a consensus that social environment is always critical, the role of induced institutional changes cannot be undermined. By meting out exemplary punishment to those abusing public authority, the available institutional mechanisms help build a momentum in the wider social milieu which, if guided properly, is likely to trigger a bigger campaign for reform in governance. Hence it is always argued that they are dialectically interconnected: institutional steps are useful inputs for social awareness, and impulses from society do not allow the institutions to remain indifferent when they are strong enough to create a momentum involving large segments of population. As history has shown, this is how the concern for ethics becomes an integral component of democratic governance in which citizens, by virtue of being its core, always remain an important source of inputs for public authority.

Concluding observations

Unlike the 1966 First Administrative Reforms Commission, the 2005 Second Administrative Commission focused on the deterioration of ethics in public governance. After having made a thorough analysis of the phenomenon, the Second Commission attributes the visible decline of ethics to a whole range of factors, including the socio-psychological decline of the individuals responsible for redrawing India's path for development. In the light of a general degradation of public administration, the Commission thus observed that 'in our case, at times public office is perceived to be an extension of one's property. That is why sometimes, public offices are a source of huge corruption and a means of extending patronage'.[118] The idea that public authority was one's personal fiefdom, which the Santhanam Committee criticized so strongly, continued to remain a constant source of irritation, even in the context of a globalizing India. This is understandable since governance is still bureaucracy controlled, though it is open to external influences that considerably weaken the bureaucratic hold over administration. The Moily report is thus a watershed, because it has articulated the newer socio-ideological concerns, meaningful in the changed milieu in conjunction with the forces supportive of a declining, but not entirely defunct, system of governance.

Similarly, the Ethics Committees of *Lok Sabha* and *Rajya Sabha* are also serious endeavours towards creating an environment by devising a long checklist of dos and don'ts for the parliamentarians. Whether mere codification of rules will yield the desired results is a debatable issue. Nonetheless, the acceptance of a code of ethics for the policy makers is, by itself, a significant development in the light of how the members of parliament recklessly exercise authority to fulfil their personal ambitions. Despite being on paper without perhaps much effectiveness, these codes can be said to have ushered in an era in which the parliamentarians are not without shackles, because the violation of the code will never go unnoticed in view of an alert civil society.

The above analysis also reveals that ethics or integrity is socio-psychological in character: social because, unless these values are socially backed, they hardly have any relevance whatsoever; and also psychological since they need to be articulated in the behaviour of those constituting a polity. It is true that the Moily Commission recommended strengthening the available institutional devices and also creating new ones if necessary; but, by insisting on developing a supportive social climate, the Commission underlines the importance of the wider social milieu in sustaining the drive for ethics in public governance. In a similar fashion, the Ethics Committees for *Lok Sabha* and *Rajya Sabha* lay down certain terms and conditions for the parliamentarians, who are not only policy makers, but are also major keys in the processes shaping India's ideological contour and depth. By seeking to train the parliamentarians in a specific way to inculcate basic values of ethics, these Committees act as their moral guardians. Whether they will achieve their desired goal is difficult to assess now, though the fact that they have become integrally connected with the parliamentary procedure in India also confirms that they cannot be so easily dismissed. Ideologically innovative, these Committees, despite not having substantial authority, are likely to be effective instruments in raising a voice in the public domain against the deviant parliamentarians, which, by itself, is a deterrent. So, in terms of what these Committees can do, there is huge potential, provided they are proactive in fulfilling their social role in a democratic political set-up. As their counterparts in the US have already shown in their history of just five decades, the parliamentary Ethics Committees in India are also potentially strong enough to fulfil their assigned task, provided it is adequately socially backed. There is thus a fundamental point that is being reiterated throughout the discussion: the dialectical interconnection between the institutional devices and the wider social environment is a key to ethically sound and contextually relevant governance, which also means that neither the institutional devices nor a sensitive social climate is independently capable of being a strong defence against tendencies towards derailing public authority. What is thus required is to create an environment in which the ideologically backed institutional devices derive sustenance from the social environment and vice versa; only then, perhaps the goal of building a robust culture of integrity can easily be fulfilled.

Notes

1 S Radhakrishnan, 'The dawn of freedom' in Rudrangshu Mukherjee (ed.), *Great Speeches of Modern India*, Random House, New Delhi, 2007, pp. 181–2.
2 Speech delivered by Rajiv Gandhi, former Prime Minister of India, on 28 December 1985 in Bombay – quoted in B P Mathur, *Ethics for Governance: reinventing public services*, Routledge, New Delhi, 2014, p. 198.
3 Tenth Five Year Plan, Vol. 1, p. 22 – quoted in B P Mathur, *Ethics for Governance*, p. 197.
4 Eleventh Five Year Plan, pp. 236–7, – quoted in B P Mathur, *Ethics for Governance*, p. 197.
5 *Report of the Committee on Prevention of Corruption*, Ministry of Home Affairs, Government of India, New Delhi, 1964, p. 2.
6 Ibid., p. 5.
7 Ibid., p. 7.
8 Ibid., p. 9.
9 Ibid., p. 117.
10 Ibid., p. 9.
11 Ibid.
12 The Licence–Quota–Permit Raj refers to a bureaucratic system drawn on the stringent government authority in granting licenses and permits for new commercial ventures. Coined by a leading nationalist C Rajagopalachari, the system remained operational till 1990 and the adoption of the New Economic Policy which, by deregulating the Indian economy, was a strong step towards making it defunct.
13 *Report of the Committee on Prevention of Corruption*, p. 12.
14 Ibid.
15 Ibid.
16 Ibid.
17 Ibid., pp. 77–8.
18 Ibid., p. 78.
19 Ibid., p. 101.

20 Ibid., p. 102.
21 Ibid., p. 104.
22 Ibid.
23 Ibid.
24 Ibid., p. 106.
25 Gunnar Myrdal, *Asian Drama: an enquiry into the poverty of nations*, Vol. II, Pantheon, New York, 1968, p. 941.
26 Era Sezhiyan (compiled and edited), *The Shah Commission Report: lost and regained*, Aazhi Publishers, Chennai, 2010, p. 46. All the quotes from the Shah Commission Report are taken from this volume, in which the original report was reproduced.
27 Ibid., chapter III of the Interim Report I, p. 9.
28 Ibid., chapter III of Interim Report I, p. 14.
29 For details on the nature of the Emergency, the following texts are very useful: Emma Tarlo, *Unsettling Memories: narratives of India's Emergency*, Permanent Black, New Delhi, 2003; W H Morris-Jones, 'Whose Emergency – India's or Indira's?', *The World Today*, XXXI, November 1975; Norman D Palmer, 'The crisis of democracy in India', *Orbis*, XIX, Summer 1975; Richard L Park, 'Political crisis in India, 1975', *Asian Survey*, XV, November 1975; S P Seth, 'Political crisis in India', *Pacific Community*, VII, January 1976.
30 Indira Gandhi's radio broadcast on 26 June 1975 – quoted in Norman D Palmer, 'India in 1975: democracy in eclipse', *Asian Survey*, 16 (2), 1976, p. 100.
31 Krishna Kumar, 'Conscience and the body politic', *The Hindu*, New Delhi, 10 July 2015.
32 Ibid.
33 Era Sezhiyan *The Shah Commission Report*, chapter V of Interim Report I, p. 23.
34 Ibid.
35 Ibid.
36 Ibid.
37 Ibid., p. 25.
38 Ibid., p. 28.
39 Ibid., p. 30.
40 Ibid., chapter VI of Interim Report I, p. 33.
41 Ibid.
42 Ibid.
43 Ibid., p. 39.
44 Ibid.
45 Ibid., p. 41.
46 Ibid., chapter XV of Interim Report II, p. 140.
47 Ibid.
48 Ibid.
49 Ibid., p. 144.
50 Ibid., chapter XXIV of Interim Report II, p. 228.
51 Ibid.
52 Ibid., p. 229.
53 Ibid.
54 John Dewey pursues this argument in detail in his *The Public and Its Problems*, Henry Holt and Company, New York, 1927.
55 Krishna Kumar, 'Conscience and the body politic.'
56 Santosh Desai, 'Trivial tales of Emergency', *The Times of India*, New Delhi, 29 June 2015.
57 Ibid.
58 Gopalkrishna Gandhi, 'Mastering the drill of democracy', *The Hindu*, New Delhi, 26 June 2015.

59 Shah Commission's Final Report III, *Economic and Political Weekly*, 6 October 1978, p. 1839.
60 Ibid.
61 Ibid.
62 Ibid.
63 *Ethics in Governance*, Fourth Report, Second Administrative Reforms Commission, Government of India, New Delhi, 2007, p. 6.
64 Ibid., p. 1.
65 Ibid., p. 2.
66 Ibid., p. 3.
67 Ibid.
68 Camilla Stivers, 'Citizenship ethics in public administration' in Terry L Cooper (ed.), *Handbook of Administrative Ethics*, Marcel Dekker Inc., New York, 1994, p. 444.
69 Terry L Cooper, *An Ethic of Citizenship for Public Administration*, Prentice Hall, New Jersey, 1991, p. 141.
70 Mohit Bhattacharya, *New Horizons of Public Administration*, Jawahar Publishers & Distributors, New Delhi, 2013, p. 273.
71 Carmen Malena, Reiner Forster and Janmejay Singh, 'Social Accountability: an introduction to the concept and emerging practice', *Social Development Papers: Participation and Civic Engagement*, The World Bank, 2004, p. 3.
72 Ibid., p. 5.
73 *Ethics in Governance*, p. 8.
74 Ibid., pp. 19–20.
75 Ibid., p. 19.
76 Ibid., p. 26.
77 Ibid., pp. 26–7.
78 Ibid., p. 35.
79 *Report of the Committee on Prevention of Corruption*, pp. 39–40.
80 *Ethics in Governance*, p. 97.
81 Ibid.
82 Ibid., p. 8.
83 Ibid., p. 9.
84 Ibid.
85 Ibid., pp. 13–15.
86 *Report of the Committee on Prevention of Corruption*, p. 139.
87 *Ethics in Governance*, p. 41.
88 Ibid., p. 43.
89 www.prsindia.org/uploads/media/vikas_doc/docs/1241499740~~DraftPublicServices Bill2006.pdf.
90 Speech by M Veerappa Moily, Chairman, Second Administrative Reforms Commission, on the occasion of the National Colloquium on Ethics in Governance – moving from rhetoric to results, 1 September 2006 – reproduced in *Ethics in Governance*, p. 223.
91 *Ethics in Governance*, pp. 78–79.
92 Ibid., p. 125.
93 Ibid., p. 127.
94 Ibid., pp. 129–30.
95 Ibid., p. 133.
96 Ibid., p. 108.
97 Ibid., pp. 115–16.
98 Ibid., p. 132.
99 Malena, Forster and Singh, p. 13.

100 John Ackerman, 'Social Accountability for the Public Sector: a conceptual discussion', Draft Paper for the World Bank, Washington DC, 2004 – quoted in Malena, Forster and Singh, p. 13.
101 Malena, Forster and Singh, p. 14.
102 www.rajyasabha.nic.in/rsnew/publication_election/ethics_committee.pdf, p. 6.
103 Ibid., p. 26.
104 Ibid., p. 28.
105 Ibid., p. 5.
106 Ibid., p. 9.
107 Ibid., p. 12.
108 Ibid.
109 *Ethics in Governance*, p. 30.
110 Ibid., pp. 30–31.
111 www.rajyasabha.nic.in/rsnew/publication_election/ethics_committee.pdf, p. 24.
112 Ibid., p. 35.
113 Resolution adopted by the Rajya Sabha on the occasion of the Golden Jubilee of Independence, 26 August–1 September 1997 reproduced in www.rajyasabha.nic.in/rsnew/publication_election/ethics_committee.pdf, p. 24.
114 Ibid., p. 25.
115 *Ethics in Governance*, p. 205.
116 Ibid.
117 Ibid., p. 31.
118 Ibid., p. 6.

6 Contemporary politico-ideological efforts towards arresting the ethics deficit in governance and corruption

The ethics deficit and corruption are dialectically interconnected. Hence it is argued that corruption is a contextual phenomenon, which means that contextual distortions due to the ethics deficit in governance provoke citizens to raise their voices. In laymen's perception, corruption is an abuse of public authority for personal gain that is largely attributed to the decline of ethics in public life. This is a commonly construed definition of corruption, which, despite being clearly spelt out, does not seem to be adequately equipped to conceptualize its complex character, given the fact that corruption is hydra-headed, and misuse of public office is only one of the forms in which it is articulated. Implicit here is the assumption that public and private interests are mutually exclusive and hence the pursuance of the latter in the name of the former will always be considered as deviant. This is well-captured by Joseph Nye, who defined corruption as 'behaviour which deviates from the formal duties of a public role because of private-regarding (personal, close family, private clique) pecuniary or state gains; or violates rules to justify certain types of private-regarding influence'.[1] Unlike the conventional conceptualization of the phenomenon, Nye sought to view corruption as a deviant function directed towards fulfilling partisan goals by resorting to means which are justified since they are connected with the public domain. In such circumstances, public servants misuse the trust reposed on them rather willingly, simply to meet private ends. In her understanding of the concept, Shumer highlighted this aspect by stating that 'one dimension of ... corruption is the privatization both of the average citizen and those in office. In the corrupt state', she argues further, 'men locate their values wholly within the private sphere and they use the public sphere to promote private interests'.[2] So corruption is a socio-psychological idea, since it derives its sustenance from a specific psychological tilt towards corrupt practices, which a complementary social climate endorses.

While seeking to locate the roots of the deviation by public servants, Shumer has drawn our attention to the wider social environment, in which deviant behaviour does not seem to be castigated as strongly as is expected. There is one related point here, which one comes across while reviewing the trajectory of corruption. Conceptually, corruption was associated in the past with the deterioration in the quality of government; gradually it became synonymous with bribery, which means that monetary transactions were a key which was recognized by Hirschman when he mentioned that 'eventually the monetary meaning drove the nonmonetary one out almost completely'.[3] One is now in a position to arrive at a definition which is reflective of the complexities of the concept both in its articulation and its substance. Corruption is a deviant exercise of power to protect private interests and in exchange for monetary benefits. This amounts to subversion of public interests by private interests, which always has wider ramifications in governance, especially when it is being manipulated to pursue partisan aims, disregarding completely the well-established rules and regulations governing public acts.

Hence it has been argued that 'private interests and public interests are both perfectly fine, as long as they stay in their proper places; but once we have the contamination of the public by the private',[4] it results in the derailment of public authority, which, if not contained immediately, will create conditions for corruption to strike at the roots of society. It is therefore important to remember that corruption hardly has a chance to flourish unless it has well-entrenched roots in the wider social milieu; once it is rooted, it creates a vicious circle, which is responsible for its survival and gradual strengthening. This is, however, not to argue that corruption is vicious everywhere; what is emphasized here is the point that, though corruption exists in all societies, 'it is also obviously more common in some societies than others and more common at some times in the evolution of a society than at other times'.[5] So, corruption is transcendental, but its intensity varies from country to country and from one historical phase to another. This also confirms the critical importance of the social climate in restraining or encouraging deviant public personnel; if the social climate is slackening, it is more likely that forces supportive of corruption will naturally be nourished. There is, however, another part of the narrative, which is, manifested in attempts to combat corruption though powerful political mobilizations for transformation. As examples from India show, there have been several campaigns to weed out corruption from public life and establish the rule of law and the basic ethical code of conduct for those holding political authority.

Corruption is driven by circumstances. According to the 1964 Santhanam Committee, corruption thrived in India, as shown in Chapter 5, because of the excessive discretionary powers that the public servants had enjoyed under the License–Quota–Permit Raj and also the absence of a permanent agency to discipline errant personnel by imposing punitive punishments. With the creation of the Central Vigilance Commission, the Committee felt that the incidence of corruption in public life was likely to be considerably reduced. It certainly had an impact, though not to the extent that was expected. Besides putting in place effective institutional mechanisms, the Committee also underlined the fact that the battle against corruption would succeed provided there existed a supportive social climate. This is most important for devising effective mechanisms for combating corruption.

As shown in Chapter 5, the 1977 Shah Commission is illustrative of how government machinery was captured by the existing political leadership to fulfil an ideological mission, in opposition to those who apparently posed a threat to the democratically elected government. The Constitution of India became sub-servient to the Congress leadership, and deviant behaviour in public life was considered as inevitable in the light of the possible devastation in the country following the massive opposition mobilization against those in power. Concep-tually, the 1975–7 Emergency is an era of political corruption in India in which public authorities were abused, beyond recognition, to accommodate the leadership-driven ideas of public well-being, which did not, however, go down well with stakeholders once implemented. The outcome was the mass campaign, led by the firebrand Gandhian leader Jayaprakash Narayan, which finally replaced the constitutional authoritarianism that the Congress supremo Indira Gandhi had imposed following the proclamation of an internal Emergency in India. By challenging the corrupt administration that thrived during the Emer-gency, the mass campaign also confirms the argument that, in a democratic polity, corruption cannot go unchecked because it creates its own enemy. The story has been repeated, it seems, in the era of economic liberalization in the wake of the outbreak of scams that seemingly have the public authority's support. Involvement of politicians was, on occasions, proved beyond doubt. Not only were they found to have abused authority, they were also reportedly bribed to extend favours to a select few at the cost of the government exchequer. Like the campaign that Jayaprakash Narayan had launched during the Emer-gency, Anna Hazare spearheaded a nonviolent movement at the behest of a polit-ical outfit, known as *India Against Corruption*, in 2011 to arrest the deterioration of governance. The campaign, however, fizzled out, as its primary goal of creat-ing a national Ombudsman, *Lokpal* in Indian parlance, remained unrealized. Nonetheless, the Anna Hazare initiative reinforces the argument that political corruption, including the embezzlement of funds, can never go unchallenged in a democratic polity that is being constantly reinvented to take care of newer public demands.

Corruption is universal, and so is the battle for its containment. This chapter therefore pursues the argument that corruption and the drive towards fighting corruption are dialectically interconnected. This is a two-dimensional claim: on the one hand, it is argued that corruption is inevitable, since human beings tend to be partisan unless there is societal pressure to be otherwise; on the other hand, elements of opposition exist which are triggered to take action for change in a conducive environment and under an able and effective leadership. As will be shown below, the campaigns that J P and Anna Hazare launched against the misuse of public authority for partisan gains are instances of powerful mass mobilizations against corruption and malpractices in governance. Along with their challenges against specific cases of abuse of authority, both J P and Anna Hazare felt that the creation of a favourable social climate was necessary to halt institutional decay, which further reinforces the idea that a meaningful contain-ment of corruption is contingent on a social environment in which ethics-driven acts are always appreciated as an antidote to corruption and misgovernance.

Jayaprakash Narayan and his battle for corruption-free governance[6]

As a Marxist, Jayaprakash Narayan (1902–79), popularly known as J P, engaged in sustained political activities to weed out corruption from public life. During the nationalist phase, he was also known as a crusader for justice for the down-trodden, a justice that was usually undermined because of the appropriation of the instruments of governance by vested interests. He was the conscience of the nationalist movement when it deviated from the well-established moral path and his Congress colleagues were reportedly appreciative of his role. Never having been a part of governance, J P always remained an outsider and yet played a very critical role when he was needed to lead movements against corrupt or deviant government. The opportunity came in 1974 when, as the Sarvadayo leader, J P gave a clarion call to fight the misrule and corruption that seemed to have crippled governance in Bihar. The movement was organized under the non-political platform, Bihar Chhatra Sangarsh Samiti, which spearheaded the campaign under J P's leadership. What had begun in 1974 spread quickly beyond Bihar and, as shown in Chapter 5, led to the imposition of the internal Emergency in 1975.

As argued above, J P's involvement in mobilization against misrule in 1975 was not an isolated case; in fact, one discerns a trend in his political life, illustrating that he was always vocal about the lack of ethics in governance, which was often reflected in the desire of the political leadership to deliberately bypass the basic code of conduct. His role in the campaign against the Emergency stood out. Given the fact that he was always associated with crusades for fair play and justice in governance, it will be enlightening to locate the campaign against the Emergency within his wider concerns for creating the social climate he considered critical for corruption-free governance. The aim here is to understand the overall theoretical predisposition that J P held, while conceptualizing his ideological priorities. In view of his sustained commitment to fight for just and fair governance, the battle in which he was involved during the Emergency was just a continuation of the desire that he had so sincerely nurtured since he had arrived on India's political scene. What J P thus provided was an ideological package which draws on the Marxist conceptualization of praxis, a creative combination of theory and practice in which neither is overshadowed by the other. The idea that runs through is also about a dialectical interconnection between what is known as derivative wisdom and practice. Drawn from what he learnt from his ideological convictions about the downtrodden, J P's model was also context driven, and is thus uniquely textured.

Plan for reconstruction of Indian polity

J P's growing frustration with the Marxian praxis and the practical manifestation of its socio-economic and political order led him to evolve an alternative order suitable to the specific requirements of the country. The adoption of the

Constitution in post-independence times was taken positively by the majority of people, in the hope that it would result in the translating of the high aspirations of the national movement. However, people like J P soon got disillusioned with the workings of democratic polity in the country. Later, J P embarked on a tour of various European countries, ostensibly to get a feel for the structure and functioning of their governments. A basic flaw discovered by J P in the structure of most of the systems of government, including the one prevailing in India after the implementation of the Constitution of 1950, was the increasing concentration of power at the higher levels of government. This appeared quite distressing to J P as, being a true democrat, he wanted the power to be vested in the hands of the people and believed that only as much power as was unavoidable needed to be transferred to the higher levels of the authority structure. Thus, in order to give a concrete shape to his ideas on the comprehensive re-conceptualizing of the nature and structure of the Indian political system, he published the book *A Plea for the Reconstruction of Indian Polity* in 1959.

In advancing his plea for the reconstruction of Indian polity J P appeared extremely influenced by the ideas of Sri Aurobindo, as he found that the 'extraordinary, intuitive sweep of his vision [that] has laid bare the true nature of the foundations of Indian polity.'[7] Following Aurobindo's line of argument J P was convinced of the veracity of the ancient Indian political order, based on the centrality of the self-governing village communities. Indeed, J P's seemingly uncritical appreciation of the ancient Indian political order was so formidable that he argued that the conceptualization of the political system in the post-independent times in India was no less than 'a question of an ancient country finding its lost soul again.'[8] Thus, J P's basic argument in calling for the reconstruction of the Indian polity was to reinvent and implant the village-based political order with the idea of decentralization underpinning the basic functional ethos and spirit of the system.

Significantly, J P called for the replacement of the prevailing politico-economic order in India, based on the parliamentary system of democracy and centralized planning, with what is called the communitarian democracy and decentralized political economy.[9] In fact, J P was a staunch critic of the parliamentary system of democracy, denouncing it from all quarters. But the most intolerable defect of such a system of democracy, to J P, was its inherent tendency towards centralism, which appears to be a contradiction in terms in itself. In other words, the notion of democracy could not be conceptualized in a way that leads to or supports any sort of centralism. As the parliamentary system of democracy invariably slips towards centralism, it could not have been the best of models of government for India.

The notion of 'communitarian democracy', as advocated by J P, carries a distinct set of political processes that is squarely different from the ones characterizing the nature of political processes in a parliamentary democracy. For instance, the essence of parliamentary democracy lies in intense competition among the political parties to seek power and establish their majority in the political system. On the contrary, J P suggests that the essence of communitarian democracy lies in cooperation and co-sharing, as such a system must afford due space for all the interests of the society to be articulated in the political decision making of the country in a harmonious manner. Naturally, in such a conceptualization of democracy, the emphasis of J P was on the moral and ethical moorings, in utter contrast to the material and power-centred nature of the parliamentary system. To J P, therefore, the fundamental task of communitarian democracy is the moral regeneration to be brought about by the example, service, sacrifice and love of scores of voluntary workers.[10]

In concrete terms, the plea of J P to reconstruct the Indian polity was principally based on the framework of a decentralized, participatory and grassroots oriented political order, as reflected in practical shape by the idea of *Panchayati Raj* as existing in the country since the ancient times. This would be an essentially pyramidal model of democracy, with the widest possible diffusion of powers at the grassroot level, making it the real level of government that matters most to the people. Thus, J P's model gives a more decentralized base to the 'four-pillar model of government', as suggested by Ram Manohar Lohia. To put it differently, while Lohia suggested villages, district, state and centre as the levels of government, J P tried to broaden the base of the local level of government by including a middle level in between the village and district levels, so that the operational imperatives of local government could be strengthened. Thus, what J P suggested was five levels of decentralized polity, consisting of village, block, district, provincial and central levels.

In J P's scheme of things, on reconstructing the Indian polity, an overwhelming emphasis was placed on reviving and reinvigorating the *Panchayati Raj* system or what he calls '*Swaraj* from below'.[11] Under this framework, the basic and lowest unit of political organization would be the *Gram Sabha* (village assembly) consisting of all the adults of the village. Primarily being a deliberative body to ensure the participation of all the adult residents of the village in the governance of their affairs, the *Gram Sabha* would elect, ordinarily by consensus, five or more members among themselves to constitute its executive committee, the *Gram Panchayat*. Thus, through these '*Panchs*' (members of the village *Panchayat*) acting as the functionaries to take care of the day to day operation of the system, the *Gram Sabha* was supposed to act as the lynchpin of the grass root democracy conceptualized by J P.

Establishing an organic link amongst the various units of the *Panchayati Raj*, J P suggested the creation of two more interlinked bodies within the system. The middle level of the *Panchayati Raj*, therefore, would be located at the block level and would be known as *Panchayat Samiti*. Consisting of the representatives of the constituent *Gram Sabhas*, the *Panchayat Samiti*'s operational area would be identical to the areas of its constituent *Gram Sabhas*. Functionally, the *Panchayat Samiti* would be entrusted with the responsibility of guiding and coordinating the activities of the *Gram Sabhas*, with particular focus on the formulation and execution of development projects. Finally, the apex of the *Panchayati Raj* was conceptualized as the District *Panchayat* or *Zila Parishad*, constituted by the members elected by the *Panchayat Samitis*. The functional domain of the *Zila*

Parishad would ordinarily remain focused on consolidating and fine-tuning the development projects initiated or approved by the *Panchayat Samitis* with a view to ensuring their technical and economic viability. The common feature underpinning all three levels of the *Panchayati Raj* would be their endeavour to provide the people with an opportunity to participate in the management of their own affairs and enjoy the spirit of true democracy.

Though the bodies of *Panchayati Raj* constituted the core of the communitarian democracy advocated by J P, he did not remain oblivious to the imperatives of the provincial and central levels of government. What was unique in his conceptualizations of these levels of government was that he wanted them to remain confined, functionally, to their stipulated domains and devoid of any temptation to bulldoze over the lower levels of democratic institution. J P thus argued for a democratic and federal structure of polity in India, so that the true spirit of democratic governance might be infused through it and afforded to the masses. Moreover, for this, he wanted the political system to be free from a party politics based on numerous primitive and sectarian motivations to serve the selfish interests of the dominant unscrupulous elements in society.

An important element of the plan of reconstruction of Indian polity, as suggested by J P, was the reconstruction of the economic system.[12] Being dead against the exploitative and competitive economic system as prevailed in capitalist societies, he argued for the reconstruction of the Indian economic system on the doctrine of cooperation, coexistence and sharing. He decried the element of centralism in the Indian planning system and argued for the remodelling of the planning system by making it decentralized and non-political. On the pattern of the grassroots orientation in the political system of the country, J P advocated a village-orientation in the planning process of the country as well. He argued that the formulation of development plans should be initiated at the level of the village with progressive integration and consolidation at the block and district levels. The planning processes at the state and national levels should confine themselves to only providing technical and logistical support for the formulation and execution of the plans at the local levels. J P also called for sectoral balance and harmony in bringing about the rapid economic development of the country. Thus, the restructured political economy of the country, in J P's view, would result in the realization of true *swaraj* for the common people of the country.

Despite the seemingly sensible and logical consistency in the plea of J P for the reconstruction of Indian polity, his scheme has been criticized by scholars as being utopian and suitable only for the wonderland of J P's imagination.[13] A common critique of J P's scheme has been its obvious focus on reviving and implanting an ancient Indian construct which might have outlived its utility in contemporary times. Moreover, the disproportionate focus on the *Panchayati Raj* as the nucleus of the post-independent Indian polity appears absurdly abstract, among other things. Thus, over the years, J P himself became quite weary of the practical utility of his plea for the reconstruction of Indian polity and shifted his focus of attention to what is known as *Sarvodaya*.

Sarvodaya

Sarvodaya was a conceptual construct J P borrowed from Gandhi to articulate his vision of a decentralized, participatory and egalitarian socio-economic and political order for the country. Delineating the core concerns of the idea of *Sarvodaya*, Vinoba Bhave wrote, 'Sarvodaya does not mean good government or majority rule, it means freedom from government, it means decentralization of power.'[14] Conceptualized so, *sarvodaya*, thus, becomes synonymous with a state of order where the bonds of being governed by a seemingly alien or outside ruler are totally absent and the people are able to enjoy their lives without any extraneous considerations. Hence, the full realization of the ideal of *sarvodaya* would necessitate the absence of government itself, yet, even if the government remains in existence, the power relations ought to be so decentralized that nobody finds themselves in any sort of subjugation to another. It is within this theoretical framework that J P outlined his vision of a *sarvodaya* social order.

In visualizing his *sarvodaya* social order, J P begins with an exploration of the innate characteristics of human nature. Though acknowledging that evil spirits and motivations exist in individuals and society, he argued that they could be overcome by the virtues of compassion and non-violence. Moreover, by inculcating the positive values of life such as cooperation, generosity, creativity and eternal joy, the good spirits and motivations of the people might be brought to the fore to make them realize the significance of such traits in securing a happy and peaceful life for themselves. Above all, if the examples of such a perspective on life become prominent and people were properly educated in this regard, they would definitely pursue noble causes and follow good men.[15] Thus, at the root of the proposed *sarvodaya* order of J P, lay his indomitable belief in the inherently noble and positive nature of the common people, which may be harnessed to secure a just, egalitarian and democratically decentralized order in India.

The social component of the *sarvodaya* order rests on an all-inclusive egalitarian social structure.[16] Social relations would be based on the principles of equality, justice and inclusion. As the society would seek the welfare of each and every individual, there would not be any place for socially degrading and discriminatory practices, rooted in the primitive and sectarian motivations of any individual. J P was quite specific about the role of various sections in society and argued for a visionary mindset and missionary zeal among the youth whose selfless and untiring efforts would be the main vehicle through which the reconstruction of society would materialize. A democratic ethos and spirit would infuse social interactions and nobody would be persuaded to do anything against their will no matter the acceptability of the task at hand. Volunteerism would be a major plank to get people to do their bit for the welfare of society.

The political dimension of *sarvodaya*, as explained earlier, would rest on the widest and most effective system of decentralized and participatory democracy, made concrete in the form of *Panchayati Raj*. What, however, was refreshing in the *sarvodaya* political order was J P's insistence on revolving his scheme of things around what is known as *lokniti* (politics of people) and *lokshakti* (power of people) in place of the existing dependence on *rajniti* (politics of power) and *rajshakti* (power of state). Despite appearing unconventional, such notions of a people-centric and society-centric perspective on Indian politics would have seemed quite natural, given J P's constant pushing for the decentralized and participatory nature of the *sarvodaya* political order. In fact, in the later years when governments in India were charged with numerous cases of corruption and high-handedness in dealing with political opponents, J P relied exclusively on powers having their roots in social and other non-governmental formations. Thus, J P conceptualized the *sarvodaya* social order as consisting of morally upright individuals having the courage to stand up for ideals such as 'self-government, self management, mutual cooperation and sharing, equality, freedom and brotherhood'.[17]

Economically, the framework of the *sarvodaya* order would seek to establish a balanced and equitable economic set-up in the country. India being a predominantly agricultural country, J P was sure to afford the first place to agricultural activities in the economic life of the people. Hence, he argued for organizing numerous collectivist farms under the collective ownership and management of the whole village. Further, J P's deep faith in the Gandhian economic perspective apparently influenced him to advocate a prime place for village and cottage industries, organized at local and regional level. However, the wave of heavy industrialization in various parts of world made him also offer a place to heavy and large-scale industries in the industrial part of the economy. Thus, in a *sarvodaya* economy, a balanced approach, according due weight to various sectors of the economy, would be followed. The net gains from the economic activities of society would be so equitably distributed that it would result in a decentralized, prosperous, distributive and participatory economic order.

Methods of realizing the *sarvodaya* order

Having conceptualized the *sarvodaya* social order in very insightful and precise terms, J P also appeared quite categorical in suggesting the appropriate methods of implementing the plan for creating such a social order in India. Quite evidently, J P's deep erudition and lived experiences of various methods and institutional arrangements to bring about drastic transformations in society made him a rebel vis-à-vis the numerous conventional methods of effecting desirable social change. For instance, he no longer favoured his old fancies about the classical Marxian prescription of changing society through revolutionary violence. Castigating the violent methods of social change, he held that such methods did not take care of the veracity of the objective in view and 'ensure the victory of the party that is more skilled in their use.' The victory ensured by such methods would invariably, as shown primarily by the Russian experiences, be authoritarian and undermine 'all attempts at democracy and the attainment of social justice or equality'.[18]

Significantly, J P was equally disillusioned with the liberal methods of social change, which sought to achieve it by legal provisions and the institutional arrangement to implement them. J P's basic critique of the parliamentary route of effecting social change was that it would not yield the desired result without mentally preparing people to accept and adapt such changes in their life styles. As he wrote eloquently,

> It is not institutions, not laws, not political systems, not constitutions that create good people. For that you require a widespread process of education understood in the widest sense of the word. Education does not mean academic education; but the improving of human beings through service, love, examples, preaching, reasoning and argument.[19]

J P also argued for the setting of concrete examples by the leaders and awakened citizens of the country, so that the masses could emulate such examples and, equipped with proper education, would be able to become the harbingers of a new *sarvodaya* social order in the country.

The cumulative impact of the twin virtues of education and concrete examples, in J P's view, would be to indelibly ingrain awareness in a person's mental and moral values, infusing him with some sort of voluntary perspective towards the prevailing problems of society and their plausible solutions. The concrete exemplification of such a moral and theoretical construct was experienced in the *Bhoodan* and *Gramdaan* movements launched by Vinoba Bhave. J P was very impressed with the idea and practice of such voluntary sharing on the part of the people and argued for the extension and strengthening of such movements by way of *sampattidaan* (sharing together of property) and the ultimate *jeevandaan* (sharing one's whole life and dedicating it to the cause of the welfare of others). J P anticipated that such voluntary sharing of the various prized possessions of life would ensure a non-violent, voluntary and democratic transformation of Indian society on the lines of the *sarvodaya* order.

Total revolution

Total revolution (*Sampurna Kranti*) was the last intellectual intervention of J P in his unending quest to seek and establish a socio-economic and political order in the country that would turn India into a democratic, federal, participatory, equitable and prosperous nation in the world. The concept of total revolution was developed for the first time by Vinoba Bhave during the 1960s to articulate his desire for a comprehensive movement in the country which would transform all aspects of life in order to 'mould a new man ... to change human life and create a new world.'[20] The idea was picked up by J P, who called upon the people in 1975 to work for total revolution in order to stem the rot creeping into all aspects of public life and create a whole new world, encompassing the basic elements of socio-economic and political order that he had been advocating in the name of *sarvodaya*.

The context of J P calling for total revolution[21] was provided by the growing authoritarianism in the functioning of the government machinery headed by Mrs

Indira Gandhi. One of the nefarious repercussions of such governance was the spreading of corruption in all aspects of political life in India. Hence, on the declaration of Emergency in June 1975, J P found it compelling to call for total revolution in the country, aimed at transforming the whole gamut of the social, economic, political, spiritual, educational and cultural life of the people. J P was convinced that piece-meal engineering would not suffice to bring about the desirable level and pace of holistic transformation in India, thereby necessitating the call for total revolution. Through his call for total revolution, J P, therefore, was not satisfied with having cosmetic changes in the outer set-up of the socio-economic and political structures of power but also called for effecting and deepening an informed consciousness in the masses to ensure the holistic transformation of the entire system. The essence of all such transformations would lie in restoring the basic spiritual foundations of all aspects of human life in the country.

J P's concept of total revolution aimed at reversing the rot taking place in the political and economic system of the country, ostensibly due to the concentration of political and economic power in few hands, and restoring the sanctity of institutions and procedures in those spheres of life by decentralizing power into the hands of the masses. In the sphere of politics, J P noted the inherent fallacies of the prevailing parliamentary system of government, as its basic characteristics such as the electoral system, party-based political processes and increasing concentration of power in the hands of one person i.e., the Prime Minister were bound to convert the system into a corrupt, tyrannical, farcical one. Hence, in his conceptualization of total revolution, J P was firm on reforming the electoral system in such a way that the people could vote in an incorruptible manner and in accordance with their free conscience. Moreover, in such a system, there would be no place for political parties and the potential concentration of power in a few hands would be effectively curbed by having the greatest possible diffusion of political power to the various levels of government.

As with political power, J P was also convinced of the perverse effects of the concentration of economic power in the hands of a few in society. He therefore also called for the total recasting of the economic system of the country. Arguing for a mixed economy framework for India, J P aspired for the economic system of the country to be able to provide for the basic necessities of the people, such as food, clothes and shelter. His idea of *sampattidaan* was nothing but a call for the sharing together of wealth and economic resources in such a way that their utilization benefitted larger sections of people rather than ensuring affluence for a few. J P visualized an economic order for the country in which there would be progressive socialization of the means of production by way of establishing cooperative societies and voluntary associations to manage the resources with a view to ensuring prosperity for all. Thus, even in the sphere of economic activities, J P's diagnosis of and cure for the ills appeared rooted in the concentration and decentralization of power respectively. He therefore suggested that the first and foremost task of the *sarvodaya* worker would be to 'diffuse political and economic power and decentralize the politico-economic structure'.[22] Indeed, decentralization, along with the people's participation, was argued by J P as the panacea for all the evils which had become deep rooted in the politico-economic system of the country.

J P's call to execute the idea of total revolution in 1975 was accompanied by some sort of blueprint for the volunteers to carry out the implementation of the scheme of holistic transformations of Indian society. He exhorted the people to rise against the authoritarian and inimical policies and programmes of the government of the day and persevere to push it back to its legitimate domain. He also called for the dissolution of the legislative bodies in the country, as they had ceased to reflect the opinion of the people by going neck deep into all sorts of political and economic corruptions. J P also pointed out the problem of price rises as a target of total revolution, since it had the potential to turn the life of the people into virtual poverty and starvation, bearing in mind their inability to pay the exorbitantly high prices of essential commodities. At the same time, he was also forthright about eradicating the existing social inequality in the country by putting a full stop to discrimination among the people on the basis of religion and caste. In a nutshell, the operationalization of the idea of total revolution in 1975 encompassed within its folds almost all the major problems facing the people before they embarked on the path of long-term revolutionary transformation, aimed at establishing the *sarvodaya* social order in the country.

In its operationalization, however, the idea of total revolution, as advocated by J P, occasionally evoked misplaced perceptions in the minds of its practitioners. For instance, it undoubtedly proved electrifying for the people and gave birth to a mammoth students' movement in many parts of the country, which was particularly formidable in Bihar in 1974. But the public perception of total revolution appeared ambivalent, as many construed it to be the total subduing of *rajya shakti* or state power at the hands of the people. However, J P was quite categorical that he did not advocate the disappearance of all political power but, rather, the placement of it where it belonged, in the hands of the people.[23] Similarly, a few people tried to have recourse to violent methods in carrying out the movement for total revolution. But J P was firm in his conviction that total revolution could be brought about only through peaceful and non-violent voluntary actions on the part of the people.

As is evident, J P had launched a successful crusade against the internal Emergency, which resulted in its revocation in 1977. The campaign was fair because it was against the efforts of a select political leadership to debase governance for its own cause. In other words, by challenging the authority that had taken away constitutionally guaranteed democratic rights, J P had articulated a voice for re-establishing the republican spirit of the Constitution. It would not be an exaggeration to suggest that the Emergency was a paradox of history since it was 'as much a constitutional response by Indira Gandhi to the constitutional means that the opposition parties had adopted to unseat her'.[24] The Emergency thus provided us with an experience that brought out very clearly that 'the Constitution contained provisions in it that could both enhance the democratic rights of the people and be used to deny [them] even the [constitutionally endorsed] fundamental rights'.[25] Nonetheless, the proclamation of the Emergency had created a context in which the issue of ethics in governance was not only raised, but was also sought to be conclusively addressed. J P can thus be said to have set in motion processes whereby the importance of a moral code of conduct for public personnel was forcefully reiterated.

The paradoxical nature of the Emergency and J P's successful mobilization against the excesses raise an open-ended question, if one seeks to comprehend those two tumultuous years in independent India's recent political history. The Emergency was a constitutional act, and so was the challenge that the opposition parties had mounted against the prevalent political authority. If the Emergency was a constitution-endorsed design of authoritarianism, it was not a deviation from the rule of law; and hence those who proclaimed it escaped condemnation. Similarly, the opposition parties were within the constitutional bounds when they protested by undertaking what the ruling authority had dubbed as unconstitutional means. A very piquant situation had emerged. Whether the governing elites indulged in unethical practices by declaring an Emergency according to the constitutional provisions is definitely a question that cannot be answered conclusively. Likewise, the fact that the mass endeavour to unseat the Congress party was based on fulfilling constitutional rights further complicates the issue. In either case, the rule of law was not grossly violated, although its application, in seeking to realize the whimsical personal preferences of the leadership, was certainly contrary to the fundamental ethical values from which the Constitution of India derives its sustenance. As shown in Chapter 5, the 1977 Shah Commission illustrates how the majority of public officials did not care about basic ethical values while executing instructions from above; not only did they personalize authority, they also indulged in activities which were contrary to their constitutional obligations. The Commission had expressed alarm at the number of instances of deliberate distortion of rules and regulations to supporting their 'misdeeds'. The government became a captive of elite interests, ignoring public outcry against the deviant public officials. J P gave powerful voice to those who, regardless of consequence, agreed to fight for the restoration of constitutional governance, which had been legitimately sacrificed, as the perpetrators of the Emergency justified it, to save the country from being devastated as a result of the organized protest by the opposition parties that had begun in Bihar in 1974. The support that J P was able to generate for his anti-corruption campaign had 'more to do with the political and economic context than Narayan's demagoguery'.[26] Plagued by social and economic underdevelopment, population pressures and underemployment in the state, the ordinary Indians seemed to have been completely disillusioned with the existing state, which led to growing hostility towards those in charge of political authority and 'their self-serving mismanagement'.[27] The movement took root in a propitious milieu and it was therefore easier for J P to mobilize the masses with a purpose. His leadership was undoubtedly a rallying point in bringing together people with contrasting ideological inclinations when he exhorted them to join him in his opposition to the Emergency.

The anti-Emergency campaign was thus as much an ideological protest against a debasing government as it was an endeavour to establish a code of ethics for those holding public authority. A fight to restore constitutional demo-cracy, J P's crusade was, in other words, an effort towards creating and consoli-dating a social climate in which concerns about ethics could strike a chord against the 'arbitrariness and reckless disregard of the rights of others and the consequent misery [which] ... terrorized citizens resulting in a complete loss of faith of the people in the fairness and objectivity of the Administration gener-ally'.[28] By contributing to the rise of a context in which government machinery was utilized to the detriment of their public aim, the two-year Emergency was also an eye-opener in the sense that it had shown, rather virulently, how an ethi-cally derailed public authority deviated from the basic code of conduct while discharging its role. Governance became highly personalized from top to bottom, and authority was exercised in a tyrannical fashion, violating, without qualms, the fundamental constitutional ethos supportive of democracy and individual rights.

The context of the 2011 Anna Hazare movement

Similar to the J P movement that had its roots in the flagrant abuse of public authority, the 2011 Anna Hazare campaign was a response to declining govern-ance in the light of the series of scams in which public officials, including minis-ters, were reportedly involved. At the behest of a non-political outfit, known as *India Against Corruption*, the 2011 anti-corruption campaign had built a mass base, rather spontaneously, not only in Delhi but also elsewhere in the country. The pace at which the campaign acquired a national character caught everybody by surprise, which perhaps confirms the mass resentment against those holding responsible positions of authority in the public domain. Outraged by the inept government, which was charged with being complicit with corrupt forces, citizens joined the campaigners in large numbers with the hope that it would not only expose the deviants, but also lay the foundation for an ethically sound polit-ical system. The fact that a large number of people, mostly the urban middle class, which had otherwise been indifferent to agitations 'landed up to protest and took the initiative through Facebook and Twitter [appears to be] a reaction to the arrogance that the leaders of the political parties displayed when Anna Hazare launched his fast unto death'.[29] Although the movement remained prim-arily a middle class assault on tainted governance, it had created conditions for change by releasing mass energies for a cause. The Anna Hazare initiative was also testimony to the fact that public outcry, despite giving an immediate jolt to the system, may not always be a source for meaningful transformation, because of its transitional character; spontaneous outbursts of public outrage do not get translated into sustained movements unless they are organizationally backed.

The Anna Hazare campaign was the culmination of mass disillusionment with the existing government, led by the United Progressive Alliance, which had begun its second term in 2009. As argued in Chapter 1, in the wake of globalization, civil society has become an integral component of governance, ascertaining conceptually the critical importance of external accountability as opposed to internal accountability, which is so commonly conceived as part of the Weberian understanding of public authority. By recognizing that 'the civil society engagements are groundbreaking initiatives that have emerged out of an urge to serve the needs of the common man',[30] the 2005 Second Administrative Reforms Commission thus underlines that

> civil society groups have put pressure on erring governments to reform corrupt practices. They have also provided monitoring mechanisms to track corruption by educating members of the public and associating them in anti-corruption efforts. They have helped generate demand for reducing corruption and introducing systemic reforms.... The successful initiatives of civil society groups [thus] underscore the criticality of educating people and raising their awareness of fighting corruption.[31]

In the context of the Anna Hazare movement, the role of civil society remained critical; not only did the civil society activists help mobilize support, they also played their part in educating the people by charting how government machinery became a captive of the corrupt and ethically derailed individuals involved in governance. It has been historically shown that 'a strong and vigilant civil society can be a check on corruption',[32] and the 2011 Anna Hazare-led mobilization proved that once again.

What was the immediate context that provoked mass outrage? A series of scams broke out during the second term of the Congress-led coalition government, which was thus labelled by the contemporary media as perhaps the most tainted government in independent India. Instead of providing an analytical account of each and every scam that has rocked India in the present century, this section focuses on two major scams – the 2010 2G Scam and the Commonwealth Games Scam – that appeared to have created massive distrust in the then government. Dubbed as number two by the *Times* magazine in its list of top ten abuses of power, the 2G Spectrum scam, in which mobile phone licenses were sold for a fraction of their value, resulted in the loss of a staggering $39 billion to the national exchequer. Not only was the loss astronomically high, the 2G scam hogged the limelight because of the involvement of key cabinet ministers, top bureaucrats and also major private players. In its audit report, the Comptroller and Auditor General of India showed how the government failure to contain corrupt ministers led to a scam of such devastating proportions. Some of those who allowed this to happen were put behind bars; some of them were given lesser punishments. By exposing the scam, the report and an alert media helped prepare the ground for the movement that was to begin in 2011.

The Comptroller and Auditor General also indicted those in charge of holding the 2010 Commonwealth Games in Delhi. The 744 page report reveals how collusion between politicians, bureaucrats and corporations resulted in a loss of almost $6 billion because of (a) the high price tag for the services and (b) the distribution of almost $2 billion which was never accounted for. The report of the V K Shunglu Committee, which was appointed to look into the excesses committed by the organizers of the Games, was most revealing. Norms for financial transactions were violated and no code of ethics was followed. 'Accountability, internal and external, was not the norm', argues the Committee.[33] Things moved in accordance with the whims of one individual, the chief of the Commonwealth Games organizing committee Suresh Kalmadi. The Shunglu Committee noted that 'all key decisions were taken by a handful of powerful loyalists to the Chairman of the Organizing Committee [disregarding completely] the presence of the Executive Board [which was] constituted for this purpose'.[34] Not only did the organizing committee operate in 'a coterie style', it included … many senior persons with questionable integrity and past records of watchdog cases. Besides cases of the blatant violation of government rules and regulations in regard to the posting and transfer of public personnel, 'there was no effective vigilance and internal audit', laments the Committee, 'to provide watchdog functions and promote compliance with propriety and ethical norms or efficiency'.[35] The wasteful expenditure could have been easily avoided had those involved in the preparation for the Games remained committed to the code of conduct for public services. The result was disastrous because, as the Shunglu Committee felt, 'the acts of commission and omission [on the part of the organizers] not only facilitated undue gains to contractors but also led to wasteful expenditure and contributed to the overall loss to the Government'.[36] Besides assigning responsibility for irregularities, which 'range from administrative misdemeanours to criminal misconduct', the Committee reveals in its report that 'the malaise runs deep and cannot be dismissed as one-off aberrations, for which relatively junior functionaries alone can be held responsible'.[37] This observation is most instructive to make the argument that corruption in governance in India is very well entrenched and cannot be removed so easily. As shown in Chapter 5, corruption was attributed to the uncontrolled discretionary power of civil servants in the License-Quota-Permit Raj, while it remained a constant source of irritation in governance in the changed environment in which the public officials' discretionary power had considerably shrunk.

So, the Anna Hazare movement unfolded in a context in which several scams had already rocked India. It was easier for the organizers to mobilize in the light of popular demand for an end to corruption. There was a common feeling that, since the government had connived with vested interests, it had simply become too inept to effectively combat corruption in governance. Added to this feeling was 'the discovery of the loot in the upper echelons of governance, by top politicians, senior bureaucrats and even the judges in the higher courts'.[38] Hazare's solution was to create a strong ombudsman, Lokpal in Indian parlance, to contain corruption, which was all that was needed 'to unleash the full benefits of liberalization in India'.[39] The institution of Lokpal was first suggested by the first Administrative Reforms Commission in 1968 and the first Lokpal bill was immediately introduced in that year. Since then, it has been introduced nine times, but never passed. Essentially a technocratic solution, the Lokpal was thus assumed to be adequately equipped to completely root out corruption. Insisting on legislation for a strong Lokpal, Anna Hazare and his colleagues appeared to have expressed complete faith in a panoptical institution, capable of fulfilling their ideological mission.

Hazare began his campaign for a strong Lokpal in April 2011, later continued by the beginning of his 'fast unto death' in August 2011. Instead of describing the movement in detail, the purpose here is to capture its nature by reference to the features that appear to be critical in comprehending its character. Hazare's movement was invariably a middle-class movement because in him the Indian middle class had found a saviour and a saint to support. By resorting to a typical Gandhian technique – fast unto death – Hazare seemed to have created an image of being Gandhian to his followers. What is striking to note is that, although he might have appropriated a Gandhian method for political mobilization, he was hardly Gandhian as his socio-political activities in Ralegaon Siddhi had shown: his support for corporal punishment for the wrong-doers was just one example to argue that his claim of being a Gandhian seems to be overstretched.

It is true that Anna Hazare's contribution to Ralegaon Siddhi's socio-economic development is phenomenal; despite being criticized for his visible patriarchal prejudices, his role in transforming the village is indisputable. In the process, he allowed a personality cult to grow around him. While he played a critical role in development, he also created a discursive reality in which the basic democratic values of live and let live were sacrificed. The idea was to create a homogeneous society, being reinforced by 'a top-down decision-making process [drawing on] ... the expectations of uncritical obedience to a supreme leader ... to whom unquestioning obedience has to be rendered'.[40] Within such conceptual parameters, Hazare created his model village, which endorsed

> physical coercion garbed as parental concerns, threats of corporal and symbolic force to reinforce authority, flogging of offenders with an army belt to make them mend their ways, and the excessive use of religious symbols to drive home lessons in a morality steeped in orthodox Hinduism.[41]

As is evident, Ralegaon Siddhi epitomized an ideal village in which deviant behaviour was not to be tolerated under any circumstances. Hazare did not find his methods wrong since they yielded results, and India, he strongly felt, needed shock therapy to create an environment in which individuals were too scared to indulge in corruption because of the adverse consequences. With the institutionalization of a system opposed to corrupt practices, it would be easier for a mindset that is appreciative of a code of ethics to strike roots. So, Anna Hazare's method is both socially endorsed and ideologically executed in circumstances in which democratic decision-making processes did not seem to have been encouraged.

A brief discussion of how Anna Hazare became a symbol of the crusade against the abuse of government authority and corruption in Ralegaon Siddhi is perfectly in order here. Steeped in poverty, unemployment, malnutrition, migration, recurring drought and environmental degradation, Ralegaon Siddhi in 1975 was just a typical village in Maharashtra. In a period of ten years, the village acquired the tag of a model village, the transformation of which was attributed to Hazare's sustained endeavour. There were *two* major steps that he undertook to create an environment in which the villagers became partners in the social cleansing that Hazare had so assiduously pursued. It was possible for the participants to get involved in social work only if they were, as Hazare insisted, rule-bound and norms-conscious. It was obvious that Hazare would remain obedient to rules and norms, because of his training as a former soldier of the Indian army. As was explained in his statement,

> the daily routine enforced in the army ... led to the development of a disciplined life, benefits of which I am availing myself of today. The habit of giving due respect and regard to the seniors by age, post or competence was inculcated in us.... This has helped me in conducting the village development work at Ralegaon Siddhi according to the rules and regulations decided by us by common consent.[42]

How to inculcate discipline if it received no takers? Hence the first solution that Hazare provided was a mixture of persuasion and physical coercion. In the process of social transformation, he believed, 'advice, persuasion or counselling do not always work and occasionally force has to be applied [because] the fear of physical force works'.[43] The application of punitive punishment was most effective when Hazare undertook a campaign against alcoholism. The decision to close down the breweries in the village was taken democratically, with the villagers consent. Once that was decided, Hazare did not hesitate to apply corporal punishment to those who violated the village diktat. It was therefore decided that anybody consuming alcohol was to be punished in public: the person caught while drinking was to be tied to a pole near the village temple and flogged to generate fear and thus restraint. This worked miracles in a very short period of time and alcoholism ceased to be a social menace in Ralegaon Siddhi.[44] What explains the popularity of such a measure was perhaps (a) Hazare's exemplary, bordering on hegemonic, control over the villagers; and (b) their appreciation of the positive social effects on family life for those who suffered terribly as a result of unrestricted alcoholism. As a result, 'flogging has become a part of everyday life and belief [and] not only has the authority employing it the sanction to use it, others legitimize its use as well'.[45] It was therefore an environment, sustained by persuasion and also coercion, if necessary, in which a new moral economy had emerged where popular consent was perhaps solicited differently. Clearly an individual-centric authority, Anna Hazare thus epitomized a wave of thinking bordering on the Gandhian emphasis on moral values by reiterating their critical salience in building a robust culture of integrity in public life.

Hazare devised his second step by charting out five universal rules which are (a) *Nasbandi* (restriction of family size), (b) *nashabandi* (ban on alcohol), (c) *charabandi* (ban on free grazing), (d) *khuraabandi* (ban on tree feeling) and

(e) *shramdan* (voluntary labour for the community).[46] This is primarily a check-list of dos and don'ts, and since the villagers accepted them as a vow, these rules were more or less carried forward. Even if there was opposition, their voices always remained subdued, since the majority of the villagers acquiesced in what was proclaimed as the village charter. Besides these five principles, Ralegaon Siddhi also follows well-defined codes of conduct to maintain the so-called purity of culture; hence not only are shops forbidden to sell *bidis* and cigarettes, film songs and movies are also prohibited. Apart from an embargo on culturally polluting influences, Hazare's diktat also forced the villagers to change their culinary preferences. Since vegetarianism creates peacefulness and does not contribute to violence, Hazare and his youth brigade in Ralegaon Siddhi engage in a relentless campaign to popularize the vegetarian diet. The campaign was effective among the *Dalits* as well, out of a symbiotic relationship that Anna Hazare had created by developing what he called, 'a faith relationship' with them. Based on this relationship, Hazare claims, there had emerged an inclination among the *Dalits* in favour of vegetarian meals.[47]

How does Hazare sustain his authority in Ralegaon Siddhi? Undoubtedly his role in addressing what ailed the village was a critical factor; he became a saviour to the villagers who were socially peripheral, economically exploited and ideologically marginalized. By dint of his sustained developmental work, especially through effective watershed management, he created good will among the villagers, which yielded positive results. It was not merely his personal popularity that endeared him to the masses, but also his acute strategic sense explains his massive popularity in Ralegaon Siddhi. Hence it was not unusual for him to resort to religious symbols and imagery to gain and consolidate a support base. The fact that most of his decisions were taken in the temple courtyard is governed by the idea that, once a commitment is given before God, it must be respected to avoid heavenly retribution. It was also felt that the 'temple has an atmosphere of purity and sanctity [and] decisions taken in a temple are believed to have the sanction of god and people are more likely to follow them'.[48] The idea was not novel, but was strategically applied to pursue an ideological goal involving the masses regardless of social, economic and political divides. As shown above, Hazare had a clear vision of what was to be done in Ralegaon Siddhi to realize its socio-economic potential in what was a completely hopeless situation. In seeking to fulfil his mission, he may have decried the democratic means which he felt were futile; nonetheless, by articulating an alternative, perhaps a powerful alternative, on the basis of his own analysis of the Indian reality, Hazare has also shown the importance of morality, ethics and integrity in shaping public life. These are values that can be inculcated in a way in which deviant behaviours are not only despised but also have no easy acceptance. Hazare's main purpose was to create 'a moral regime, not only to get rid of liquor, smoking or non-vegetarianism, but also to exercise control over the private and the public, the personal and the political'.[49] His idea of morality is thus reflective of what he believed in personal life. Critical of western influences for their pernicious impact on Indian culture, Hazare was also vehemently opposed to indecent cinemas and television shows, which were impediments to the growth of a healthy moral culture. Hence, in Ralegaon Siddhi, film songs and movies (except specific religious films) were strictly forbidden. Along with maintaining the high moral standards of the villagers, these restrictions, if applied at the national level, would surely arrest 'the falling moral standards of the nation'.[50] As is evident, Anna Hazare is also a moral crusader who sought to govern Ralegaon Siddhi in accordance with well-defined codes of moral conduct which needed to be imposed to avoid India's degeneration. That he managed to create a solid moral order in the village confirms how important a leader could be in fulfilling specific tasks. The fact that the radical transformation of Ralegaon Siddhi was absolutely individual driven may have given Hazare tremendous confidence in the ability of a morally upright and impeccably honest individual to do miracles. This is perhaps the reason why he favoured the creation of an absolutely powerful Lokpal who, if endowed with the quality that he insists, could be an effective instrument not only for combating corruption but also for building a society appreciative of the values of integrity and ethics in governance.

Support base of the Hazare campaign for Lokpal

A scan of the social background of the supporters that thronged to back up the campaign for a strong Lokpal reveals that it was a middle class-dominated affair. An aspiring middle class, comprising almost one-third of India's total demography, which came into being in the wake of economic liberalization found in the Hazare-sponsored Jan Lokpal bill an effective device to take care of bureaucratic red tapism, to mete-out maximum punishment for the corrupt politicians and officials and to weed out roots of corruption to a significant extent. Those supporting the India Against Corruption campaign were persuaded to believe that a parliamentary law had the capacity to effectively mitigate corruption in public life. The creation of an effective Lokpal, it was believed, was an antidote to corruption. His followers were led to believe, a commentator thus argues, that 'a powerful individual with a reputation for honesty [with substantial power] would eradicate corruption, without the need for changing the prevailing system'.[51] The idea seemed to have created a hope which was reflected in the swelling of mass support that was witnessed during the fast that Hazare had undertaken to force the government to initiate steps for effective legislation.

It was the campaign of a well-off Indian middle class. *The Economic Times* thus argues that

> if you needed evidence that the Anna Hazare movement had a large element of middle-class support, you need to look no further than the parking lot at the India Gate, New Delhi; it was full of [luxury cars] ... which Anna Hazare's supporters had driven in from far flung areas to express their support.[52]

Although the middle class had constituted the core of his support base, the movement also inspired people from different walks of life, as was evident when

Mumbai's *Dabbawallas*, (a unique service industry for delivering boxed-lunches to the office-goers in the city), for example, went on strike for the first time in 120 years to protest about Hazare's arrest. Besides the *Dabbawallas*, student groups, farmer groups, senior citizen societies, the sex workers' union, the taxi drivers' union and the small vendors' association supported the campaign as it picked up following the arrest of Hazare on 16 August 2011. The arrest can thus be said to have set off a groundswell of protest across the country. Mainly a middle-class outcry, the Hazare campaign gradually gained momentum, because it articulated the mass resentment with those usurping public authority for partisan gains. The campaign created an optimism in a context in which the existing Congress-led coalition government had lost its credibility, given the involvement of its members in various scams. It has thus been argued that Anna Hazare is significant because

his fast unto death catalyzed the exasperation and the anger of Indian citizens. The sight of hundreds of people holding candles in their hands [to show solidarity with Hazare] transmitted a simple but powerful message: citizens have a right to demand that the taxes that are extracted from them are spent for the public good and not private gains.[53]

Hazare's public image as being honest also helped the campaign to instantaneously create a support base among the youth who, like Hazare, felt that the immediate need was for a legally backed strong institution. So, opinion seems to have converged on the formation of a Leviathan-type *Lokpal* to meaningfully counter corruption and to establish a robust culture of integrity in governance. Hazare also defended the stance by saying that 'a strong *Lokpal* is needed and the corrupt should be put to jail or better still, hanged to the death'.[54] How did a Gandhian justify being in favour of capital punishment? He himself explained by stating that 'the need is not of Mahatma Gandhi but of Chhatrapati Shivaji' (who resorted to violent means to combat the ruthless Mughal emperor in Maharashtra).[55]

What is noteworthy is the fact that the initial low key mobilization led to a massive movement, following Hazare's fast-unto-death pledge, that 'had sprouted in urban centres across the country [and] nowhere did anyone plan the protest, [people] gathered around spaces connected with Gandhi'.[56] It became an all-India movement which had no parallel because, for the first time, the use of social media was widespread. Twitter, Facebook and You Tube became important tools of mobilization and activism along with candle light vigils, which also cemented a bond among the participants. It was as if an Arab Spring was being enacted on Indian soil, especially in the light of the techniques of mobilization, which were novel. Anna Hazare gave a powerful voice to the disgruntled middle class while the 2010–12 Arab Spring translated the participants' revolutionary fervour into movements against authoritarian regimes. Hence it has been argued that

the modus operandi and the engine behind the revolutionary uprisings [in the Arab world] is a mode of delayed defiance that results in the gradual appearance of a new imaginative geography of liberation in which ideas of freedom, social justice and human dignity are brought forth to the collective imagination.[57]

The comparison of the Arab Spring with the Hazare campaign may not be apt: there is, however, a sense in which one argues that the latter became a vehicle of mass protest, like the former, since the prevalent political regime lost its credibility, to a significant extent, following the unearthing of scams confirming the charges of the embezzlement of tax payers' money and also abuse of government authority for private enrichment. Hazare's clarion call for radical institutional changes which he articulated by insisting on a Leviathan-type *Lokpal*, thus immediately created a constituency of support among those of the middle class who did not seem to have reaped the benefits of economic liberalization to the extent they had expected, because of misgovernance which so far remained almost unaddressed in the absence of a strong institutional mechanism.

But Hazare's insistence on a draconian Lokpal seemed to have caused a fissure even among those who also felt that corruption needed to be curbed to ensure public well-being in the real sense of the term. The most articulate critique of the Lokpal bill happens to be the one that Arundhati Roy had provided by saying that

> while his means may be Gandhian, Anna Hazare's demands are certainly not. Contrary to Gandhiji's ideas about the decentralization of power, the Jan Lokpal Bill is a draconian, anti-corruption law, in which a panel of carefully chosen people will administer a giant bureaucracy, with thousands of employees, with the power to police, everybody from the Prime Minister, the judiciary, members of Parliament, and all of the bureaucracy, down to the lowest government official. The Lokpal will have the power of investigation, surveillance and prosecution. Except for the fact that it won't have its own prisons, it will function as an independent administration, meant to counter the bloated, unaccountable, corrupt one that we already have. Two oligarchs, instead of just one.[58]

So, the creation of 'a Leviathan-like Lokpal, based on the concept of ombudsman in Western societies',[59] is contrary to the basic ethos of democracy which builds a collective will through contestations, deliberations and negotiations. By arguing for creating a centralized institution of the state, the Jan Lokpal Bill seems to have drawn on Anna Hazare's personal experience at Ralegaon Siddhi where he, being projected as a messiah, rose to become an undisputed leader who was barely challenged by his followers. This is also undemocratic because 'messianism substitutes the collective subject, the staple in democracy, by an individual subject, the messiah'.[60] The argument was further pursued by the analyst who stated that

> the people may participate in large numbers, and with great enthusiasm and support in the activities undertaken by the messiah, as they are doing

reportedly at Anna Hazare's fast..., but they do so as spectators. The action is of the messiah; the people are only enthusiastic and partisan supporters and cheerleaders. If at all they ever undertake any action on the side, this is entirely at the messiah's bidding, its ethics, rationale and legitimacy never explained to them (no need is felt for doing so); whenever they march it is only in support of the messiah, not for specific demands that they have internalized and fell passionately about. When they gather [around Hazare], for instance, the occasion is not used to enlighten them, to bring home to them the nuances of the differences between the government's Lokpal Bill and the Jan Lokpal Bill, so that they could act with discrimination and understanding. On the contrary, the idea is to whip up enthusiasm among them without enlightening them, through the use of meaningless hyperbole like 'the government bill is meant not for the prevention but for the promotion of corruption' and 'Anna is India and India is Anna'. If the venue was one where discussions, debates and informative speeches were taking place, the matter would [have been] different, but those alas have no place in the political activity around messianism.[61]

This is a core structural limitation of the campaign that Hazare had launched to weed out corruption, which was defined too narrowly, as 'a moral problem to be addressed only at the level of individual'.[62] Also, it was assumed that, being an unchallenged messiah, the image that Hazare had built in Ralegaon Siddhi was adequately equipped to force the state to accept the Jan Lokpal Bill in its undiluted form. In the process, not only are the values of democracy compromised by encouraging the role of a messiah, the issue of structural inequality contributing to the glaring socio-economic imbalances becomes peripheral, if not entirely insignificant, in what is redefined as democratic struggles in the elite discourse.

Is corruption just a matter of legality, of financial irregularity and bribery, or is it the currency of a social transaction in an egregiously unequal society, in which power continues to be concentrated in the hands of a smaller and smaller minority?

asks the socio-political activist, Arundhati Roy.[63] In his scheme of things, the wider social context seems to have been entirely ignored, because Hazare felt that substantial social progress could be achieved once the evil politicians and their cohorts in government administration were shown the door. He was thus criticized for being silent when 'reckless and rapacious economic transformations had proceeded unchecked ... [through] illegal mining and land acquisitions for special economic zones ... [at the cost of] marginal farmers and indigenous communities'.[64] It is true that he had just one objective – the creation of a powerful Lokpal – with other issues remaining peripheral. That, however, does not mean that they were not important in his ideological preferences, as his statements following the fast had shown. Within a week of his fast, Hazare had broadened his demands beyond corruption to issues such as farmers' rights to land, the rights of labourers to humane conditions of works and even nuclear non-proliferation, which did not seem to please his supporters among the Hindu right wing.[65] He acquired important allies, such as social activist Medha Patkar, who is known for her guiding role in the Narmada Bachao Andolon (Save Narmada Movement), a social movement opposed to the construction of an ecologically destructive mega-dam on the Narmada river. Patkar is also a key organizer for the National Alliance for People's Movements, a broad alliance of social movements that has resisted various initiatives of the post-liberalized Indian state through the use of Gandhian means. Patkar's steadfast support has lent the Hazare movement a measure of credibility that other high profile allies (including the Bollywood stars or sports personalities) could not possibly provide. In a statement pledging support to Hazare, Patkar and her colleagues connected the battle against corruption with 'wider struggles against corporatization, capitalism, communalism, casteism, patriarchy, criminality and consumerism'.[66]

In his battle against corruption, Hazare, unlike his militant counterparts, always remained true to the fundamental ethos of parliamentary politics. Accepting parliament as supreme in democratic governance, he thus made an appeal to the parliamentarians to make a stringent law to contain corruption. He never called for 'regime change' nor did he dispute 'the parliament's authority to make laws'.[67] The Jan Lokpal remains, so far, shelved largely due to the absence of a consensus among the civil society activists and also the government over its authority, despite the agreement that India needs a strong ombudsman. The idea has, in other words, an appeal among the political parties, cutting across ideological preferences though when it is sought to be articulated in the form of an institution they do not seem to hold identical views. There can be plenty of reasons. One of them is perhaps the lack of moral courage to allow an institution of governance to exercise legal and also substantial authority, given the public backing over especially the errant politicians to arrest deviation from the established code of conduct. By recognizing moral values as critical to governance, the Lokpal is thus a powerful ideological voice in favour of a political system that will be resilient enough to counter the rise of Frankenstein's monster.

Besides giving a jolt to the system of governance, the Anna Hazare campaign catapulted the issue of corruption onto the centre stage of Indian politics. There is no denying the fact that the issues were always there in the public domain, but did not receive the limelight that they did following the 2011 India Against Corruption movement. Hence it is argued that what Hazare had initiated with his fast-unto-death vow in 2011

> will be remembered for forcing doors when no one else would – for jolting India into starting a countrywide discussion on corruption, of a scale that small, locally rooted civil society groups could not possible hope to initiate. Team Anna could certainly pave the way for change on a grand scale by building a multifaceted and inclusive alliance against corruption, not only

individual acts of corruption by unethical public servants, but also processes that have precipitated some of the most injurious forms of corruption adversely affecting India's moral fabric.[68]

The movement fizzled out and the goal remains elusive. Yet, the Hazare campaign brought refreshing insights in Indian politics not only in its nature but also in how it was articulated. With the involvement of the middle class and its critical role in ideologically charting the course of action for the campaign, Anna Hazare can be said to have created a format of politics in which the role of the numerically strong and financially well-placed middle class is formally recognized. It has thus been aptly suggested that the 2011 campaign was able 'to employ Gandhian motifs to popularize an urban middle class worry that has had, until now, less currency in India'.[69] Their presence, both at the level of leadership and also as participants became an important source of strength which confirms that socially they need to be taken seriously, especially when they are united over an issue. Corruption brought the disgruntled middle class together and Anna Hazare became their messiah. By being integral to the campaign, the middle class also seems to have regained the lost ground in Indian politics. They are now not being led, but are also capable of being a leader, if necessary. This is perhaps the most valuable contribution of the 2011 India Against Corruption campaign. Today, it is corruption that created a platform; tomorrow it could be the reckless extraction by foreign multinational corporations of minerals from across the country, which, if allowed, would surely affect the middle class in view of its overall impact on economic growth. So, the middle class cannot remain immune, once the paradigm of growth-at-any-cost is accepted as inevitable. In that respect, the 2011 Anna Hazare campaign is a milestone in contemporary Indian politics because, not only has it brought the issue of corruption in public life into common reckoning, it has also created a legitimate space for the middle class which did not seem to have played a critical role in India's development trajectory especially in the aftermath of the acceptance to the 1991 policy of economic liberalization.

Concluding observations

Corruption seems to be instinctively linked with human nature; so are the efforts to weed out its roots. The dialectical interconnection between corruption and the consolidation of public opinion needs to be understood to conceptualize the phenomenon in a historical perspective. This is articulated in the argument that, while corruption, in one form or another, has always existed, there have always been well-defined policy measures that have made a significant dent in it. Implicit here is the fact that corruption cannot be completely ruled out; what is feasible is to contain the incidence by creating an environment in which values of ethics, integrity and morality are deeply rooted. It is true that institutionalized legal means are a deterrent to corruption; they cannot, however, be sufficient to substantially weaken its base unless a propitious environment complements the endeavours. The ideological milieu that the 1975 J P movement had created was translated in the repeal of a large number of draconian laws (codified in the 1977 Forty-Second Amendment Act) through the *Forty-Third* and *Forty-Fourth Amendment Acts* in 1978. In other words, the fact that mounting public pressure resulted in the abrogation of laws supporting authoritarianism also confirms the critical role that social context plays in shaping a specific ideological stance. Similarly, the insistence on a strong *Lokpal* by those involved in the India Against Corruption campaign of 2011 can also be said to have its roots in the movement that Hazare had launched against the debilitating impact of corruption in India's public life.

There is one fundamental conceptual point here: corruption and the decline of ethics are dialectically inter-connected; while the former has had 'variegated incidence in different times at different places, with varying degrees of damaging consequences'[70] the latter also unfolds gradually and is thus contingent on specific mindsets which either remain indifferent or supportive of 'some sort of malfeasance for private enrichment'.[71] There can thus hardly be a universal explanatory model because this interrelationship is also context-driven. For instance, in the erstwhile Licence–Quota–Permit Raj guaranteeing massive discretionary power to those holding public authority, corruption was considered to be 'the much needed grease for the squeaking wheels of rigid administration'.[72] Gradually the idea seems to have lost steam. In the mid-1970s, the efforts towards utilizing government machinery for personal gain provoked mass consternation, which was reflected in the 1975 J P movement. Challenging the ideological design of those in power, the campaign for J P's total revolution created, rather instantaneously, a constituency of support in the country because of the abuse of authority by the powerful at the cost of the ordinary citizen. This was the main factor behind the massive campaign that J P had spearheaded in collaboration with political forces with incompatible ideological predilections. By the time the Anna Hazare led the campaign for the Jan Lokpal Bill in 2011, it was clear that public offices were utilized for personal gains with the revelation of scams involving the transaction of huge financial benefits for those in governance. What is striking is the fact that those who are responsible for managing governance in India tend to be corrupt because of the excessive importance of public authority in India's development trajectory. It is true that the state seems to have lost its determining role in the economy in contrast with what it had in the earlier dispensation of state-driven economic development; nonetheless, even in the changed socio-ideological milieu, the Indian state continues to remain a significant player, especially in disbursing money for development and also in extending favour to the private operators to initiate business ventures in exchange for kickbacks. The 2G spectrum scam and illegal appropriation of government funds to prepare for the 2010 Commonwealth Games in Delhi are illustrative here. The Hazare movement may not have achieved its goal, but it fulfilled a historical mission by articulating the middle-class frustration in the form a nation-wide campaign against corruption.

There is a continuing thread linking the 1975 J P movement with its 2011 counterpart, led by an army subaltern, Anna Hazare. As shown above, in the battle against the derailment of public authority in two different phases of India's recent political history, both J P and Hazare emerged as undisputed leaders holding hegemonic control over the movement for probity in governance. They became, in other words, messiahs to save Indians from crises. By encouraging individual-based leadership, these movements were criticized as undemocratic in character; there was not a mechanism to replace the hegemonic individual leaders because of their charismatic ability to guide their massive followers in accordance with what they felt appropriate at the particular historical juncture. This is definitely a bad side of messianism that creates a situation in which the will of the leader is carried forward since he/she has a majority to back his/her claim even at the cost of the constitution and institutions of parliamentary governance. Neither the Constitution of India nor the constitutionally guaranteed institutions can be overturned by the wishes of the majority at a particular time. 'If perchance', thus argues an analyst, we

> accept messianism out of expediency, it would be violating the spirit of the Constitution and undermining democracy. Besides, any such licence will make multiple (quasi-religious) messiahs sprout, who compete and collude, as oligopolists do in the markets for goods, to keep people in thralldom.[73]

Nonetheless, it is fair to argue that the campaigns that J P and Anna Hazare had spearheaded were a product of circumstances in which public frustration reached its zenith. It was possible for them to trigger movements, given their unassailable public images. They became messiahs in the absence of leaders who had the Gandhian capability of uniting socio-economically and also ideologically disparate masses for a common cause. One of the reasons which sustained their popularity was perhaps the use of civil disobedience methods and also the invocation of Gandhi who continues to remain ideologically inspiring, especially in movements challenging an authoritarian state or tendencies of political authorities towards being authoritarian. So, at a particular point of history, messiahs are required to quell anti-democratic forces, despite the fact that there is always an implicit danger, as history has demonstrated, in uncritically championing messianism in political mobilization.

Notes

1 Joseph Nye, 'Corruption and political development: a cost-benefit analysis' in Arnold J Heidenheimer, Michael Johnston and Victor T LeVine (eds), *Political Corruption: a handbook*, Transaction Publishers, New Brunswick, 1989, p. 966.
2 Sara Shumer, 'Machiavelli: republican politics and its corruption', *Political Theory*, 7 (1), 1979, p. 9 – quoted in Peter Bratsis, 'Corrupt Compared to What? Greece, capitalist interests and the specular purity of the state', discussion paper no. 8, London School of Economics and Political Science, 2003, www.eprints.lse.ac.uk/5696/1/corrupt_compared_to_what.pdf, p. 9.
3 Albert Hirschman, *The Passions and Interests*, Princeton University Press, Princeton, NJ, 1977, p. 40.
4 www.eprints.lse.ac.uk/5696/1/corrupt_compared_to_what.pdf. Peter Bratsis, 'Corrupt Compared to What?, p. 16.

5 Huntington, Samuel. 1989. 'Modernization and corruption', in Heidenheimer, Johnston and LeVine, p. 377.
6 This section is drawn on Bidyut Chakrabarty and Rajendra Pandey, *Modern Indian Political Thought: text and context*, Sage, New Delhi, 2009, pp. 109–20, unless otherwise stated.
7 Jayaprakash Narayan, *A Plea for the Reconstruction of Indian Polity*, Akhil Bharat Sarva Seva Sangh, Kashi, 1959, p. 22.
8 Ibid., p. 26.
9 Ibid., pp. 66–8.
10 Ibid., p. 107.
11 See Jayaprakash Narayan, *Swaraj for the People*, Akhil Bharat Sarva Seva Sangh, Varanasi, undated, chapter 2.
12 Ibid., chapter 3.
13 For a lucid and representative critique of J P's plan for reconstruction of Indian polity, see, W H Morris-Jones, *Politics Mainly Indian*, Orient Longman, Bombay, 1978, pp. 97–106.
14 Vinoba Bhave, *Democratic Values*, Sarva Seva Sangh Prakashan, Kashi, 1964, p. 3.
15 Jayaprakash Narayan, *A Picture of Sarvodaya Social Order*, Sarvodaya Prachuralaya, Tanjore, 1961 p. 6.
16 Jayaprakash Narayan, *From Socialism to Sarvodaya*, Akhil Bharat Sarva Seva Sangh Prakashan, Kashi, 1959, pp. 39–41.
17 Ibid., p. 40.
18 *A Picture of Sarvodaya Social Order*, pp. 4–5.
19 Ibid., p. 151.
20 Vinoba Bhave, *Revolutionary Sarvodaya*, Bhartiya Vidya Bhavan, Bombay, 1964, p. 1.
21 See Jayaprakash Narayan, *Total Revolution*, Sarva Seva Sangh Prakashan, Varanasi, 1975.
22 Jayaprakash Narayan, *Towards Total Revolution*, vol. 3, Richmond Publishing Co., Surrey, 1978, p. 79.
23 Dennis Dalton, 'The ideology of Sarvodaya: concepts of politics and power in Indian political thought', in Thomas Pantham and Kenneth L Deutsch (eds), *Political Thought in Modern India*, Sage, New Delhi, 1986, p. 292.
24 Ananth V Krishna, *India since Independence: making sense of Indian politics*, Pearson, New Delhi, 2011, p. 143.
25 Ibid.
26 Mathew Jenkins, 'Anna Hazare, liberalization and the careers of corruption in modern India: 1974–2011', *Economic and Political Weekly*, 16 August 2014, p. 44.
27 John R Wood, 'Extra-parliamentary opposition in India: an analysis of populist agitations in Gujarat and Bihar', *Pacific Affairs*, 48 (3), 1975, p. 319.
28 Era Sezhiyan (compiled and edited), *The Shah Commission Report: lost and regained*, Aazhi Publishers, Chennai, 2010, Third and Final Report, chapter XXIV, p. 228.
29 V Krishna Ananth, 'Lokpal Bill campaign: democratic and constitutional', *Economic and Political Weekly*, 16 April 2011, p. 21.
30 *Ethics in Governance*, Fourth Report, Second Administrative Reforms Commission, Government of India, New Delhi, 2007, p. 127.
31 Ibid.
32 Speech by M Veerappa Moily, chairman, Second Administrative Reforms Commission, on the occasion of the National Colloquium on Ethics and Governance – Moving from rhetoric to results, 1 September 2006 – reproduced in *Ethics in Governance*, p. 223.
33 The report is quoted from *The Hindu*, New Delhi, 31 March 2011.
34 Ibid.
35 Ibid.

36 Ibid.
37 Ibid.
38 Sumanta Banerjee and Anna Hazare, 'Civil society and the state', *Economic and Political Weekly*, 3 September 2011, p. 12.
39 Mathew Jenkins, 'p. 48.
40 Neera Chandhoke, 'Our latest democratic predicament', *Economic and Political Weekly*, 7 May 2011, p. 19.
41 Ibid.
42 Anna Hazare, *Ralegaon Siddhi: a veritable transformation*, Ahmednagar, 1997, p. 114 – quoted in Mukul Sharma, 'The making of moral authority: Anna Hazare and watershed management programme in Ralegan Siddhi', *Economic and Political Weekly*, 20 May 2006, p. 1984.
43 Mukul Sharma, p. 1983.
44 Drawn on Mukul Sharma, p. 1983.
45 Mukul Sharma, p. 1983.
46 Ibid., p. 1984.
47 Drawn on Mukul Sharma, p. 1984, unless otherwise stated.
48 Mukul Sharma, p. 1984.
49 Ibid., p. 1985.
50 Ibid., p. 1986.
51 Sumanta Banerjee, p. 13.
52 *The Economic Times*, New Delhi, 20 August 2011.
53 Neera Chandhoke, p. 19.
54 Anna Hazare's statement in *The Times of India*, New Delhi, 3 September 2011.
55 Ibid. Fond of Shivaji, a devout Hindu king who always gave a befitting reply to the Mughal authority in the battle field, Hazare admired him for the sacrifice he made 'for the uplift and welfare of the ordinary people'. Anna Hazare, *Ralegaon Siddhi: a veritable transformation*, Ahmednagar, 1997.
56 V Krishna Ananth, p. 20.
57 Hamid Dabashi, *The Arab World: the end of postcolonialism*, Zed Books, London and New York, 2012, 'p. 226.
58 Arundhati Roy, 'I'd rather not be Anna', *The Hindu*, New Delhi, 21 August 2011.
59 Mitu Sengupta, 'Anna Hazare and the idea of Gandhi', *The Journal of Asian Studies*, 71 (3), August 2012, pp. 596–97.
60 Prabhat Patnaik, 'Messianism versus democracy', *The Hindu*, New Delhi, 24 August 2011.
61 Ibid.
62 Mitu Sengupta, 'Anna Hazare's anti-corruption movement and the limits of mass mobilization in India', *Social Movement Studies*, 13 (3), p. 408.
63 Arundhati Roy, 2011.
64 Mitu Sengupta, 'Anna Hazare's anti-corruption movement', p. 408.
65 Ibid., p. 409.
66 Medha Patkar's statement is quoted in Mitu Sengupta, 'Anna Hazare's anti-corruption movement', p. 409.
67 Mitu Sengupta, 'Anna Hazare and the idea of Gandhi', p. 598.
68 Ibid.
69 Vinay Senapati, 'What Anna Hazare's movement and India's new middle classes say about each other', *Economic and Political Weekly*, 23 July 2011, p. 43.
70 Pranab Bardhan, 'Corruption and development: a review of issues', *Journal of Economic Literature*, Vol. XXXV, September 1997, p. 1320.
71 Ibid., p. 1321.
72 Samuel P Huntington, *Political Order in Changing Societies*, Yale University Press, New Haven, CT, 1968, p. 386.
73 Prabhat Patnaik, 2011.

Conclusion

I

There are two major arguments that appear to have shaped our thinking on ethics in governance: first, 'the publicness' of public administration is fully articulated if the administrators remain sensitive to their ethical commitments of contributing to the public well-being. This is easier said than done, given the political complexities in which administration is located. There has been a continuous decay in the traditional moral code as a result of 'the falling away' from religious belief. What appears to have significantly dented public administration is a decline in three moral qualities in relation to the conduct of governance, which are: 'optimism, courage and fairness tempered by charity'.[1] This is elaborated further by Dwight Waldo in seeking to conceptualize public morality in governance. By providing a list of 12 obligations,[2] Waldo defined 'public morality' as:

> (1) obligation to the constitution, (2) obligation to law, (3) obligation to nation or country, (4) obligation to democracy, (5) obligation to organizational–bureaucratic norms, (6) obligation to profession and professionalism, (7) obligation to family and friends, (8) obligation to self, (9) obligation to middle-range collectivities, (10) obligation to public interest or general welfare, (11) obligation to humanity or the world, (12) obligation to religion or God.

Given the contextual nature of public administration, one has also to be careful in articulating 'public well-being', which is subject to change in view of new demands on governance. Since public administration is constantly being reinvented, it is theoretically impeding and empirically inconceivable to think of a universal model capable of providing a meaningful explanation of the reality.

The second argument relates to the hegemonic presence of corruption in public administration all over the world. Regardless of various control-mechanisms, corruption is 'a particularly viral form of bureaupathology', which is 'debilitating' and also 'contagious'.[3] This needs to be treated before it causes devastation to the organization. One can possibly think of specific administrative steps that evolve internally, but may not be adequate to conclusively root out the sources of corruption in administration, because of the prevalence of a well-entrenched mindset supporting deviation from established norms of public morality. Administrative reform is transitional, if not futile, unless it is backed by meaningful efforts at changing the overall political environment in which administration is grounded. So what it means is the dialectics of change involving administration and the socio-economic milieu, each shaping the other.

The elaborate discussion of ethics in governance in India demonstrates that the issue has 'a much wider import than what happens in the different arms of government [and] ... an across-the-board effort is [thus] needed to fight deviations from ethical norms'.[4] Reiterating that mere internal intervention cannot be conclusive in eradicating the source of the administrative ills, the Second Administrative Reforms Commission, like its first counterpart, attributes the decline of ethical values in administration to the overall decadence of moral values in India's politics since independence. Besides the pernicious impact of colonialism on independent India's administration, there is no denying that public governance has become a casualty, largely due to its appropriation by narrow, partisan and sectional interests. Nonetheless, there have been serious endeavours in recent times not only to identify the sources of decadence, but also to devise mechanism for arresting such a decline. One can possibly refer to the political institutions like the Election Commission or the Supreme Court of India, among others, which have taken several steps since the late 1980s in an attempt to eliminate the sources of the abuse of power by the powerful. Similarly, the civil society clamour for cleansing the political system is another seriously pursued endeavour to challenge corruption in public life. These attempts shall yield results in a conducive environment because 'in the long run', as the Santhanam Committee concludes, 'the fight against corruption will succeed only to the extent to which a favourable social climate is created'.[5] Ethics in governance is thus a goal that will remain elusive unless it is conceptualized and articulated in the overall political environment that critically influences Indian administration and its voice.

II

The idea of constitutional morality holds the key to comprehending ethics in governance, where ethics is understood as critical moral values shaping a specific mindset, and being appreciative of responsibility and accountability. Given the fact that, in democracy, public functionaries are 'trustees of the people',[6] the former is dialectically connected with the latter. The authority exercised by those in governance is thus not arbitrarily exercised, but is conceptually drawn from public interests. For a morally sensitive political order, appropriate laws and rules need to be made, and the public functionaries are also to be imbued with the required moral values, allowing the system to remain viable. The concern for public well-being is a key to perfect governance, which is conceivable if those responsible for governance are also made aware of their constitutional obligations when in power. This is possible in two ways: on the one hand, an alert citizenry will not allow them to be deviant; on the other hand, stringent laws will be uniformly applied if the charge of the abuse of authority is proved beyond doubt. Laws are undoubtedly effective preventive instruments provided they are not short-circuited by the intervention of political bigwigs. It is true that punitive measures are restraining devices; they also create an environment in which civic virtues for upholding constitutional values are nurtured. The basic purpose is to generate an impulse for constitutional morality as perhaps the most reliable shield against an ethics deficit in governance. This was a belief that B R Ambedkar held dear even as early as when he presented the 1950 Constitution of India to the nation. It was John Dewey of Columbia University who provided him with ideological support in favour of his argument for social democracy, which was wider in connotation than political democracy. Like his academic mentor, John Dewey, Ambedkar also believed in the supremacy of constitutional values in democratic political systems. Mere codification of laws was not enough, as Ambedkar argued, unless 'there is public conscience to behave in accordance with Constitutional provisions [which] is more important that the Constitution itself'. In continuation of the argument, he further stated that 'the principles of democracy are for the people to respect the system of formation of Government, observance of laws, habit of independent thinking and observance of laws of the majority'.[7]

What was critical for the survival of democracy was civility, a Dewey conceptualization that Ambedkar held dear while discharging his historical role. It called for tolerance, restraint and mutual accommodation in public life. Civility was thus 'a moderating influence which acts against the extremes of ideological politics'.[8] In his perception, without civility, 'democracy becomes defunct' and he was also aware that the lack of a living democratic tradition in India was a serious deterrent in the context of rigid caste hierarchy. To transform a society of caste and communities into one of citizens was not an easy task. Nonetheless, he fulfilled his role by seeking to create 'a sense of constitutional morality' while defending his liberal agenda.[9] Here too, Ambedkar was indebted to a classicist, George Grote,[10] whom he quoted extensively in his speech of 4 November 1948 in the Constituent Assembly. Institutions of governance in a democracy, felt Grote,

> lose salience [unless] there is diffusion of constitutional morality, not merely among the majority of any community, but throughout the whole ... since any powerful and obstinate minority may render the working of a free institution impracticable, without being strong enough to conquer ascendancy for themselves.[11]

By constitutional morality, Grote meant

> a paramount reverence for the forms of constitution, obedience to authority acting under and within these forms, yet combined with the habit of open speech, of action subject to definite legal control and unrestrained censure

of those in public authorities ... with a perfect confidence amidst bitterness of party contest that the forms of constitution will not be less sacred in the eyes of his opponents than his own.[12]

This long quote from Grote's writings was surely an aid to Ambedkar when he defended a liberal democratic framework of constitutional governance in India, though he was aware that it was difficult to instil a sense of constitutional morality in India because democracy which 'complements constitutional morality ... is only a top-dressing on an Indian soil which is essentially undemocratic'.[13] In the absence of constitutional morality, the operation of the constitution, no matter how carefully written, 'tends to become arbitrary, erratic and capricious'.[14] How to make the constitution an effective instrument of governance in such circumstances, asked Ambedkar? He was in favour of detailed provisions in the constitution to scuttle efforts at derailing it and challenging the fundamental constitutional values from which it derived its sustenance. In his defence, he thus argued that 'one can take the risk of omitting from the Constitution details of administration and leaving it for the Legislature to prescribe them ... if the people are saturated with Constitutional morality such as the one described by Grote'.[15] As is evident, Grote provided Ambedkar with an intellectual justification for a liberal constitution in a context in which basic liberal values of human dignity were brutally bypassed in favour of perhaps the most ruthless form of social segregation. So, the idea of constitutional morality was a powerful device which allowed Ambedkar to knit together liberal constitutional principles despite strong opposition by the Gandhians in the Constituent Assembly, who insisted that 'instead of incorporating Western theories the new Constitution should have been built upon village *panchayats* and district *panchayats*'.[16]

For constitutional morality to put down organic roots, Ambedkar insisted on obedience to

> constitutional methods of achieving our social and economic objectives [which meant that] we must abandon ... the method of civil disobedience, non-cooperation and satyagraha [because], when constitutional methods are open, there can be no justification for unconstitutional methods ... and the sooner these unconstitutional methods are abandoned, the better for us.[17]

The Gandhian Satyagraha was, according to him, a form of coercion. This is an assessment that probably reflects serious political differences that Ambedkar had had with Gandhi since the 1932 Poona Pact that deprived the Untouchables of separate electorates in the *Government of India Act 1935*. The defence for his opposition to Satyagraha was based on his commitment to constitutional morality, which was a key to the success of the constitution. As one who was influenced by Edmund Burke too, Ambedkar was also convinced that violence could never be a permanent solution to human problems because 'the forceful subjection of any community always leads to resentment [which was enough] ... to cause a severe dent to the democratic ethos'.[18] Ambedkar thus provided a typical liberal solution by suggesting that the issues of discontent could be resolved by a strong legal system along with the desire to sort out differences through dialogues and deliberations. Besides being appreciative of fundamental democratic means, Ambedkar also found in constitutional morality a powerful means to contain the decline of ethics in governance. For him, constitutional morality acquired organic roots in democracy because the latter creates an environment in which public functionaries cannot afford to ignore the public, since they owe their existence to them. So, once democracy is strengthened whereby the public voice gets reinforced, the chances of misuse of governance are likely to be less. The argument insisting on empowering the citizens as perhaps the most effective challenge against the ethics-deficit can easily be substantiated with the consolidation of public opinion in contemporary India against corruption per se, and particularly against the forces thriving on corruption. Constitutional morality may not be adequate to contain corruption because it draws on the individual inclination towards ethics-driven conditionalities; but a nation-wide democratic movement involving people cutting across social barriers, as was witnessed recently in the wake of the 2011 Anna Hazare campaign, nurtures not only a mass drive for opposition to corrupt practices, but also creates an environment in which demands for ethics in governance are forcefully made. It is therefore fair to argue that sustained campaigns against the misuse of public authority is perhaps the best option to organically create a proactive mindset which will be a deterrent against deviant acts by those involved in governance. This is also an ideologically meaningful design, in which the idea of constitutional morality is as critical as the challenges by the masses for evolving an environment that insists on obedience to fundamental ethical values by the public functionaries while in governance.

III

Civil society is now integral to governance. That it is a contested terrain adds a new twist to its relationship with governance. Civil society, just like the state, is a site of power relations. So the tendency to treat civil society as benign is theoretically misleading and empirically wrong. Civil society cannot be depoliticized, simply because one cannot wish away the contradictory relations along class, caste or gender axes, for instance, along which it is articulated. Furthermore, civil society can never be a universal category since it is specific to historical circumstances. Hence the assumption of shared meaning seems to be futile for two reasons: first, since civil society is specific to the cultural context of the country in question, it cannot be translated comfortably into other languages and social milieux; second, in many state-directed economies, where the state played a key role in development and governance, civil society may not be an accepted partner simply because it has no antecedent, in the sense that organizations outside the state were always a suspect. In a nutshell, what it suggests is the difficulty in conceptualizing civil society as a universal category, because the history of state–society relations differs profoundly from one society to another.

As argued in the book, ethics and governance is enmeshed in a very complex manner in which the former determines the shape of the latter and is also shaped in the process. Dialectically construed, this interrelationship is a very useful conceptual aid to comprehend how ethics is built and articulated in public governance. There is no denying the fact that fundamental codes of ethics cannot, at all, be compromised; otherwise, governance will just become an act of personal aggrandizement. In today's context of mass awakening, as the 2010–12 Arab Spring shows at the global level and the 2011 Anna Hazare campaign in Delhi articulates the message at the national level in India, those in governance cannot afford to be indifferent to the public demands. This is a new environment, in which governance is not merely governmental, but a design that is both market-driven and civil society-induced. Market redefines citizens as clients or consumers, while civil society expands the public sphere by including a whole range of civic actions that hardly figured in the bureaucratic model of public administration. Civil society is also the arena in which social movements become organized. Representing diverse and even contradictory social interests, civil society is a space that generally articulates responses reflecting the social base, constituencies and thematic orientations of the concerned group.[19] The civil society can thus be most effective in governance by mediating between citizen and state, by articulating the citizen's interests to government, by inculcating participatory norms and by restricting government by citizen involvement in its day-to-day functioning. Drawn from the shared accountability of stakeholders, the new governance paradigm secures accountability by reducing discretion or delegation in public bureaucracy through collaborative governance. This also makes participation meaningful and effective, in the sense that the involvement of the stakeholders in the decision making brings about changes in the organizational structure from a hierarchical, centralized form to a more decentralized and flexible form for enhancing self-management.

The growing importance of civil society in governance can be traced back to three sources: first, civil society is critical in reducing 'the governmental overload', especially in the developed countries where governments were downsized to achieve the goal; second, the role of civil society is justified as pertinent in governance in the World Bank's 'good governance' policy of aid-conditionality, focusing on transparency, human rights and accountability; third, civil society gains salience in the developing countries because the state-directed development paradigm fails to a large extent to eradicate poverty and also to contain the emergence of 'an insensitive' and also mechanical bureaucracy. Civil society contributes to the consolidation of decentralized bottom-up people-centric grass-roots governance. It works in two complementary ways: on the one hand, there seems to be a growing realization that wider social space is available outside the governmental institutions for autonomous social action; as a result, the dependency syndrome (or dependence on government) seems to have, on the other hand, evaporated and people are drawn into the processes of development, no longer as 'mere target groups', but as active participants, shaping the course of development. In the changed environment, civil society organizations, commonly defined as non-governmental or voluntary organizations, are crucial aids to governance especially in areas such as the environment, human rights, gender and transparency in public administration, to name a few. Civil society is thus not only a powerful force against governmental excesses but also a site for people's participation in the development process. In that perspective, civil society makes participation in governance people centric and also development oriented.

IV

One of the core issues of governance reform is accountability of those involved in public affairs.[20] Lack of accountability defeats the primary goal for which governance is seen as an appropriate model in public administration. In most of the developing countries, this deficiency results in 'misguided resource allocation and arbitrariness and corruption in government [that] have deterred private sector investment and slowed growth and poverty-reduction efforts in numerous settings'.[21] Historically, the liberal-democratic set-up evolved basic mechanisms of accountability such as ministerial control, parliamentary debate, legislative committees, media security and the ombudsman system. In recent times, there have been some major changes – a sort of paradigmatic shift – in the mode of public governance under the rubric of 'new public management', 'reinventing government' or 'reengineering government'. In essence, what is being advocated is a market-centred, neo-liberal approach to governance under which its objectives are shifted to economic growth and productivity, and its normative standards are redirected toward efficiency, competition, profit and value for money. The standards that are being set for public governance are those of business management. This marks a radical departure from the traditional norms and objectives of governance as enhancing human progress, maintaining law and order, removing poverty and unemployment, providing public welfare, ensuring impartiality and equal treatment, safeguarding citizens' rights and guaranteeing justice and fairness.

A critical evaluation of accountability in the context of the World Bank's strategy of governance reveals the extent to which this idea is linked with the contemporary neo-liberal agenda of the developed world. In the entire gamut of World Bank-inspired thinking on administrative reform, accountability is a most crucial dimension. The primary concern here is to do away with 'dysfunctional and ineffective public institutions – broadly defined to include all institutions that shape the way public functions are carried out – [that] are seen to be at the heart of the economic developmental challenge'.[22]

V

Accountability, though simple sounding, is an extremely complex concept. Traditional public administration considered it basically as an internal organizational issue, seeking to bring about a congruence between top-down policy and bottom-line implementation. There have been many constitutional and institutional changes to enhance public accountability of government agencies. In the developed countries initially, and later in the developing nations as well, the philosophy of 'new public management' has undergone a radical change, although the focus has continued to remain on the 'management'. For the developing 'third world' in the grip of serious debt crisis, the World Bank came out with the new 'good governance' prescription with its accompanying micro-accountability and macro-accountability formula. Institutional capacity-building became the central point and the Bank's primary objective has been to promote sound development management by removing, as far as possible, the possibilities of 'capture' of benefits by the socially powerful. This is of crucial significance, because the third world has inherited a colonial administrative model that is hard to destroy. Administrative hegemony has been further reinforced by a powerful socio-economic elite that is as keen as the administrative class to 'privatize' government. Accountability-enforcing institutions such as the legislature and the judiciary are too distant and cumbrous to bring about any real pro-people accountability climate in governance. Decentralization has been formally (constitutionally) assured and philosophically celebrated. But the grassroots institutions are yet to grow as autonomous institutions in a hostile and vertically divided caste-ridden Indian society, which is being complemented by a centralizing administration and inequitable resource distribution. Accountability has thus remained so far, in any variant, a managerial concept for application by 'external' managers, be it the internal organizational managers or outside donors like the World Bank. This runs contrary to what is critical to democratizing administration by empowering people. Nonetheless, it has raised new issues in the debate on accountability, which is not merely structural but also sociological, involving those who matter in a specific administrative context.

The question that is now being raised by quite a few social activists and civil libertarians is: can there be, as an alternative, a people's campaign for transparency and accountability? One such example of a search for grassroots accountability is the Mazdoor Kisan Shakti Sangathan (MKSS), which is just one or many such people's organizations growing up in different parts of India to transform public administration into a truly people's administration. To quote the proceedings of the MKSS, the effort has been to transform the demand for a right to livelihood, wages and employment into a demand to know from the government agency/*Panchayat* how much money was allocated and where and how it was spent. It was aptly articulated in the slogan: '*Hamara paisa, hamara hisab* [Our money, our accounts]'. Through people's awakening, the institution of *Jan sunwaii* or public hearing turned out to be an effective forum where the people could speak and be heard. 'The public hearings on development expenditure at the *Panchayat* level have', argue the main architect of the MKSS campaign, 'led to a crystallization of issues and given a tangible quality to the abstract notion of transparency and the right to information'[23] From the very modest beginning in the villages in Rajasthan, the success of MKSS has been a source of inspiration to activists in India and throughout the world. It led to 'the genesis of a broader discourse on the right to information in India'.[24] After dithering over this issue for years, the central government finally introduced the Freedom of Information Bill in Parliament on 25 July 2000. The bill was certainly a significant step in the process of democratization though Madhav Godbole apprehended that the 'the bill, as presented in parliament, [was] hardly [adequate] to bring transparency to issues of governance'.[25] This bill finally became the Freedom of Information Act, 2002 that has now been replaced by the RTI, which seeks

> to provide setting out the practical regime of right to information for citizens to secure access to information under the control of public authorities, in order to promote transparency and accountability in the working of every public authority, the constitution of Central Information Commission and State Information Commission and for matters connected therewith or incidental thereto.[26]

The Right to Information is derived from part III of the Constitution of India guaranteeing freedom of expression under Article 19. Hailed as the Magna Carta of freedom,[27] this Act is the codification of a right that empowers citizens to requisition information within a specific time frame of 30 days. As a 'path to swaraj',[28] as the act is characterized in the media, this is an important pillar of democracy in ensuring 'transparency' and 'accountability'. There are, however, doubts about the extent to which this Act will help the people in getting the information they seek, despite the institution of the Central Information Commission and State Information Commission, because 'of the typical colonial mindset of the bureaucracy' which, by denying access to information to the people, seems to sustain its hegemony in public administration. The validity of the *Official Secrets Act 1923*, even after the passing of the RTI Act, seems to be puzzling though the Act suggests punitive measures to check 'the errant officers' that will hardly be effective unless the mindset is less 'bureaucratic' and more 'developmental'.

VI

As the unearthing of scam after scam reveals, there has been a massive ethics deficit in governance. Public authority is being misused for personal enrichment. Despite being challenged, those abusing authority are hardly restrained. The situation does not seem to be as dismal as it is made out, in view of the growing civil society activism as an antidote to malpractices in governance. There are occasions when parliamentarians raise the issue, that have always been addressed by reiterating the importance of creating a vibrant political culture, opposed to tendencies towards appropriating public machinery for personal gain. There is a serious lacuna in this argument because (a) it cannot be done overnight and (b) those who insist on developing a fair culture are also allegedly involved in malpractices, as shown in Chapter 6. As a result, the concern that the parliamentarians had shown did not appear to have evoked a positive response from the stakeholders. However, the parliamentary decline seems to have been matched by the ascendancy of other political institutions of Indian democracy. For instance, the President, Supreme Court of India and the Election Commission have, among others, shown a remarkable resilience in upholding some of the intrinsic constitutional values that are critical to ethics in governance. It is now increasingly being felt that these important political institutions have a role in reversing the trend, by being true to the value system that the founding fathers had left for posterity. This argument is sought to be substantiated below by assessing the role of these selective constitutional institutions in events when the constitutional propriety was infringed.

India's President no longer remains an ornamental head of state. In the context of the decline of single-party rule, the first citizen of the country seems to have redefined his/her constitutional role by being more pro-active than before. Article 53 of the Constitution vests 'the executive power of the Union ... in the President'; as constitutional head of state he/she is expected to act as an agent of the political executive, namely the council of ministers or cabinet. The rise of coalition government and the spread of corruption – in the political executive, legislatures and civil services – have created a legitimate space for other constitutional functionaries, including the presidency, 'to act as guardians of fairness and constitutional balance'.[29] That the President was not a mere 'rubber stamp' was evident when the late K R Narayanan prevented the Uttar Pradesh Governor Ramesh Bhandari from arbitrarily dismissing the Kalyan Singh-led BJP government and replacing it with Jagdambika Pal's Congress–Samajwadi coalition. Bhandari dismissed the Singh government without giving the chief minister an opportunity to prove his majority on the floor of the assembly, which Narayanan thought was both 'unconstitutional' and 'partisan', designed to help the ruling United Front–Congress in the forthcoming election.[30] A landmark Supreme Court judgment 'reinstalled' the BJP government, justifying K R Narayanan's intervention for constitutional propriety since there was 'widespread disenchantment ... with the excessive use of the President's rule for partisan purposes'.[31] Similarly, Narayanan's reluctance to endorse the decision of V C Pande, the Bihar governor, to appoint the Nitish Kumar-led minority government immediately after the 2000 state assembly election would have led to a serious constitutional crisis had Nitish Kumar not resigned. The fact that the Rabri Devi-led RJD coalition won the vote of confidence 'intensified the clamour against the governor's precipitous and apparently partisan action'.[32] President A P J Abdul Kalam's refusal to approve the 2006 Office of Profit bill when it was sent to him after its endorsement by both houses of parliament redefined the role of this institution in the changed socio-political environment. Although the President had no alternative but to grant assent once the bill was approved by the parliament for a second time, the episode is nonetheless reflective of the growing independence of India's highest constitutional authority. Three important principles were consolidated in the wake of this controversial office of profit episode: first, the underlying principle debarring the holder of an office of profit under the government from being a member of parliament is drawn on a foundational principle of the doctrine of separation of powers, namely, that there should be a demarcation of authority and power between executive and legislature to avoid 'misappropriation of authority and power' by these two wings of government. The famous 1973 Kesavananda Bharati judgment of the Supreme Court endorses this principle as part of the Basic Structure of the Constitution of India. Second, the President's reluctance to approve the bill is also suggestive of the fact that there should be uniformity in interpreting the law as regards the office of profit. In fact, given the Supreme Court ruling on this, there is no scope for different interpretations and, as the top judicial institution in the country, the Supreme Court is constitutionally authorized to enforce uniformity in this regard. Finally, by sending the bill back to parliament for reconsideration, the President also upheld the judicial sanctity of the criteria that the Supreme Court devised to settle the controversy. These criteria are: (a) it must be a post, created by and under the control of the government, (b) the appointee to the post should also be under governmental control, (c) the holder of the post must be entitled to some profit or benefit other than compensatory allowance, whether he/she takes it or not, and (d) there is power/authority attached to that position that can be exercised by the holder.[33] It is true that the controversy was finally resolved not by following the judicial wisdom, but by political considerations. Nonetheless, this episode established beyond doubt a healthy trend, which is constitutionally creative and politically challenging in so far as the institutions of governance are concerned. The bill was therefore a significant intervention in redefining the political, which is located in the institutions that had creatively responded to the issues, perhaps linked with the deepening of democracy by meaningful participation of 'the people' in the political processes.

Similarly, the Supreme Court in the famous Bommai judgment of 1994 radically altered the complexion of the debate on the basic structure of the constitution. Critical of the indiscriminate application of Article 356 to dismiss the duly elected state governments, the Supreme Court came out heavily against the Union government. B R Ambedkar was confident, as his statements in the Constituent Assembly endorse, that Emergency provisions in the Constitution of India would rarely be invoked and, as Indian democracy matured, the need to do so would be less compelling, reducing Article 356 to 'a dead letter'. However, by 1994, this provision had been applied more than 90 times, the Supreme Court noted, and thus made this Article 'a death letter', rather than 'a dead letter', as the founding fathers foresaw. The judgment put to rest all speculation regarding the 'delicate balance of powers in a federal polity' by saying that 'federalism envisaged in the Constitution is a basic structure.... The state *qua* the Constitution is federal and independent in its exercise of legislative and executive power'. It is true that the Constitution prefers an arrangement that is tilted in favour of the centre. But that does not mean that 'the States are mere appendages of the Centre. Within the sphere allotted to them, States are supreme. The Centre cannot temper with their powers'. Simultaneously, by clarifying the constitutional status of the States, the judgment also redefined the role of the President who is not a mere stooge of the Union Government by underlining that

the provision requires that the material before the President must be sufficient to indicate that unless a proclamation (under Article 356) is issued, it
is not possible to carry on the affairs of the state as per the provisions of the
Constitution. It is not every situation arising in the State but a situation
which shows that constitutional government has become an impossibility,
which alone will entitle the President to issue the proclamation.[34]

B R Ambedkar was right when he suggested that growing democratization
would make the Emergency Provision redundant. The Supreme Court is certainly an important component in this process. By creatively interpreting the
constitutional provisions, the top court contributed to the redrawing of the basic
contours of Indian federalism that have, with their roots in the 1935 constitutional structure, evolved organically out of an engagement with the constantly
changing social, economic and cultural milieu. The Bommai judgment is a
watershed, perhaps the most significant, in the evolution of an organic federalism
in India, which is surely a break with the past.

The revival of the Election Commission as a political watchdog is a remarkable development, supporting the growing democratization of Indian politics.
Established in 1950, the Election Commission was set up as a constitutional
agency and entrusted, according to Article 324 of the Constitution, with the task
of superintendence, direction and control of all national and state level elections.[35] The Commission holds substantial power in so far as the procedural
aspects of the elections are concerned. In fact, it derives its strength from the
code of conduct, formulated by the political parties participating in the election
generally by consensus. There is no doubt that, by its sincere involvement in the
processes of elections, starting from the preparation of the voters' roll to the declaration of the poll outcomes, the Commission has played a critical role in redefining politics in today's India. The role of the Commission in the state election
in West Bengal in 2006 is illustrative here: with the announcement of the dates
of elections, the Commission took control of the election machinery of the state
in an unprecedented manner. First, it took ample care to revise the voters' roll,
since the incumbent Left Front government was charged with manipulating the
voters' list. The Election Commission found a large number of them in various
districts. During the clean-up operation, the observer found an alarmingly huge
number of false names[36] in the list of voters, and struck them off. Hence the
charge seemed authenticated and the media thus attributed the sustained electoral victory of the Left Front to 'the bogus voters'. Second, following its success
in Bihar in holding a free and fair election under the strict surveillance of the
state-controlled coercive forces, the Commission decided to conduct the poll on
five fairly dispersed dates, stretching over almost two months. The Commission
requisitioned police and paramilitary forces from outside the state, simply
because the state police did not appear to be reliable. Because the dates were dispersed, it was possible to get adequate numbers of them to supervise the voting
on the day of election. It was a remarkable election in West Bengal, which was
held under the strict control of an Election Commission that implemented its

authority strictly in accordance with its constitutional obligation to Indian demo-cracy.[37] Although the electoral outcome brought back the incumbent Left Front government to power, unlike in Bihar where a new government was installed replacing the government that held power for more than 15 years, the Commission provided critical inputs to the processes of democratization by empowering the ordinary voters, who now became part of 'the movers and shakers' of Indian democracy, who can be ignored only at the cost of the political parties seeking political power. In other words, the voters are not merely seasonal participants; they have also been made to feel their importance in political processes that hardly mattered so far in their everyday life.

VII

The study is both exploratory and explanatory: exploratory because the purpose here is to understand the context in which the ethics deficit is so well entrenched that India's resilience as a constitutional democracy seems be fast disappearing; explanatory because, on the basis of an analytically drawn exploratory exercise, the study provides an explanation, linking the decline of ethics in governance with India's overall moral decadence, visible everywhere. There is a historical reason, since one cannot deny the pernicious impact that colonialism had in India's development trajectory and, similarly, the granting of excessive discretionary power to those holding public authority in the wake of the Licence–Quota–Permit Raj. The system that had emerged not only contributed to an arrogant civil service, it had also created circumstances for abuse of authority. Despite having understood the complex roots of corruption in India, the 1964 Santhanam Committee did not go beyond suggesting the creation of a Central Vigilance Commission, besides strengthening the system of internal account-ability in the line of Weberian thinking. Corruption did not subside to the extent that was expected. The 1975 internal Emergency was the pinnacle in the sense that the abuse of public authority for biased ideological gain reached its zenith. As shown in Chapter 6, the 1977 Shah Commission report graphically illustrated how public authority was abused to deny citizens of their basic fundamental rights. What it confirms is the fact that a powerful state may not always work as an antidote to the tendencies contributing to the ethics deficit; instead, it created, as demonstrated by the Santhanam Committee and Shah Commission, a propitious environment for corruption to spread its tentacles.

The situation did not seem to have changed in the new environment of economic liberalization. There have been innumerable instances where even the ministers were involved in plundering public money for partisan gains. The state seemed to have been helpless or complicit with those misusing their authority as public personnel. Like the J P movement that successfully challenged the atrocious Emergency regime that Indira Gandhi led, the 2011 Anna Hazare India-Against-Corruption campaign raised a powerful voice against those who had no qualms in bending, if not bypassing, rules and regulations for personal enrichment. Despite having charged the emotions, the Hazare movement, unlike the

J P campaign, failed to achieve the goal; nonetheless, it was a fruitful campaign because it once again catapulted corruption as a core issue in the public domain. Despite being critical of the parliamentarians for their deviant behaviour, Hazare approached, rather ironically, the same set of parliamentarians to create a Leviathan-like Lokpal by approving the Jan Lokpal Bill. The Lokpal is still a distant goal though a law to that effect was passed in 2013. What is significant here is the fact that the role that Hazare played cannot be so easily dismissed, since he created a mass momentum against corrupt politicians who seem to have been accustomed so far to not taking into account the public mood, especially in between elections. The idea is changed now, to a significant extent, and those in public authority are aware that there is a price, perhaps a heavy price, if the code of ethics is violated by them while fulfilling their well-defined constitutional obligations.

The study also confirms that the abuse of authority for personal benefits can never go unchallenged, especially in a democracy that thrives out of a very intense civic engagement. Whenever attempts were made, as the past has shown, to thwart public institutions, there have been serious public protests. A custodian of democratic values, an alert citizenry always puts hurdles, if not checks, in the way as soon as efforts towards misappropriating public authority are made. This is the lesson of history. Examples from India – starting from the 1974 J P movement to the 2011 Anna Hazare drive for a strong Lokpal – have proved the point beyond doubt. In recent years, there may not have been nation-wide campaigns against corruption, as was seen in 2011, though one can refer to innumerable instances showing that the abuse of authority usually provokes immediate opposition, because of the citizens being always vigilant. The purpose here is not to provide a detailed account of the scams that India confronted in recent years, but to conceptualize the dialectics involving corruption and citizens. As it has been argued, corruption is integral to governance, though it can be considerably contained if the citizens discharge their role effectively by being tuned to the fundamental ethos of democratic governance. This can be done in two complementary ways: on the one hand, tendencies towards overrunning the available institutions of authority need to be checked by applying the existing laws without discrimination or favour; on the other hand, simultaneously, serious efforts are to be made not only to create but also to sustain and consolidate a social climate appreciative of a fundamental code of ethics for articulating democracy in governance. What is critical here is the idea that corruption can never be effectively contained by legislative means unless they are supported by a propitious social climate, because this is where the mindset is built. As shown in this book, given the relentless efforts by both official agencies and civil society in India, the situation seems to be changing, with the corrupt and deviant being taken to task, suggesting perhaps a significant transformation in the social climate as well. This is most enlightening, since the idea that corruption is not insurmountable appears to have gained ground in contemporary India.

Notes

1 Stephen K Baily, 'Ethics and the public service' in Roscoe C Martin (ed.), *Public Administration and Democracy*, Syracuse University Press, Syracuse, 1965.
2 Elaborated in Richard J Stillman II (ed.), *Public Administration: concepts and cases*, Houghton Mifflin Company, Boston, 1996, pp. 462–5.
3 Gerald E Caiden, 'Dealing with administrative corruption' in Terry L Cooper (ed.), *Handbook of Administrative Ethics*, Marcel Dekker Inc, New York, 1994, p. 320.
4 *Ethics in Governance*, Fourth Report, Second Administrative Reforms Commission, Government of India, New Delhi, 2007, p. 5.
5 *Report of the Committee on Prevention of Corruption*, Ministry of Home Affairs, Government of India, New Delhi, 1964, p. 101.
6 *Ethics in Governance*, p. 19.
7 B R Ambedkar, lecture in the legislative assembly, Trivandrum, 10 June 1950 – reproduced in Narendra Jadhav, *Ambedkar Speaks: political speeches*, Vol. III, Konark Publishers Pvt. Ltd, New Delhi, 2013, p. 537.
8 Andre Beteille, 'Constitutional morality', *Economic and Political Weekly*, 4 October 2008, p. 42.
9 Pratap Bhanu Mehta makes this point in his 'What is constitutional morality', *Seminar*, November 2010, pp. 17–24.
10 George Grote (1794–1871), an English radical who wrote the *History of Greece* (four volumes) during 1846–56 was influenced by liberals such as Ricardo, James Mill and Jeremy Bentham.
11 B R Ambedkar speech before the Constituent Assembly on 4 November 1948, *Constituent Assembly Debates*, Vol. VII, p. 38.
12 Ibid.
13 Ibid.
14 Andre Beteille, p. 36.
15 B R Ambedkar speech, p. 38.
16 Ibid.
17 B R Ambedkar speech before the Constituent Assembly on 25 November 1949, *Constituent Assembly Debates*, Vol. X, p. 978.
18 B R Ambedkar, speech at the Round Table Conference, London Plenary session, 20 November 1930 – reproduced in Narendra Jadhav, *Ambedkar Speaks: political speeches*, Vol. III, Konark Publishers Pvt. Ltd, New Delhi, 2013, p. 107.
19 For details of this argument, see J L Cohen and A Arato, *Civil Society and Political Theory*, The MIT Press, Cambridge, MA, 1992.
20 In the World Bank's 1994 report *Governance: the World Bank's Experience*, 'good governance is epitomized by predictable, open and enlightened policy-making (that is transparent processes); a bureaucracy imbued with a professional ethos; an executive arm of government accountable to its actions, and a strong civil society participating in public affairs, and all behaving under the rule of law'.
21 *Reforming Public Institutions and strengthening governance: main strategy*, A World Bank Strategy, November 2000, Public Sector Group, Poverty Reduction and Economic Management (PREM) Network, p. 1.
22 Ibid.
23 Aruna Roy, Nikhil Dey and Shanker Singh, 'Demanding accountability', *Seminar*, April 2001.
24 Working paper entitled 'National level R[ight] T[o] I[nformation], Commonwealth Human Rights Group, 2005, p. 2.
25 Madhav Godbole, 'Unending struggle for Right to Information', *Economic and Political Weekly*, 12 August 2000, p. 2899. Godbole further observed that

> through five years of dithering over the bill on the right to information, the position of the central governments which have been run by two United Fronts, the

BJP and its allies, has remained the same. [It] is disconcerting that in this important area of governance, the interests of bureaucracy and the ruling elite seem to converge against the empowerment of common man.

26 The Gazette of India, Part II (section 1), Ministry of Law and Justice, Government of India.

27 Working paper entitled 'National level R[ight] T[o] I[nformation], p. 2.

28 *The Hindu* characterized the Right to Information as 'a path to Swaraj', *The Hindu*, New Delhi, 7 October 2005.

29 L I Rudolph and S H Rudolph, 'Redoing the constitutional design: from an interventionist to a regulatory state' in Atul Kohli (ed.), *The Success of India's Democracy*, Cambridge University Press, Cambridge, 2002, p. 141.

30 For details of the UP case, see A G Noorani, *Constitutional Questions in India*, Oxford University Press, New Delhi, pp. 328–39.

31 James Manor, 'The Presidency' in Devesh Kapur and Pratap Bhanu Mehta (eds), *Public Institutions in India: performance and design*, Oxford University Press, New Delhi, p. 116.

32 L I Rudolph and S H Rudolph, p. 150.

33 While elaborating on the office of profit controversy, I have drawn on an unpublished article by J S Verma, the former chief justice of India. I am thankful to Justice Verma for having shared this unpublished article, a part of which was printed in *The Times of India*, 4 September 2006.

34 S R Bommai Vs. Union of India, *AIR*, The Supreme Court of India, December 1994.

35 For a very persuasive descriptive account of the Election Commission, see Ujjwal K Singh, *Institutions and Democratic Governance: a study of the Election Commission and electoral governance in India*, Monograph, Nehru Memorial Museum and Library, New Delhi, 2004; Manjari Katju, 'Election Commission and functioning of democracy', *Economic and Political Weekly*, 29 April 2006.

36 Sumanta Banerjee, 'Assembly Polls, 2006: elections, *jatra* style, in West Bengal', *Economic and Political Weekly*, 11 March 2006, p. 864.

37 I have dwelled on the role of the Election Commission in the 2006 West Bengal assembly election at some length in my 'Left Front's 2006 victory in West Bengal: continuity or a trendsetter', *Economic and Political Weekly*, 12 August 2006.

Bibliographical notes and a select bibliography

It is very difficult to prepare an exhaustive bibliography on a vast subject such as ethics in governance. Given the dialectical interconnection between the decline of ethics and corruption, it is also easily conceivable why the subject has attracted wider attention. There is hardly a country in the globe now which is not affected by these twin factors of an ethics deficit and the consequent rise of corruption. As a result, not only has it provoked vast academic interest, it has also become a source of concern for the policy makers both at the global and national levels. One has thus to be aware of the context that has critically influenced the way these phenomena are sought to be understood. There is one unique feature of this exercise: corruption is not merely an academic phenomenon; it is also reflected in both national and global policy priorities. Hence the bibliography contains three types of work. First, there are fully fledged books and papers on the topic. The list is pretty long, which confirms that the phenomenon of the ethics deficit and its adverse consequences have attracted considerable academic attention. The second type is articles and essays in reputed peer-reviewed journals, which are well researched and thought provoking. Some of the articles/essays were later expanded into full-length studies. Besides these academic exercises, the third type, listed separately at the end of the bibliography, is policy studies, which are equally research based and conceptually well directed. They cannot be said to have emerged exclusively out of the normative concern for creating corruption-free societies; instead, these policy-driven analyses have also clear policy objectives, because most of these policy briefs are utilized by probable investors before they launch their business ventures. For instance, the assessment of Transparency International, the World Bank, the United Nations Development Programme and other global/multinational agencies always remain critical sources of useful information for investors in the contemporary globalized world. Besides being indicative of the nature of the political system in specific countries, these reports have also enough inputs to understand how governance is articulated. For instance, in the context of the License–Quota–Permit Raj, corruption was considered to be a useful device to get things done, especially at the lower level of Indian bureaucracy; similarly, in the changed environment of economic liberalization, the decline of ethics seems to have reached an alarming height with the involvement of those at the highest level of governance, as the revelations of scams involving massive misappropriation of public funds for private gain shows. These examples direct our attention to the fact that there can hardly be universal models for conceptualizing the ethics deficit and corruption, since these are context-dependent phenomena. As examples from India show, while the granting of excessive discretionary power led to corruption in public life, an uncontrolled privatization is not a panacea either, given the rising incidence of corruption in the context of India's market-driven economy. These reports are thus very useful not only in conceptually comprehending the idea but also to understand its actual articulation in specific circumstances.

The bibliography may not be exhaustive, but it is certainly directional for those seeking to explore the ethics deficit and corruption in their most complex manifestations. The most fundamental lesson that one draws out of this list of texts is about the critical importance of the context in which the issues of ethics and its derailment are conceptualized and elaborated. In that sense, each of the texts is unique, despite being helpful in comprehending the complexities of the unfolding of processes, integrally connected with the decline of ethics in governance and its concomitant fall-outs. The idea is not novel, but is being reiterated here to dissuade efforts to seek to build universal models for these phenomena. Given the obvious contextual roots of these impediments to rule-bound governance, the following bibliography is not at all prescriptive, but is clearly suggestive of well-informed texts which are useful to conceptualize and understand the complex unfolding of corruption in a specific milieu, which is usually attributed to the decline of ethics in public life.

Ackerman, John, 'Social accountability for the public sector: a conceptual discussion', draft paper for the World Bank, Washington DC, 2004.

Agarwal, Chetan, 'Right to information: a tool for combatting corruption in India', *Journal of Management & Public Policy*, 3 (2), June 2012.

Agarwal, U C (ed.), *Public Administration: vision and reality*, Indian Institute of Public Administration, New Delhi, 2003.

Ambedkar, B R, lecture in the legislative assembly, Trivandrum, 10 June 1950 – reproduced in Narendra Jadhav, *Ambedkar Speaks: political speeches*, Vol. III, Konark Publishers Pvt. Ltd, New Delhi, 2013.

Anderson, Thomas Barnebeck, 'E-government as an anti-corruption strategy', *Information Economics and Policy*, 21, 2009.

Appleby, Paul, *Public Administration in India: report of a survey*, the Ford Foundation, Delhi, 1953.

Appleby, Paul, 'History and precedent vs. reform' in U C Agarwal (ed.), *Public Administration: vision and reality*, Indian Institute of Public Administration, New Delhi, 2003.

Appu, P S, 'The all-India services: decline, debasement and destruction', *Economic and Political Weekly*, 26 February 2005.

Avasthi, A and S R Maheswari, *Public Administration*, Lakshmi Narain Agarwal, Agra, 2010.

Baily, Stephen K, 'Ethics and the public service' in Roscoe C Martin (ed.), *Public Administration and Democracy*, Syracuse University Press, Syracuse, 1965.

Banerjee, Sumanta, 'Assembly Polls, 2006: elections, *jatra* style, in West Bengal, *Economic and Political Weekly*, 11 March 2006.

Banerjee, Sumanta and Anna Hazare, 'Civil society and the state', *Economic and Political Weekly*, 3 September 2011.

Bardhan, Pranab, 'Corruption and development: a review of issues', *Journal of Economic Literature*, Vol. XXXV, September 1997.

Bardhan, Pranab, 'An economist's approach to the problem of corruption', *World Development*, 34 (2), 2005.

Bardhan, Pranab, Sandip Mitra, Dilip Mookherjee and Abhirup Sarkar, 'Local democracy and clientelism: implications for political stability in West Bengal', *Economic and Political Weekly*, 28 February 2009.

Beteille, Andre, 'Constitutional morality', *Economic and Political Weekly*, 4 October 2008.

Bhatnagar, Subhas, 'Administrative corruption; how does e-government help?' *Global Corruption Report*, 2003, Transparency International, New York, 2003.

Bhatt, Anil, 'Colonial bureaucratic culture and development administration: portrait of an old-fashioned Indian bureaucrat', *Journal of Commonwealth and Comparative Politics*, 17 (3), 1979.

Bhattacharya, Dwaipayan, 'Of control and factions: changing party-society in rural West Bengal', *Economic and Political Weekly*, 2009.

Bhattacharya, Mohit, 'Voluntary associations, development and the state', *The Indian Journal of Public Administration*, July–September 1987.

Bhattacharya, Mohit, *New Horizons of Public Administration*, Jawahar, New Delhi, 2008.

Bhattacharya, Mohit, *New Horizons of Public Administration*, Jawahar, New Delhi, revised edition, 2013.

Bhave, Vinoba, *Democratic Values*, Sarva Seva Sangh Prakashan, Kashi, 1964.

Bhave, Vinoba, *Revolutionary Sarvodaya*, Bhartiya Vidya Bhavan, Bombay, 1964.

Brass, Paul R, 'Foucault steals political science', *American Reviews of Political Science*, 3, 2000.

Bratsis, Peter, 'Corrupt compared to what? Greece, capitalist interests and the specular purity of the state', discussion paper no. 8, London School of Economics and Political Science, 2003.

Brautigam, Deborah, 'Governance and economy: a review', Working Papers, Policy and Review Departments, The World Bank, December 1991.

Brown, Mark Malloch, 'Can ICTs address the needs of the poor?', *UNDP Choices*, 10 (2), 2001.

Brueckner, Jan, 'Fiscal decentralization in the LDCs: the effects of local corruption and tax evasion', Department of Economics, University of Illinois, Urbana-Champion, 1999.

Bull, Martin J and James L Newell, *Corruption in Contemporary Politics*, Palgrave Macmillan, London, 1997.

Bussell, Jeniffer, 'Why get technical? Corruption and the politics of public service reform in Indian states', *Comparative Political Studies*, 43 (10), 2010.

Bussell, Jeniffer, *Corruption and Reform in India: public services in the digital age*, Cambridge University Press, Cambridge, 2012.

Caiden, Gerald E, 'Development administration and administrative reform', *International Social Science Journal*, 2 (1), 1969.

Caiden, Gerald E, 'Dealing with administrative corruption' in Terry L Cooper (ed.), *Handbook of Administrative Ethics*, Marcel Dekker Inc, New York, 1994.

Caiden, Gerald E, 'Administrative reform – proceed with caution', *International Journal of Public Administration*, 22 (6), 1999.

Celarier, Michelle, 'Privatization: a case study in corruption', *Journal of International Affairs*, 50, 1997.

Chakrabarty, Bidyut, 'Left Front's 2006 victory in West Bengal: continuity or a trendsetter', *Economic and Political Weekly*, 12 August 2006.

Chakrabarty, Bidyut, *Reinventing Public Administration: the Indians experience*, Orient Longman, New Delhi, 2007.

Chakrabarty, Bidyut and Rajendra Pandey, *Modern Indian Political Thought: text and context*, Sage, New Delhi, 2009.

Chandhoke, Neera, 'Our latest democratic predicament', *Economic and Political Weekly*, 7 May 2011.

Cohen, J L and A Arato, *Civil Society and Political Theory*, The MIT Press, Cambridge, MA, 1992.

Cooper, Terry L, *An Ethic of Citizenship for Public Administration*, Prentice Hall, Englewood Cliffs, NJ, 1991.

Crook, Richard and James Manor, *Democratic Decentralization*, OED Working Paper Series, No. 11, The World Bank, Washington DC, 2000.

Dabashi, Hamid, *The Arab World: the end of postcolonialism*, Zed Books, London, 2012.

Dalton, Dennis, 'The ideology of Sarvodaya: concepts of politics and power in Indian political thought', in Thomas Pantham and Kenneth L Deutsch (eds), *Political Thought in Modern India*, Sage, New Delhi, 1986.

Das, S K, *Public Office, Private Interests: bureaucracy and corruption in India*, Oxford University Press, New Delhi, 2001.

Dasgupta, Rajarshi, 'The CPI (M) machinery in West Bengal: two village narratives from Koochbehar and Malda', *Economic and Political Weekly*, 28 February 2009.

David, Jennifer, 'Corruption in public service delivery: experience from South Asia's water and sanitation sector', *World Development*, 32 (1), 2004.

Dehejia, Vivek H, 'Escaping India's gilded age', *New York Times*, 15 April 2011.

Department of Information and Publicity, Government of Delhi, *Bhagidari: the citizen–government partnership: some preliminary observations*, Delhi 2012.

Desai, Santosh, 'Trivial tales of Emergency', *The Times of India*, New Delhi, 29 June 2015.

Dewey, John, *The Public and Its Problems*, Henry Holt and Company, New York, 1927.

Dey, Bata K, 'E-governance in India: problems, challenges and opportunities – a future vision', *Indian Journal of Public Administration*, XLVI(3), July–September 2000.

Dicey, A V, *Lectures on Relation between Law and Public Opinion in England during the Nineteenth century*, London, Macmillan, 1948 (2nd edition). Drawn on 'Governance barometer: policy guidelines for good governance', prepared by the National Party of South Africa, *www.gdrc.org/u-gov/governance-understand.html*, accessed on 3 August 2015.

Friedrich, Carl J, 'Corruption concepts in historical perspective', in Arnold J Heidenheimer, Michael Johnston and Victor T LeVine (eds), *Political Corruption: a handbook*, Transaction Publishers, New Bruswick, 1989.

Gandhi, Gopalkrishna, 'Mastering the drill of democracy', *The Hindu*, New Delhi, 26 June 2015.

Ghertner, Asher D, 'Gentrifying the state, gentrifying participation: elite governance programs in Delhi', *International Journal of Urban and Regional Research*, 35 (3), 2011.

Gill, S S, *The pathology of Corruption*, Harper Collins, New Delhi, 1998.

Godbole, Madhav, 'Unending struggle for Right to Information', *Economic and Political Weekly*, 12 August 2000.

Gorwala, A D, *Report of Public Administration* and also *Efficient Conduct of State Enterprises*, Government of India, New Delhi, 1951.

Healy, Patsy, *Collaborative Planning: shaping policies in fragmented societies*, UBC Press, Vancouver, 1997.

Heywood, Paul M and Staffan Andersson, 'The politics of perception: use and abuse of Transparency International's approach to measuring corruption', *Political Studies*, 2008.

Heywood, Paul M and Jonathan Rose, 'Close but no cigar: the measurement of corruption', *Journal of Public Policy*, 34 (3), 2014.

Hirschman, Albert, *The Passions and Interests*, Princeton University Press, Princeton, NJ, 1977.

Huntington, Samuel P, *Political Order in Changing Societies*, Yale University Press, New Haven, CT, 1968.

Huntington, Samuel, 'Modernization and corruption', in Arnold J Heidenheimer, Michael Johnston and Victor T LeVine (eds), *Political Corruption: a handbook*, Transaction Publishers, New Brunswick, 1989.

Innes, Judith E and David Booher, *Planning with Complexity: an introduction to collaborative rationality for public policy*, Routledge, Oxford, 2010.

Jenkins, Matthew, 'Anna Hazare, liberalization and the careers of corruption in modern India: 1974–2011', *Economic and Political Weekly*, 16 August 2014.

Jenkins, Rob (ed.), *Regional Reflections: comparing politics across India's states*, Oxford University Press, New Delhi, 2004.

Jenkins, Rob, 'Democracy, development and India's struggle against corruption', *Public Policy Research*, September 2006.

Jenkins, Rob and Anne Marie Goetz, 'Accounts and accountability: theoretical implications of the Right-to-Information movement in India', *Third World Quarterly*, 20 (3), 1999.

Kamarck, Elaine, 'Government innovations around the world', Faculty Research Working Paper Series, John F Kennedy School of Government, Harvard University, 2004.

Kangle, R P, *The Kautilya Arthasastra*, Part II, University of Bombay, Bombay, 1972.

Kapoor, Jagdish C, 'IT and good governance', *Indian Journal of Public Administration*, XLVI (3), July–September 2000.

Katju, Manjari, 'Election Commission and functioning of democracy', *Economic and Political Weekly*, 29 April 2006.

Khan, Mohbbat, *Bureaucratic Self-Preservation: failure of major administrative reform effects in the civil service of Pakistan*, University Press Limited, Dhaka, 1980.

Kirlin, Jonh J, 'The big question in a democracy', *Public Administration Review*, September–October 1996.

Kohli, Atul, *The State and Poverty in India: politics of reform*, Cambridge University Press, Cambridge, 1989.

Kohli Atul, *State-Directed Development: political power and industrialization in the global periphery*, Cambridge University Press, Cambridge, 2004.

Koreth, George and Kiron Wadhea, *Building a Citizens' Partnership in Democratic Governance: the Delhi Bhagidari process through large-scale group dynamics*, Sage, New Delhi, 2013.

Krishan, Ananth V, 'Lokpal bill campaign: democratic and constitutional', *Economic and Political Weekly*, 16 April 2011.

Krishna, Ananth V, *India since Independence: making sense of Indian politics*, Pearson, New Delhi, 2011.

Kumar, Krishna, 'Conscience and the body politics', *The Hindu*, New Delhi, 10 July 2015.

Kundu, Debolina, 'Elite capture in participatory governance', *Economic and Political Weekly*, 5 March 2011.

Kurer, Oskar, 'Definitions of corruption' in Paul M Heywood (ed.), *Routledge Handbook of Corruption*, Oxford, 2015.

Leftwich, Adrian, 'On the primacy of politics in development' in Adrian Leftwich, (ed.), *Democracy and Development: theory and practice*, Polity Press, Cambridge, 1996.

Lyer, Lawrence E, Jr, Carolyn J Heinrich, and Carolyn J Hill, *Improving Governance: a new logic for empirical research*, Georgetown University Press, Washington DC, 2001.

Machiavelli, Niccolo, *The Prince*, Penguin Classics, Penguin, Suffolk, 1979.

Mahalingam, Sudha, 'Vigilance commission: issues for vigilance', *Frontline*, 15(19), 1998.

Maheshwari, S R, *Administrative Reforms in India*, Macmillan, New Delhi, 2002.

Maine, Henry S, *Village Communities in the East and West*, Henry Elliot Company, New York, 1876.

Malena, Carmen, Reiner Forster and Janmejay Singh, 'Social accountability: an introduction to the concept and emerging practice', *Social Development Papers: Participation and Civic Engagement*, The World Bank, 2004.

Manor, James, 'The Presidency' in Devesh Kapur and Pratap Bhanu Mehta (eds), *Public Institutions in India: performance and design*, Oxford University Press, New Delhi.

Mansukhani, H L, *Corruption and Public Servants*, Vikas Publishing House, New Delhi, 1979.

Mansuri, Ghazala and Vijayendra Rao, *Localizing Development: does participation work?* The World Bank, Washington DC, 2013.

Marx, Fritz Morstein, 'Administrative ethics and the rule of law', *The American Political Science Review*, 43, 1949.

Mathur, B P, *Ethics for Governance: reinventing public services*, Routledge, New Delhi, 2014.

Mehta, Pratap Bhanu, 'What is constitutional morality', *Seminar*, November 2010.

Minogue, Martin, 'Changing the state: concepts and practice in the reform of the public sector' in Martin Minogue, Charles Polidano and David Hume (eds), *Beyond the NPM: changing ideas and practice in governance*, Edward Elgar, Cheltenham, 1998.

Mitra, Chandan, *Corrupt Society: the criminalization of Indian politics from independence to nineties*, Viking, New Delhi, 1997.

Mohanty, Aditya, 'From Bhagidari to Mohalla Sabhas in Delhi: when participation trumps governance', *Economic and Political Weekly*, 5 April 2014.

Morris-Jones, W H, *Politics Mainly Indian*, Orient Longman, Bombay, 1978.

Morrow, William L, *Public Administration: politics and the political system*, Random House, New York, 1980.

Myrdal, Gunnar, *Asian Drama: an inquiry into the poverty of nations*, Vol. II, Pantheon, New York, 1968.

Narayan, Jayaprakash, *A Plea for the Reconstruction of Indian Polity*, Akhil Bharat Sarva Seva Sangh, Kashi, 1959.

Narayan, Jayaprakash, *From Socialism to Sarvodaya*, Akhil Bharat Sarva Seva Sangh Prakashan, Kashi, 1959.

Narayan, Jayaprakash, *A Picture of Sarvodaya Social Order*, Sarvodaya Prachuralaya, Tanjore, 1961.

Narayan, Jayaprakash, *Total Revolution*, Sarva Seva Sangh Prakashan, Varanasi, 1975.

Navlakha, Gautam, 'Lokpal movement: unanswered questions', *Economic and Political Weekly*, 5 November 2011.

Nelissen, Nico, Marie-Louise Bemelmand-Videc, Arnold Godfroij and Peter De Goede (eds), *Reinventing Government: innovative and inspiring visions*, International Books, Netherlands, 1999.

Nilekani, Nandan, *Imagining India: the idea of renewed nation*, Penguin, New Delhi, 2009.

Noorani, A G, *Constitutional Questions in India*, Oxford University Press, New Delhi, 2000.

Nye, Joseph, 'Corruption and political development: a cost-benefit analysis' in Arnold J Heidenheimer, Michael Johnston and Victor T LeVine (eds), *Political Corruption: a handbook*, Transaction Publishers, New Brunswick, 1989.

Osborne, David and Ted Gaebler, *Reinventing Government: how the entrepreneurial spirit is transforming the public sector*, Prentice Hall of India, New Delhi, 1992.

Palmer, N D, 'India in 1975: democracy in eclipse', *Asian Survey*, 16(2), 1976.

Palmier, L, *The control of Bureaucratic Corruption: case studies in Asia*, Allied Publishers, New Delhi, 1985.

Park, Richard L, 'Political crisis in India, 1975', *Asian Survey*, 15(2), 1975.

Patnaik, Prabhat, 'Messianism versus democracy', *The Hindu*, New Delhi, 24 August 2011.

Paul, S and M Shah, 'Corruption in public service delivery' in S Guhan and S Paul (eds), *Corruption in India: agenda for action*, Vision Books, New Delhi, 1997.

Penttinen, Elina, 'Capitalism as a system of global order' in Henri Goverde, Philip G Cerny, Mark Haugaard and Howard Lentner (eds) *Power in Contemporary Politics: theories, practices, globalizations*, Sage, London, 2000.

Philip, Mark, 'The definition of political corruption' in Paul Heywood (ed.), *Routledge Handbook of Political Corruption*, Routledge, Oxford, 2015.

Prasad, Kamala, *Indian Administration: politics, policies and prospects*, Pearson-Longman, New Delhi, 2006.

Quah, J S T, *Curbing Corruption in Asia: a comparative study of six countries*, Eastern Universities Press, Singapore, 2003.

Quah, J S T, 'Curbing corruption in India: an impossible dream', *Asian Journal of Political Science*, 16(3), December 2003.

Ramchandran, V, 'A chronic aberration', *Economic and Political Weekly*, 7–13 May 2005.

Richardson, T, 'Foucauldian Discourse: power, truth in urban and regional policy making', *European Planning Studies*, 4 (3), 1995.

Robson, W A, *The Governors and the Governed*, George Allen and Unwin, London, 1964.

Rouband, Luc (ed.), *Citizens and The New Governance*, IOS Press, Amsterdam.

Roy, Aruna, Nikhil Dey and Shanker Singh, 'Demanding accountability', *Seminar*, April 2001.

Roy, Arundhati, 'I'd rather not be Anna', *The Hindu*, New Delhi, 21 August 2011.

Roy, Sanjit (Bunker), 'Voluntary agencies in development – their role, policy and programmes', *Indian Journal of Public Administration*, July–September 1987.

Roychowdhury, Supriya, 'Globalization and decentralization', *The Hindu*, 5 January 2002.

Rudolph, L I and S H Rudolph, 'Redoing the constitutional design: from an interventionist to a regulatory state' in Atul Kohli (ed.), *The Success of India's Democracy*, Cambridge University Press, Cambridge, 2002.

Sachdeva, Sameer, '*White paper on E-governance Strategy in India*', World Bank, Washington DC, December 2003 (unpublished).

Sagar, T, *Communicative Planning Theory*, Avery, Aldershot, 1994.

Salskov-Iversen, Dorte, Hans Krause Hansen and Sven Bislev, 'Governmentality, globalization and local practice: transformation of a hegemonic discourse', *Alternatives: social transformation and human governance*, April–June 2000.

Sanchez, Andrew, 'Criminal entrepreneurship: a political economy of corruption and organized crime in India' in Paul M Heywood (ed.), *Routledge Handbook of Corruption*, Oxford, 2015.

Sarkar, Abhirup, 'Political economy of West Bengal', *Economic and Political Weekly*, 28 January 2006.

Sengupta, Arjun, 'Delivering the right to the development: ESCR (economic, social and cultural rights) and NGOs', *Economic and Political Weekly*, 9 October 1999.

Sengupta, Mitu, 'Anna Hazare and the idea of Gandhi', *The Journal of Asian Studies*, 71 (3), August 2012.

Sengupta, Mitu, 'Anna Hazare's anti-corruption movement and the limits of mass mobilization in India', *Social Movement Studies*, 13 (3), 2014.

Seth, S P, 'Political crisis in India', *Pacific Community*, Vol. VII, January 1976.

Sezhiyan, Era, *Members of Parliament Local Area Development Scheme (MPLADs): concepts, confusion, contradictions*, Institute of Social Sciences, New Delhi, 2005.

Sharma, Arvind, 'Administrative reforms in India: a synoptic view' in Pradeep Sahni and others (eds), *Governance and Development: issues and strategies*, Prentice Hall, New Delhi, 2003.

Shumer Sara, 'Machiavelli: republican politics and its corruption', *Political Theory*, 7 (1), 1979.

Shungly, V K, 'India's anti-corruption strategy' in *Combating Corruption in Asian and Pacific Economics*, Asian Development Bank, Manila, 2000.

Singh, Amita, *Public Administration: roots and wings*, Galgotia Publishing, New Delhi, 2002.

Singh, Digvijay, 'Public ownership of reforms: the experience of Madhya Pradesh', in Stephens Howes, Ashok Lahiri and Nicholas Stern (eds), *State-level Reforms in India: towards more effective government*, Macmillan, New Delhi, 2003.

Singh, Gurharpal, 'Understanding political corruption in contemporary India politics' in Paul Heywood (ed.), *Political Corruption*, Blackwell, Oxford, 1997.

Singh, Ujjwal K, *Institutions and Democratic Governance: a study of the Election Commission and electoral governance in India*, Nehru Memorial Museum and Library, New Delhi, 2004.

Sinha, Jayant and Ashutosh Varshney, 'It is time for India to rein in its robber barons', *Financial Times*, 6 January 2011.

Sitapati, Vinay, 'What Anna Hazare's movement and India's new middle classes say about each other', *Economic and Political Weekly*, 23 July 2011.

Spector, Bertram (ed.), *Fighting Corruption in Developing Countries: strategies and analysis*, Kumarian Press, CT, 2005.

Stillman, Richard J, II (ed.), *Public Administration: concepts and cases*, Houghton Mifflin Company, Boston, 1996.

Stivers, Camilla, 'Citizenship ethics in public administration' in Terry L Cooper (ed.), *Handbook of Administrative Ethics*, Marcel Dekker Inc., New York, 1994.

Tarschys, Daniel, 'Wealth, values, institutions: trends in government and governance' in *Governance in the 21st Century: future studies*, OECD, 2001.

Taub, R P, *Bureaucrats under Stress: administrators and administration in an Indian state*, University of California Press, Berkeley, 1969.

Thampi, G K, *Corruption in South Asia: insights and benchmarks from citizen feedback surveys in five countries*, Transparency International, Berlin, 2002.

Tocqueville, Alexis de, *Democracy in America*, Vol. 1, Vintage Classics, New York, 1990.

Tummala, K K, 'Corruption in India: control measures and consequences', *Asian Journal of Political Science*, 10 (2), 2002.

Tummala, K K, 'Combatting corruption: lessons out of India, *International Public Management Review*, 10 (1), 2009.

Varshney, Ashutosh, 'A republic of greed: why Narendra Modi must crack the whip on India's snowballing corruption'. *The Times of India*, New Delhi, 17 July 2015.

Viswanathan, Shiv and Harsh Sethi, *Foul Play: chronicles of corruption*, Banyan Books, New Delhi, 1998.

Vittal, N, *Corruption in India: the roadblock to national prosperity*, Academic Foundation, New Delhi, 2003.

Wood, John R, 'Extra-parliamentary opposition in India: an analysis of populist agitations in Gujarat and Bihar', *Pacific Affairs*, 48 (3), 1975.

World Bank, The, *The World Bank in Governance: the World Bank Experience*, Washington DC, 1992.

World Bank, The, *Deterring Corruption and Improving Governance in the Electricity Sector*, April 2009.

Yiftachel, O, 'Planning as control: policy and resistance in deeply divided societies', *Progress in Planning Series*, Vol. 44, Pier Gammon Elsevier, Oxford, 1995.

Zakaria, Fareed, *The Future of Freedom: illiberal democracy at home and abroad*, Penguin, New Delhi, 2003.

Reports

Citizen Centric Administration: the heart of governance, Second Administrative Reforms Commission, Twelfth Report, Government of India, February 2009.

Committee on Civil Service Reform, Government of India, New Delhi, 2004, available at http://darpg.gov.in/darpgwebsite_cms/Document/file/CivilServiceReforms2004.pdf, accessed on 8 August 2015.

Corruption in India: an empirical study, Transparency International, available at www.transparency.org/policy_research/surveys_indices/cpi/2007, accessed on 30 August 2015.

Corruption Perception Index for 2014, Transparency International, available at www.transparency.org/cpi2014/results, accessed on 30 August 2015.

Ethics in Governance: Second Administrative Reforms Commission, Government of India, New Delhi, 2007.

Governance and Development, The World Bank, Washington DC, 1992.

Human Development in South Asia: the crisis of governance, Oxford University Press, Oxford, 1999.

India Corruption Study 2005: To Improve Governance: Volume I – Key Highlights New Delhi, Transparency International India. 30 June 2005.

Local Governance: an inspiring journey into the future, Second Administrative Reforms Commission, Government of India, New Delhi, 2007.

Principles for Managing Ethics in Public Services, OECD, PUMA policy brief no. 4, 1998, available at www.oecd.org/gov/ethics/1899138.pdf, accessed on 8 August 2015.

Reconceptualizing Governance, UNDP discussion paper 2, New York, January 1997.

Reforming Public Institutions and Strengthening Governance: a World Bank strategy, Public Sector Group, The World Bank, 2000.

Refurbishing of Personnel Administration: scaling new heights, Second Administrative Reforms Commission, Government of India, New Delhi, 2008.

Report of the Committee on Prevention of Corruption, Ministry of Home Affairs, Government of India, New Delhi, 1964.

Report of the Fifth Central Pay Commission, Government of India, New Delhi, 1997.

Report of the Sixth Central Pay Commission, Government of India, New Delhi, 2008.

The Shah Commission Report: lost and regained, Sezhiyan Era, (compiled and edited), Aazhi Publishers, Chennai, 2010.

Index

For Product Safety Concerns and Information please contact our EU
representative GPSR@taylorandfrancis.com
Taylor & Francis Verlag GmbH, Kaufingerstraße 24, 80331 München, Germany